This volume explores the rise of Celtic-speaking societies in Europe. It covers both prehistoric and historic cultures, from the early Iron Age Celtic peoples of continental Europe (800–400 BC) to the eighteenth-century Scottish clans defeated by the English at the Battle of Culloden in 1746. Interweaving archaeological and textual evidence, the result is an interdisciplinary study of state formation, never before attempted on such a wide scale, which contributes to our understanding of social complexity in Celtic Europe, and, more generally, to the processes underlying social transformation.

NEW DIRECTIONS IN ARCHAEOLOGY

Celtic chiefdom, Celtic state

Editors

Wendy Ashmore
Department of Anthropology, University of Pennsylvania

Françoise Audouze
Centre de Recherches Archéologiques,
Meudon, France

Richard Bradley
Department of Archaeology, University of Reading

Joan Gero
Department of Anthropology, University of
South Carolina

Tim Murray
Department of Archaeology, La Trobe University,
Victoria, Australia

Colin Renfrew
Department of Archaeology, University of
Cambridge

Andrew Sherratt
Department of Antiquities, Ashmolean Museum,
Oxford

Timothy Taylor
Department of Archaeology, University of Bradford

Norman Yoffee
Department of Anthropology, University of Arizona

Celtic chiefdom, Celtic state

The evolution of complex social systems in prehistoric Europe

Edited by
BETTINA ARNOLD
University of Minnesota
and
D. BLAIR GIBSON
University of California at Los Angeles

Published by the Press Syndicate of the University of Cambridge
The Pitt Building, Trumpington Street, Cambridge CB2 1RP
40 West 20th Street, New York, NY 10011–4211, USA
10 Stamford Road, Oakleigh, Melbourne, Victoria 3166, Australia

First published 1995
Reprinted 1996

A catalogue record for this book is available from the British Library

Library of Congress cataloguing in publication data

ISBN 0521 464692 hardback
ISBN 0521 585791 paperback

Transferred to digital printing 1999

To Susan L. Saul Gibson and Thomas H. Hruby,
without whose help and support none of this would
have been possible

Contents

Illustrations

Contributors

BETTINA ARNOLD
Department of Anthropology
University of Minnesota

PATRICE BRUN
Centre Nationale de Recherches Scientifiques (CNRS),
Paris

OLIVIER BÜCHSENSCHÜTZ
Centre Nationale de Recherches Scientifiques (CNRS),
Paris

JOHN COLLIS
Department of Archaeology
University of Sheffield

CAROLE L. CRUMLEY
Department of Anthropology
University of North Carolina-Chapel Hill

MICHAEL DIETLER
Department of Anthropology
Yale University

ROBERT A. DODGSHON
Institute of Earth Studies
University College of Wales

SEAN B. DUNHAM
Interdisciplinary Archaeological Studies
University of Minnesota

FRANZ FISCHER
Institut für Vor-und Frühgeschichte
University of Tübingen

D. BLAIR GIBSON
Department of Anthropology
University of California at Los Angeles

COLIN HASELGROVE
Department of Archaeology
University of Durham

NERYS THOMAS PATTERSON
Assistant Warden
15 Shepard Street
University of Wales, Bangor

PETER S. WELLS
Department of Anthropology
University of Minnesota

Acknowledgments

We would like to thank the following friends, family members and colleagues for their help and support: Sinéad Ni Ghabhláin for her superb translating job; Timothy Earle for his suggestions and for serving as discussant at the original conference session which produced this volume; Françoise Audouze for her useful editorial suggestions; Susan L. Saul Gibson for technical support and editing (especially the index, which was a Herculaean task and could not have been completed without her help); Baelyn Neff and Lisa Keeley for their help with the index; and Thomas H. Hruby for computer expertise, editing, encouragement and good food. Any errors or omissions probably can be attributed to the dark forces of the Celtic underworld, but the responsibility is ours alone.

1
Introduction. Beyond the mists: forging an ethnological approach to Celtic studies

BETTINA ARNOLD and
D. BLAIR GIBSON

[A]rchaeology alone, without the texts, in the rustic farmsteads and peasant hamlets; the forts and strongholds of chieftains and tribes; the barbaric panoply of parade and war; even the evidence for rituals including human sacrifice and head-hunting, shows us a picture of a society barbarous and uncivilized in its essentials however much the superficial veneer may have been acquired by exceptional individuals and societies in for instance Gaul. And that we have read the archaeological evidence correctly, the texts amply confirm
(Piggott 1968:46).

Why the Celts?

To the modern culturally sensitive intellectual it may seem like an exercise in ethnocentric vanity: a group of European and Euroamerican authors coming together to produce a book on the political achievements of the Celts. However, to those of us engaged in Celtic studies, this work marks a sort of emergence from the humanist ghetto – an effort to establish a rapport with those individuals working in the mainstream of the social sciences.

The study of Celtic peoples has been characterized by both insularity and disciplinary fragmentation. This situation is partly due to the extraordinary richness of the material remains of these peoples. In the periods prior to Roman expansion the Celts had spread throughout most of central and western Europe and the British Isles, and came to occupy parts of eastern Europe, central Italy and Anatolia. The often impressive material remains of their cultures have busied antiquarians and archaeologists for over two centuries. Celtic cultures persisted intact beyond the Roman conquest on the fringes of Europe in the British Isles and Brittany. The languages and folklore of the modern Celtic peoples, as well as the written texts of their historic ancestors, have become the province of linguists and philologists. Scholars working in these various disciplines have not really perceived any need to coordinate their researches or to exchange information.

In the past archaeologists were justified in restricting their attention to excavation and the description of artifacts, even in areas where early texts were available. The Celtic texts were and are difficult to read and interpret. Trustworthy translations of many of the important texts, such as the Irish and Welsh law-tracts and annals, have only appeared in a trickle over the past century. Perceived cultural differences between the Celts of the British Isles and the Continent made it seem unlikely in any case that the materials from one area would have any bearing on other Celtic cultural areas (see Patterson, this volume).

We feel that after over a century of work enough archaeological data have accumulated, and a sufficient number of texts have been edited and translated, to warrant synthetic analyses. Indeed, it seems clear that further progress in understanding Celtic Europe will only result from interdisciplinary collaboration. To the editors of this volume, and to many of the contributors, the intimidation that we might have felt in the face of the "problems" of the data has given way to a feeling of anticipation as we have come to realize the potential in the diverse records of the Celts. These sources will permit analyses that will make substantive contributions to the debates on many of the great questions of the historical social sciences.

Despite their common linguistic stock, the Celtic peoples came to exhibit tremendous diversity in subsistence adaptations not only across Europe, but even within regions such as the British Isles. The various Celtic groups exhibit great variation in social integration, as well as in the kinds of social and economic institutions they possess. This diversity is what makes this area an exciting place to initiate research. Like Polynesia, Celtic Europe is a fertile place within which to investigate questions involving the factors which effect and affect social development, as well as the process of social and economic "adaptive radiation." Indeed, a number of the authors represented in this volume (Brun, Collis, Dietler, Haselgrove, Wells) have chosen to examine the variation in social configurations within and between Celtic societies.

It is too much to expect that this volume will influence all scholars in the various fields of Celtic studies to turn their backs on entrenched academic traditions and divisions that are over a century in the making. However, this volume demonstrates the willingness of several researchers to initiate paradigm changes in their respective fields. It is hoped that research projects testing explicit behavioral models in the later prehistoric and proto-historic periods will be carried out in Europe in the near future.

A question of identity: defining "Celtic"

The book's title contains three troublesome terms which many readers may question. What precisely is meant by the rubric "Celtic" in the context of this volume? It can be taken to mean a Boston basketball team, or existing groups of modern-day Gaelic speakers, or all Frenchmen, past and present.[1] The adjective "Celtic" has been applied to peoples from Ireland to Czechoslovakia, from the Urnfield period to the present day. It has many different meanings in different contexts, and some will inevitably contradict others. Linguists, social anthropologists, archaeologists, historians, folklorists and sports writers all lay claim to the term, and all use it differently.

The first recorded use of the term "Celts" is usually attributed to Herodotus' description of peoples encountered by Greek traders to the north of Massalia in the fifth century BC. He refers to these peoples as "Keltoi". It is possible that this was a more or less accurate rendering of the term used by the local peoples to refer to themselves, but it is unlikely that the term would have been familiar to contemporary peoples living just slightly further north, much less to groups living in completely different geographic areas in earlier or later times. Celticists assign primarily linguistic significance to the term "Celtic" (Dillon and Chadwick 1972:2–3; Evans 1977:67) and in this sense it is taken to mean those groups of historic peoples known to have spoken Celtic languages. Included in this group are the inhabitants of Ireland, Scotland, Wales, Brittany, Cornwall, and the Isle of Man. This language family affiliation may well indicate a common Celtic identity which transcended local polities at various times. For most archaeologists, however, the term "Celtic" refers to peoples sharing a common material culture and a distinctive art style. Included are those areas of central Europe and the British Isles which share these archaeological characteristics, beginning in the late Hallstatt period and continuing until Roman contact. For some archaeologists the time frame is broader, incorporating the whole span of time between the Neolithic and the early medieval period in Ireland, Wales and Scotland (Burgess 1980: 177; Renfrew 1987: 245; Harding 1990).

The term "Celtic," then, appears to be almost dangerously non-specific when applied indiscriminately to what, to some researchers, are different cultural and socio-political groups (see Collis, this volume). In a sense its

incorporation into so many different disciplines is an extreme example of "lumping," and one which seems inadequate to the task of accurately representing the disparate groups to which it is applied. On the other hand, its pervasiveness requires some explanation other than simple expedience. While it may never be possible to prove conclusively that the prehistoric "Celtic" peoples spoke Celtic languages, certain aspects of material culture, art style, and ideological constructs referred to as "Celtic" by archaeologists, linguists, and historians do reflect a remarkable temporal and spatial continuity.

Definitions: chiefdom/state

Most anthropological research on social evolution has been conducted on non-western societies, and models derived from such studies have then been applied to the reconstruction of European prehistory with varying success (Renfrew 1976; Milisauskas 1978; van de Velde 1979). It seemed both necessary and desirable to present in one volume research which considers how social evolution and political systems might be conceptualized utilizing historic and prehistoric evidence from western Europe. The aim is to bring studies of Celtic civilization into the cross-cultural theoretical mainstream.

The terms "chiefdom" and "state" are almost as problematic as the term "Celtic." Service (1971; 1975) and Sahlins (1958; 1968) are of course the classic sources for definitions of both terms, but the literature on this subject is rife with studies debunking all or parts of the original definitions and assumptions (Webb 1973; Peebles and Kus 1977; Lewis 1978; Sanders and Webster 1978; Carneiro 1981; Feinman and Neitzel 1984; Upham 1987). Though these studies have pointed out many glaring deficiencies in the formulation of a linear social typology, they have not managed to suggest a convincing alternative approach to the study of social evolution.

The static and bounded nature of the developmental stages represented by these types poses difficulties in interpreting and understanding the transitions from one "stage" to the next.[2] Not surprisingly, this is where most attention has been focussed (Sanders and Marino 1970; Sanders 1974; Isaac 1975; Kristiansen 1982; Johnson and Earle 1987). How does a "developed chiefdom" differ from an "early state," and can the two "stages" be distinguished from one another archaeologically? According to Carneiro,

Our task is to draw lines at different points through this continuum to set off significantly different parts of it. Although this is partly arbitrary, it is not entirely so. Only if the lines between stages are drawn at appropriate points will the most salient features between contrasting forms stand out (1981:67).

This passage illustrates the dilemma posed by the use of an evolutionary typology. How are the "appropriate" points at which the "lines of demarcation" are drawn determined? And what distinguishes a "salient" feature from a non-salient one? The procedures by which these divisions are identified and, too often, codified, vary from author to author, and the decision-making process involved is seldom justified or even delineated in detail. Two of the few points on which there is general agreement are that "chiefdoms are poorly defined and understood" (Earle 1978:6), and that "our most pressing need . . . is for a detailed comparative study of chiefdoms from all parts of the world and at all levels of development" (Carneiro 1981:71).

Refining our models of political organization, rather than rejecting out of hand the use of concepts such as segmentary society, chiefdom, or primitive state, is imperative if progress is to be made in unravelling the past history of the world's polities. Some form of typological control is necessary if only to advance critical thinking on these concepts. Organizational constructs defining the elements of social evolution (such as the degree of social complexity) are essential, or cross-cultural comparisons cannot be carried out. When simple foragers are placed on the same level as complex chiefdoms, or a segmentary society is considered to be equivalent to a state, it is impossible to generate interpretations regarding the significance of any cultural practice or social institution.

The models of political systems discussed above are recent creations of American anthropologists, which have been taken up by processualist archaeologists. However in Europe Celtic political systems have been evaluated within a distinctly different scholarly tradition, a tradition that is also represented in this volume (see Büchsenschütz, Fischer). This school of thought is an outgrowth of history and the study of Classical civilization, and arrives at interpretations of the past primarily through the direct historical approach and inductive reasoning. A brief history of archaeological research on the Celts concentrating on the motivations and methodologies of different European theoretical schools follows in the next section.

Perspectives on Celtic political systems: the direct historical approach

The operating assumption of the direct historical approach is that it is possible to trace back the history of a people in a particular area from the present into the past,

moving from the historical sources to the archaeological record without forfeiting continuity or traversing a theoretical threshold in the process. It is an approach favored by many European archaeologists studying the prehistoric Iron Age, and has been applied, for example, by Pauli (1978) in his study of the early Iron Age salt mining community on the Dürrnberg near Hallein in Austria, as well as by various researchers attempting to connect the early medieval period directly with the early Iron Age in southern Germany, with the Classical sources acting as a segue (Fischer 1982; Kimmig 1983a, among others). This approach treats the archaeological record in western Europe like a river of continuous linear development, which can be traced to its source even when it has dried to a trickle and vanishes with the appearance of written records. It is assumed that the trajectory and the people remain the same, and that the gap between history and prehistory can be bridged without requiring a change in the techniques of investigation, or in the analytical approaches applied.

The direct historical approach originated within the context of the intellectual tradition of European archaeology in which a direct link is perceived between the subjects of archaeological inquiry and the researchers themselves. Several citations serve to emphasize this point. Peter Goessler: "Prehistory is an historic discipline, not a natural science . . . and it serves historic goals even if its sources are generally quite different ones" (1950:7). Hans Jürgen Eggers: "There is only one history, and prehistory is part of it in its entirety. These two types of scholarship differ only in their different sources: on the one hand written texts, on the other material culture" (1986:16).

There are several problems with the direct historical approach, but perhaps the most telling is its dependence on the written word as the final authority on the actions and lifeways of people in the past. The archaeological record is rarely allowed to speak for itself, and when it contradicts the written sources, or the reconstructions derived from the written sources, such irregularities are simply explained away as minor detractions from the overall pattern of continuity. In theory, the concept is laudable, for the direct historical approach is in some ways a form of ethnoarchaeology. In practice, however, the direct historical approach denies the archaeological record primary validity, and often overestimates the value and dependability of written sources at the expense of the material record.[3]

The European approach to archaeological interpretation has continued to be primarily inductive. Pauli states this very clearly in the following passage:

I attempted at that time [in 1978] to combine all the facts available up to that point based on preliminary studies of my own rather than on models borrowed from elsewhere. In the interests of clarity, and in order to bring the details and general patterns of such processes into greater relief for myself, I compared the results with relevant examples from other places and time periods wherever possible. For this reason, which simultaneously reflects the course of my own scholarship, "models" or "case studies" are applied to my work only after the archaeological microanalysis has been done. And that is the way it will stay. (1984:49–50)

The emphasis in west central European archaeology since 1945 has been primarily on gathering and cataloguing information, rather than on its interpretation from a social or processual perspective. One approach has been to map different categories of grave goods, creating pan-European distribution patterns which tell us very little about the people and processes which produced them;[4] another has been to analyze regional sequences with a view primarily to establishing chronologies that tell us even less about cultural process.[5] Both approaches have concrete if limited utility, but unfortunately answer few of the questions which most interest us if we are attempting to understand cultural change and the development of social complexity. Those "old school" European researchers who have the most comprehensive grasp of the material are often the least able to see the forest for the trees.

In archaeology, as in most other disciplines, moderation and a willingness to accept alternative perspectives are the key to developing a more integrated theoretical approach, combining elements of both inductive and deductive reasoning (which are generally present to some extent in all theoretical approaches, even when they are not explicitly identified). In order to realize the potential of the sources for the late prehistoric/early historic periods of Europe, an analytical approach must be developed that integrates questions regarding the social and cultural existence of the Celts with the historical and archaeological data. The data are certainly rich and varied enough to support the kinds of investigations that have been carried out on more historically recent peoples of the non-western world, and we see no reason why the Celtic sphere cannot be scrutinized in the same fashion.

The ethnoarchaeology of Celtic peoples: *potential for Celtic ethnology*

At the dawn of written history, speakers of Celtic languages occupied most of present-day Europe. Though the demise of Gaelic culture commenced with the military defeats of the Cisalpine Gauls at the hands of the Romans at the beginning of the second century BC, the last of the independent Gaelic polities in the British Isles did not succumb until the eighteenth century AD. The protracted interactions of the non-literate Gaelic-speaking peoples of western and central Europe with the literate Mediterranean civilizations, and the lengthy persistence of Gaelic polities at the fringes of Europe beyond the reach of Roman and German expansion, have resulted in a temporally and spatially diverse textual record of their cultures.

The Celtic cultures of the Continent figure among the earliest and most durable subjects of the West's original anthropologists, the classical geographers. These include Poseidonius, Strabo, Caesar, Tacitus, Diodorus Siculus and Pliny (see Tierney 1960; Piggott 1968: Ch. 1; Crumley 1974; Champion 1985). Ethnographic accounts of the insular Celts also survive from non-Gaelic writers of the medieval period such as Giraldus Cambrensis (1978a, 1978b, 1982) and Geoffrey of Monmouth (1929). Of significance equal to or greater than this legacy of ethnographic writing is the enormous and diverse body of ethnohistoric writing produced by Irish and Welsh *literati* between the eighth and seventeenth centuries AD. The most prolific and reliable sources on Gaelic social institutions are the Irish and Welsh law texts, produced by a class of native jurists. Next to these in usefulness are the annals and genealogies, which supply much chronological, historical, and social information. And lastly, the mythological cycles, hagiographies, and other literary works inform on ideology, ritual, ethics, and morality of the insular Celts, and give an indication of the significance of roles and institutions such as fosterage, feasting, and chieftainship.

The information contained in the ethnographic and ethnohistoric texts of the Celts, supplemented by over a century of archaeological investigations, is as complete as the sources available for cultural areas more familiar to the modern anthropologist such as Mesoamerica, East Africa, the North American Woodlands, the Pacific Northwest Coast, or Polynesia. The traditional social structures of all of the latter culture areas have been eclipsed in part or in whole by contact with modern state systems, and the cultures themselves were dramatically transformed through their relations with economic and social institutions of European origin. The ethnographic and ethnohistoric records we possess for these cultures exhibit limitations and deficiencies equivalent in magnitude and kind to the deficiencies of the Celtic sources from earlier centuries. The cultures that existed within all of these regions exhibit comparable diversity in social complexity, in social and cultural institutions, and in economic adaptations. These regions are also fundamentally similar in that the observations made on specific cultures, such as the Tlingit, Iroquois, Maori, or Irish were made over an extended period of time, and so reflect much *in situ* cultural change. Clearly then there are no qualitative peculiarities of the data base of the Celtic cultures that preclude either the application of the techniques of ethnology, or the use of these data in cross-cultural comparisons.

One would think that the copious and often dramatic remains of the societies of later prehistoric Europe would offer much incentive for theory building in the area of political systems. However, as the next section indicates, much of the past and current thinking on the structure of the societies of the Late Hallstatt and early La Tène periods of west central Europe is rather murky. An ethnological approach to the situation could offer a firmer basis than the limited strategies discussed above for attempting social reconstructions.

The potential of the archaeological record for Celtic ethnology: studies of late Hallstatt period social organization and political systems

As far back in prehistory as archaeological cultures can be identified with the speakers of Celtic languages, their social units and networks were regional in extent. This is not to claim that the Celtic-speaking groups were the first in Europe to achieve a measure of social complexity. Indeed, regionally integrated sodalities can probably be identified as early as the late Neolithic of northern Europe, if not before (Milisauskas and Kruk 1984; Renfrew 1973).

Researchers in several European countries have proposed the appearance of chiefdoms in northern, western, and eastern Europe in the early Bronze Age (Randsborg 1974; Renfrew 1979; van de Velde 1979; Kristiansen 1982). There is tangible evidence that social complexity increased throughout the Bronze Age in Europe. Ostentatious objects in bronze and gold increase in size, number, and degree of elaboration. What this trend no doubt signifies is the expansion and increasing reliability of trade networks in raw materials, and vertical and horizontal expansion of chiefly aristocracies. As the sphere of influence of these aristocracies increased, they would be better able to mobilize and expend capital on the production of sumptuary crafts.

Greater social complexity is more directly manifested in regional florescences in social integration during the later Bronze Age, as is evidenced by the establishment of substantive settlements in the Lusatian area of Poland, in Switzerland, in the eastern Hallstatt Zone, as well as in northern Italy. This trend culminated in west central Europe in the appearance of highly stratified polities during the period 600–400 BC (Hallstatt C, D; La Tène A). So uniform are the cultural manifestations associated with this late Hallstatt florescence that the region over which they are distributed has come to be called the West Hallstatt Zone.

This late Hallstatt cultural florescence is characterized by large fortified hilltop settlements and lavish burials in tumuli. Imported pottery wine vessels, as well as large and exquisitely crafted vessels of bronze, bear testimony to mercantile and/or political contacts with Italy and Greece. Craft production became more intensive and specialized with some products, such as sheet metal work in gold and bronze, clearly sponsored by the elites for their exclusive consumption. Iron was introduced during this period, and supplanted bronze as the material for tools. Pottery production reached new heights with a profusion of forms being produced at *Fürstensitze* such as the Heuneburg. The greater care invested in late Hallstatt ceramics is evident in the finer wares, which are often finely painted polychrome or delicately stippled vessels. The few pieces of fabric that have been preserved in the tombs also show that intricate, multi-colored designs were woven for the aristocrats.

Some writers who have recently addressed the question of the nature of the Celtic political systems on the European continent have refused to see anything like a state or chiefdom in the archaeological Hallstatt Celtic polities, consigning them instead to the ambiguously defined category of *Stammesorganisation* ("clan" or "tribal organization"; see for instance Bittel 1981b:15; Hingley 1984; Fischer, this volume). In the anthropological literature of the present day, however, the notion of the "tribe" has a heavily circumscribed meaning. When it is used at all, it is generally applied only to those societies such as the Yanomamö which have populations gathered into villages, but which lack segmentary organization and big men. So conceived, it is clear from the information we have on the societies of the late Hallstatt and late La Tène periods that their polities were simply too large and complex to be called "tribal."

If we take issue with the position of the "tribal"

structure of the political systems of the late La Tène period Celts, how should their polities be characterized? An awareness on the part of some researchers that the Hallstatt polities were regionally integrated entities is expressed in synthetic examinations of the site record that have associated the enclosed hilltop settlements, called in German *Fürstensitze* ("princely seats"), or *Adelssitze* ("aristocratic seats"; Kimmig 1969:95), with the large tumuli (*Fürstengräber*). In most cases the geographical focus of these treatments has covered the western Hallstatt area in its entirety (Kimmig 1969, 1983a; Frankenstein and Rowlands 1978; Bintliff 1984b). Wolfgang Kimmig was the first to demonstrate that the *Fürstensitze*, taken together with nearby tumulus cemeteries, constituted the focal points of a number of small polities (1969). However, when seeking to explain the nature of these late Hallstatt polities, Kimmig fell back upon familiar historical systems out of Europe's more recent past.

> This suggestion gives rise to the consideration, whether or not in fact it is possible that behind the above mentioned areas where "aristocrat's graves" are concentrated noble territories emerge in outline. If this is the case, then at least in the region of the northwest Lower Alps during the late Hallstatt period a map is produced which may only be compared with a corresponding map of the small German principalities from the time following the Thirty Years' War. (Kimmig 1969:108)

This "feudal model" of West Hallstatt society is another product of the direct historical approach, though it must be said that it is less a coherent model than a collection of appelations. Kimmig never bothered to elaborate his conjectures in any detail, and later proffered a different set of terms. In his 1983 treatment of the results of the Heuneburg excavations, the most important hilltop sites became *Dynastensitze* (dynastic seats), the capitals of *Dynastengeschlechte* (dynastic lineages). Proceeding from his impressions of differences in site size, the number of associated exotic Mediterranean finds, and the trappings of tombs, Kimmig proposed three gradations of late Hallstatt aristocrats: *Burgherren* or *große Herren* (castle or great lords), *kleine Häuptlinge* (small chieftains) and *Bauernadel* (peasant nobels) (1983a:147). Under the rule of the aristocrats were peasants and clients (p. 151; Pauli 1985:30). These terms communicate Kimmig's conviction that late Hallstatt society was variably stratified across the Western Zone, but little else.

The popularity of the feudal model has resulted in a sort of theoretical stagnation in Iron Age studies (Oeftiger 1984:98). Steuer has criticized this "feudal fixation" as obstructing the interpretation of "real" conditions during the early Iron Age (1979:602). It would certainly be of interest to learn whether the polities of late medieval Germany bear anything beyond a mere formal resemblance to the political systems of the western Hallstatt Zone, but those who advocate this scenario have not attempted a structured comparison.

A few investigations into the social structure of late Hallstatt society have been undertaken that proceed from the prolific burial data (Kossack 1959; Kilian-Dirlmeier 1970; Pauli 1978; Hodson 1977, 1979). The artifact assemblages associated with the burials have been analyzed to determine the sex, age, kin-group affiliation, and social ranking of the dead. These studies are difficult to equate as their premises and objectives are so varied. The burial analyses of Pauli and Kilian-Dirlmeier do, however, point toward the existence of polities of regional extent – polities that can be delineated through the distributions of distinctive patterns of style and form in material culture, as well as by peculiarities of the burial ritual. Variations in the position of a grave within a tumulus, and in the quantity of accompanying grave goods, imply the stratification of the polities of the West Hallstatt Zone into nascent social classes.

More recently Heinrich Härke has undertaken a comprehensive examination of the settlement record of the later Hallstatt periods (1979). Though it was not a stated goal of his study, he attempted to estimate the territorial extent of the Hallstatt polities, and put forward some estimates of the gross configurations of the society that produced the settlement record. Both Kimmig's and Härke's studies are premised upon the implicit assumption that the *Fürstensitze* and their associated tumuli constituted political capitals. Härke eschews the 'feudal' model of Hallstatt society, but stops short of offering an explicit alternative (1979:135–6, 1989:185–94).

In their influential paper, Frankenstein and Rowlands applied dependency models, a combination of Wallerstein's core/periphery model and Ekholm's prestige goods system concept, to the West Hallstatt case (1978). Their arguments are premised upon the existence of a four-tiered hierarchy of chieftains, consisting of a paramount chieftain, "vassal chiefs," "sub-chiefs," and "village chiefs." Paramount chieftains became ascendant in the hierarchy by acquiring exotic items from the south that figured in social transactions. Their increased social stature enabled them to sponsor the production of other prestige goods, such as glass and bronze jewelry, that were distributed to their aristocratic subordinates. This explanation of the origin of the Hallstatt polities has been justly criticized by Bintliff (1984:167), who points out the fact that Mediterranean imports are relatively rare finds on Hallstatt *Fürstensitze* sites, and that the exotic bronze vessels often have the appearance of heirlooms – being consigned to burial only after several generations of use. However, he finds no fault with Frankenstein and Rowlands' model of Hallstatt political structure:

> [I]n this phase the spacing of centres suggests large territories and even "proto-state" structures, to be linked perhaps to the emergence of paramount chiefs or princes from an aristocratic stratum scattered throughout the region. The paramounts associated with the major putative centres and their particularly impressive prestige burials, seem to have dominated numerous district chiefs whose rich tumuli are found at various points around the suggested territory of each princedom. (1984:165)

The reasoning of Frankenstein and Rowlands is fundamentally similar to Kimmig's in that both stress the importance of exchange in wealth items in generating the perceived social structure.

The West Hallstatt polities: chiefdoms or states?

It is clear from the foregoing cursory synopsis of past research and thinking upon the political systems of the West Hallstatt Zone that early Iron Age polities of regional scale can now be recognized in the European archaeological record with certainty, even if their exact dimensions are unknown. The most prominent signature of these earlier, archaeological polities of the Hallstatt period are the sizeable elevated fortified settlements, the *Fürstensitze*. These settlements advertise their likely role as former political capitals by virtue of their size (1–11 ha), their strategic location at the confluence of major waterways, architectural features such as large enclosing earthworks or walls, and the remains of buildings located both within and outside the walls, as well as by the proximity of these sites to groupings of large burial mounds. Sumptuary Mediterranean imports within the central burials of these tumuli can be taken as sure indicators that members of the ruling kin groups were interred within them.

A "political capital" in the sense used above refers to a site or assemblage of sites that function as the integrative focus or foci of a polity. Polities such as chiefdoms and primitive states are integrated by a variety of forces, manifesting themselves both physically and psychologically, implemented through institutions of leadership. The leaders of chiefdoms and states establish the legitimacy of their rule by acting as mediators in a cult of aristocratic ancestors (see Firth 1936), as well as through

attendant notions of sacredness attaching to their person as a result of this role (e.g. *mana* in Polynesia, *neimed* in early medieval Ireland).

Chiefdoms and primitive states are also integrated economically by means of networks consisting of the economic needs, rights, privileges, and obligations that bind aristocrats to craftsmen, freemen, and dependants. Such polities are paradoxically no less integrated through the factions of kinsmen and adherents that cluster around the leading aristocrats. These stand behind and support aristocrats in their bids for power, constitute fighting forces in the pursuance of military goals, and intimidate or physically suppress malcontents and rivals (see Dodgshon, this volume).

All of these elements which serve to integrate polities are given a tangible focus in monuments which concentrate and express them. These monuments may consist of any number of constructions in differing cultural contexts: tombs, memorial markers, temples, or special settlements. Invariably, however, their construction is initiated and sponsored by the leading elements of the society, and so often they communicate and reinforce the legitimacy of this group to lead. A political capital, then, should not be construed as being solely and invariably the *residence* of a ruling kin group, though a royal or chiefly residence may constitute a significant element of the capital. Capitals may consist in part of the cemeteries of aristocrats, religious centers (temples or cathedrals), and craft working centers. These individual elements may be concentrated in one locale or dispersed throughout a territory (see Crumley 1976, and Gibson, Crumley, this volume).

Though no *Fürstensitze* have been completely excavated, the extensive investigation of the Heuneburg in southern Germany has demonstrated that the site was intensively occupied, and contained substantial buildings. The finds from this settlement are evidence for a great range and intensity of craft production. The presence of Mediterranean imports in the form of ceramic vessels from Greece for the drinking ritual and the large exotic vessels of bronze that have been recovered from tumulus burials associated with this and other *Fürstensitze*, as well as other objects and materials such as coral and ivory from the Mediterranean, attest to the substantive contacts that must have existed between the aristocrats of the West Hallstatt Zone and their counterparts in Greece and Etruria.

The large tumuli that occur in the vicinity of the *Fürstensitze* often contain the remains of one or two individuals buried with sumptuary goods in the central chamber.[6] These *Fürstengräber* are tangible evidence of the considerable power that accrued to a narrow class within Hallstatt society, consisting of the ruling elites and their families. These manifestations of personal political power point to the existence of a sharply defined aristocracy (see Fischer 1981b:77–84). Such stark social divisions stand in sharp contrast to the finer gradations in rank which one encounters in simpler chiefdoms, and would seem to indicate that the social landscape of the West Hallstatt Zone was dominated by either complex chiefdoms or primitive states (Bintliff 1984b; van de Velde 1985; Pauli 1985:31).

Primitive states, like those of medieval Europe, of the interlacustrine region of eastern Africa in the precolonial period (e.g. Rwanda, Bunyoro, Baganda, Nkore), and throughout Asia, exhibit a central authority with sweeping personal power.[7] The king's authority is manifested in his ability to appoint local administrators, and to exert his rule through a nascent bureaucracy (Maquet 1961; Johnson and Earle 1987:246). Behind the king's authority stands a permanent body of warriors, giving force to his rule.

In primitive states the aristocracy and commoners are sharply distinguished; ties of kinship between the aristocracy and commoners, fictive or otherwise, no longer exist. The king and his family take on a life that is both spatially and socially segregated from the populace. They are distinguished by great affluence, through their possession of sumptuary and ritualistic paraphernalia restricted to their rank and office, and by adherence to a distinct behavioral code. The comportment of the king is meant to communicate his rank and the sacredness of his person. This latter quality is promulgated through rituals that are meant to maintain the state through his special relationship with the supernatural. Many of these aspects of kingship are perceptible in the archaeological record of the West Hallstatt Zone.

Sumptuary restrictions, involving both food and drink, seem to have been one of the distinguishing features of West Hallstatt elites. Analyses of the skeletal remains recovered from the West Hallstatt zone indicate that both male and female elites were often of above average height (Arnold 1991a), indicating possible dietary differences. The aristocratic burials are distinguished by the presence of feasting equipment such as cauldrons and drinking horns. These demonstrate the position of these leaders at the apex of the pyramid of social and ritual exchanges (see Dietler, this volume).

Evidence of the sacerdotal character of leadership in the Hallstatt period is circumstantial but strong nevertheless, consisting as it does of the lavish treatment afforded the chiefly dead. In addition to the inclusion of equipment appropriate to feasting and drinking rituals found in the tombs of leaders, four-wheeled wagons were also frequently interred, and it is certain that these possessed an important ritual function attendant to their association with kingship.[8] Anthropomorphic statues were erected on the tops of some tumuli in southern Germany. The famous ithyphallic statue on top of the Hirshlanden tumulus wears a torc and conical hat, objects found in the Hochdorf central burial which may have been symbols of kingship. Torcs are found on depictions of gods, such as the representation of Cernunnos on the Gundestrup cauldron.[9] Kurt Bittel (1981c:93–5) and Kimmig (1983a) have also noted that several Hallstatt tumulus cemeteries (Heiligkreuztal, Obermachtal, Hohmichele) have adjacent *Viereckschanzen* (Bittel 1981c:93–5, Kimmig 1983a:219). *Viereckschanzen* are now understood to be enclosures where religious rituals were conducted, identified with the *temenos* of the historical sources. Those that have been excavated date to La Tène times, but Bittel and Kimmig argue that they must have Hallstatt precursors, and Bittel suggests their connection to a cult of the ancestors (1981c:93–5).[10]

At this juncture it is difficult to identify the residences of leaders on the nucleated settlements, though a case can be made for the larger, enclosed house at the Goldberg, located not far from the Ipf *Fürstensitz*, and the large house in the Heuneburg outer settlement (Audouze and Büchsenschütz 1992:214–17; Arnold, this volume). The preservation of this house *underneath* a tumulus within a tumulus cemetery could be taken as evidence of ancestor worship, as a house of a dead king could have become sanctified space. Thus it would seem that the late Hallstatt leaders segregated and elevated themselves and their families from the populace spatially, socially, and ritually. If all of these indications cannot be taken to prove the attainment of the socio-cultural level of the primitive state by polities of the Western Zone by late Hallstatt times, the possibility must at least be admitted.

Prospects

From an ethnological perspective, the artifacts, ecofacts, and settlements of complex societies are viewed as pathways to understanding the structure and behavior of the societies, social groups, and individuals that produced them. The ethnological perspective in archaeology encompasses the *region* as the primary unit of investigation, as the cultural systems and processes that we wish to understand were regional in extent. Archaeologists can only ignore the region at their peril, as social integration is a significant causal factor in the production of material culture. Behind the adoption of a regional framework for the study of Celtic societies lies the tacit assumption that important behaviors and stimuli which had an impact at the level of the community or family originated at the supralocal level. To accept this statement of fact is to abandon the concept of local self-sufficiency. If one embraces this position, then it is necessarily incumbent upon the researcher to consider the potential impact of supralocal influences – whether they be social, economic, or ideological – when explaining phenomena at the individual, household, or community levels.

The regional approach is not directed to prove the existence of regionally integrated groups among the Celts, but to gain an understanding of their structure and constitution, and of the nature of the relationships that existed between them. Moreover, though the Celts were of the same broad linguistic stock and possessed many cultural institutions in common, they were distributed over a vast area with widely ranging geographical and ecological properties. Both the archaeological and the historical evidence suggests that the variation in social complexity and structure among the hundreds of polities in contemporary existence across Europe at any time during the Hallstatt–La Tène periods was considerable. An important application of the regional approach should be to further the examination of inter-group variation in social structure and complexity in Celtic Europe (Murray 1994).

The challenge then is to approach the recovery of archaeological data in a manner that addresses issues such as the course of social development, variation in the social constitution of groups across Europe and across time, the configuration of economic systems, the division of labor, the operation of ideological systems, and the transmission of ideas. We argue that research programs and strategies must be designed at the outset to identify and recover the data relevant to these issues in a systematic fashion. The initiation of archaeological research projects configured to the discovery of social behavior at the regional level of integration should steer archaeologists away from the detailed, particularistic perspective which tends to overemphasize minutiae at the expense of general patterns. Likewise the regional approach should supersede the panglossian surveys of artifact or feature types that, by default, contribute to the false impression of an artificially uniform social landscape. A regional approach could lead to the creation of novel methodologies for the resolution of problems in the areas of human behavior and social evolution.

The papers collected here do not represent the first steps taken upon the path toward a realization of an ethnological approach to the study of the Celts. Rather, this volume brings together several conflicting approaches and agendas for the interpretation of the remains of "Celtic" societies across Europe. The impetus for assembling this varied collection of works was to initiate a dialogue between otherwise isolated national schools, as well as between segregated disciplines. The operating assumptions of each paper are explicitly defined, and in a few instances contrast with other approaches. If scholars in different countries, working with different data sets, can be made aware of the work of others, and if a dialogue is established between them as a result, we will have gone no small distance toward a more unified approach.

Notes

1 Carole Crumley has discussed the Celtic character of French nationalism, and the use of topographic features and archaeological sites associated with the Celtic past of France for political purposes. François Mitterand's delivery of a major policy speech on the summit of the Aeduan stronghold of Bibracte in 1985 (Marquardt and Crumley 1987) is a case in point. "The French were not all Gaullists, but they are all Gallic, insofar as Celtic values define the French nation-state" (Crumley 1988: 8).

2 Tolstoy addresses this problem briefly in his review of Jones and Kautz's 1981 volume *The Transition to Statehood in the New World* when he refers to recent applications of non-linear differential equations, describing the phenomenon known as "chaos," to the study of social evolution (1989:72, 78).

3 These pitfalls in the use of historical analogy were pointed out some time ago by Binford (1967).

4 This ultimately positivist and particularist approach has been described by Herbert Jankuhn as "stamp collecting" (Härke 1989:407).

5 Many regional chronologies have been produced over the past few decades, as the following references illustrate: Zürn 1952; Uenze 1964; Joachim 1968; Haffner 1965; Schaaf 1969; Sangmeister 1969; Kilian-Dirlmeier 1970; Liebschwager 1972; Parzinger 1986, among others.

6 Not all late Hallstatt era tumuli are associated with *Fürstensitze*, and not all *Fürstensitze* have tumulus cemeteries. The Magdalenenberg and the Hochdorf tumuli stand either alone or near open settlements, while the Ipf *Fürstensitz* lacks an associated cemetery.

7 It is ironic that given our familiarity with state structure, the literature on the organization of simple states in anthropology is scanty. Here we have utilized the term "primitive state," which we have borrowed from

Service (1975), in preference to the terms "formative state" (Steward 1979:186), "early state" (Claessen and Skalník 1978b), and "archaic state" (Johnson and Earle 1987). These latter two terms seem to refer to a heterogeneous group of structures which are only linked by the factor of historical antiquity. The term "primitive state" does not connote the antiquity of the polity under question, but refers instead to the degree of organizational complexity of the unit.

8 From the European Bronze Age we have models of four wheeled wagons bearing sun discs, and from the late Hallstatt period from Strettweg, Austria, there is the famous bronze four-wheeled wagon bearing the likeness of a goddess presiding over a stag hunt. Kossack (1959) was the first to recognize that the Hallstatt four-wheeled wagon was an object that signified high social rank.

9 Similar statues occur throughout western and central Europe during the Iron Age (Bittel et al. 1981:121, 164).

10 In a recent paper, Matthew Murray (n.d.) has evaluated these monuments and argues for their significance as places for holding feasts connected with funerary rites. As such, *Viereckschanzen* would have seen only intermittent use.

PART I

Celtic political systems: research paradigms

2
From chiefdom to state organization in Celtic Europe

PATRICE BRUN
Translation: Sinéad Ni Ghabhláin

Introduction

State-level organization emerged in the Celtic world during the second and first centuries BC as the end result of an evolutionary process of increasing social complexity. This process, whereby the state replaced already distinctly stratified social formations resembling chiefdoms, seems to conform to typologies elaborated by neo-evolutionist anthropologists (Fried 1960; Service 1971, 1975). This model is however too sketchy. Historical records of the Iron Age suggest that the mechanical and irreversible character of this model should not be overemphasized. Chiefdoms are revealed as quite diverse and, above all, fragile. They form in one place, only to disintegrate a little later and then reappear elsewhere.

My aim is to propose a formal model concluding that the emergence of Celtic states represents a significant qualitative change. Evolutionary theory suggests that external factors can have effects on the social dynamic only if internal factors (technical innovations and intensification of production) are locally present. We may succeed in detecting the necessary conditions, but not the extent of those conditions; the choices between the various possible solutions go beyond organizational difficulties and remain impenetrable. We can suppose that researchers engaged in an information processing capacity and in the study of chaotic systems are confronted with the same kind of phenomena, and will soon allow us to surmount this difficulty.

The identity of the Celts

The historical sources identify as Celts the bearers of the archaeological culture called La Tène. The human groups called Celts, who invaded the north of Italy in the fourth century BC, carried the same equipment as those who lived in the North-Alpine zone (Fig. 1.1). The same observation can be made of the groups who came to cohabit with the Ligurians and who occupied the coasts of Languedoc in the south of France in the second century BC. The term "Celt" designates with certainty the La Tène cultural complex from 400 BC on. At first the terms Celt and Gaul are used interchangeably in the texts, then later, the term Gaul tends to designate a sub-group of the Celtic entity. The bearers of the La Tène culture are clearly Celts. This culture covers the same geographical area as the Hallstatt culture which preceded it. In addition, nothing in the assemblage of the La Tène culture indicates an immigrant population. It has been generally accepted for a number of years that the bearers of the Hallstatt culture were the antecedents of those of the La Tène culture. These two terms are, unfortunately, ambiguous. Therefore, it is necessary to reserve their use to qualify simple chronological periods. The cultural homogeneity of the North-Alpine zone, the seat of the culture identifiable as Celtic, goes back, in fact, to the first half of the second millennium. Following Clarke, I have called this assemblage the "North-Alpine Complex" (Brun 1988a, 1988b). The following traditional stages are involved: the Tumulus culture of the Middle Bronze Age, the Urnfield culture, the Hallstatt and the La Tène cultures. The geographical extent of this entity expands and contracts over time but retains the same initial area of influence.

Chiefdoms, or socially stratified formations

The Bronze Age – age of ambiguity

The principal characteristics of the Bronze Age appear during the middle of the third millennium BC. The Beaker phenomenon is the vector, or one of the expressions, of quite important changes. These include the generalized use of copper across the Continent and the practice of constructing a circular tumulus for an individual burial, sometimes accompanied by a rich assemblage in copper, gold, and amber. Social change is manifested, above all, by the individualization of political power. No longer is it segments of society, such as lineages, that are demonstrating their status through funerary monuments, but rather individuals and their immediate relations. From the beginning of the Bronze Age, certain children's tombs are furnished with symbols of high social status. Status is therefore probably transmitted through heredity. The dominant social stratum also seems to have preferential access to copper objects.

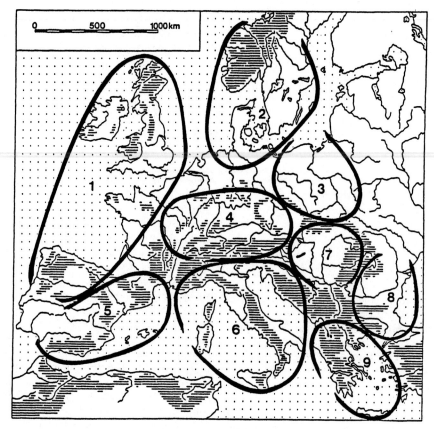

2.1 European cultural complexes. 1. Atlantic Complex, 2. Nordic Complex, 3. Lusatian Complex, 4. North-Alpine Complex, 5. Iberian Complex, 6. Italian Complex, 7. Carpathian Complex, 8. South-oriental Complex, 9. Grecian Complex.

The available historical sources, the spatial distribution of social groups, and their anthropological correlates suggest that they were, for the most part, integrated at an intermediary scale between the local (the site and its immediate catchment area) and the regional levels. Each autonomous political community consisted of around a hundred people on average, distributed in five to eight small settlements. Hereditary transmission of leadership roles is the principal argument for classifying these forms of social organization as chiefdoms. The other argument – socio-economic centralization, which implies the redistributive role of the chief (Renfrew 1973) – remains difficult to use outside of Wessex as the scale of integration is generally barely above the local level.

This is important because, in effect, it signifies the first stage in the emergence of political organization operating beyond the descent system. If kinship organization offers lineage societies the opportunity of agglomeration, for example in the case of war, this aggregation would dissolve once its goal had been attained. This principle based on kinship must be contrasted with the more durable principle of integration based on territory, or co-residence (Sherrat 1984). The Wessex communities seem to have succeeded in organizing polities 1000 km² in extent on this territorial principle (Renfrew 1973). Evidence of similar polities is very rare in Europe during the same period. The large territories which characterized the Wessex chiefdoms (Renfrew 1973) were not any more durable than chiefdoms documented in other contexts. This level of integration remained markedly intermittent during the Bronze Age.

The available data, then, do not conform to the classical model of centralized territories. The data do support the centralization of power but only at a restricted scale and in three forms (Brun and Pion 1992): 1. A cluster of dispersed farms gravitate around a monument, a sort of tomb-sanctuary, which symbolizes the unity of the territorial community. This community is ruled by a chief who occupies one of the farms. 2. A cluster of farmsteads polarized by a village, near which is found the territorial sanctuary. These clusters should be composed of more numerous agricultural units than the preceding case (paradoxically the disparity of wealth is less evident). 3. Identical in organization to #2, but the central role of the village is held by a fortification. It appears that this type of settlement owes its existence to the control it exerted over long-distance exchange, especially over exchange in metal. This was a phenomenon of marginal zones where exchange between cultural complexes could take place outside the constraints of community laws.

Each politically autonomous territory measured from 7 to 15 km in diameter during the whole period, except during periods of temporary expansion. Variation in territorial extent could be conditioned by other factors, of course – geomorphological, pedological, and topographic. All things considered, social stratification did not succeed in stabilizing Bronze Age polities. The polities existed, but remained unstable. Thus, the mode of organization of Bronze Age societies retained many of the characteristics of the late Neolithic period.

Stabilization of political territories
During the Hallstatt B2/3–C periods (900–600 BC), the settlement pattern changes markedly. There is a great increase in the number of fortified sites. Small cemeteries of tumuli appear, often close to the fortifications. Typologies of ceramic and metal objects indicate the fragmentation of previous cultural units. Bronze hoards become more numerous – they are larger and their composition is more varied. Iron working becomes widespread. Rare earlier, iron objects increase rapidly in number during the ninth and eighth centuries BC. The phenomena noted above seem to imply social reorganization on a centripetal principle. A small fortification, the seat of the local aristocracy, polarizes each politically autonomous territory. The neighboring group of tumuli corresponds to a cemetery for the local aristocratic dynasty.

During the same period, products from central Italy are beginning to be found north of the Alps. Most of the products of this region, a region undergoing urbanization, had traveled through the eastern group of cultures of the North-Alpine Complex. Baltic amber took the same routes in the other direction. The opulence of the eponymous cemetery of Hallstatt during the eighth and seventh centuries BC is explained not only by the exploitation of the salt deposits at the site, but also by its location near the most important east Alpine passes. It is in Bavaria, Franconia, and Bohemia that a dense concentration of tombs which produced horse trappings has been found (Kossack 1954). Chariot burials are especially numerous there during this period (Kimmig and Rest 1959; Piggott 1983).

Hallstatt is not unique in its intensive exploitation of salt. The majority of rock salt beds began production during this period. The marshes of the Seille in Lorraine are a good example. Excavation has revealed that certain artificial islands composed of the residues of salt domes belonging to this period were up to 15 m deep. The volume has been estimated at 3 million cubic meters. This implies specialized mining communities. The same characterization also applies to certain copper mines in upper Austria. There are also indications of economic specialization in animal herding. In Switzerland, lakeside stations practiced animal herding dominated by cattle rearing, while others specialized in sheep rearing. At Choisy-au-Bac in the Paris basin, the proportion of pigs in the faunal assemblage reached 60 percent with females predominating – an indication of particularly intensive specialized breeding (Meniel 1984).

Economic specialization increased not only at the inter-community level, but also within each community. The forge took its place beside the bronze workshop. Iron working requires the availability, knowledge, and expertise of full-time specialists. The presence of another kind of specialized craftsman – the carpenter-wheelwright – is evident in the ceremonial chariots. These craftsmen must have collaborated closely with the ironsmiths. It is during the same period that sophisticated looms first appeared. These allowed the execution of twilled weaving, a more sophisticated weaving technique which employs chevron and lozenge motifs of varied colors and of great delicacy; in short, they made possible the production of luxury cloths and tapestries. The existence of other craft specialists is implied by these great vertical looms. It should be emphasized that these craftsmen depended on the aristocracy, as the principal, if not only, consumers of their products. We must wait until the sixth century BC to see iron play a significant role in tool kits; up until then, it was used primarily for the production of weapons.

During Hallstatt D times (600–450 BC), contact with the Graeco-Etruscan world was instrumental in bringing about important changes in the social organization of west central Europe. During the two preceding centuries a north–south axis of exchange gradually superseded all other axes. This involved, principally, the eastern part of the North-Alpine Complex. During the sixth century BC, the demands of the Mediterranean cities were increasingly felt in central Europe – but henceforth, in the western part, in association with the foundation of the Greek settlement of Massalia. The chiefs that were located directly on the principal communication routes obtained more Mediterranean diplomatic gifts. In the framework of a prestige economy, they gained in power, reinforcing their control of exchange with the Mediterranean civilizations, monopolizing redistribution, and finally subjugating neighboring chiefs. In this manner, centralized political units of a scale previously unknown in Europe were formed.

These princedoms disintegrated in the fifth century BC, whereas the intermediary role seems to have been transfered to the Tessin community on the one hand, and to the communities situated at the north-western periphery of the area held by the princedoms on the other – the Hunsrück-Eifel, Aisne-Marne, and Berry regions. This competition destabilized the "princes," whose power remained very fragile because it depended totally on their contacts with the exterior. The zones in which diplomatic gifts were henceforth concentrated offer a contrasting image. They manifest structural analogies with the princedoms; with the exception of the region of Bourges (Fig. 1.2), these cultural groups do not seem to be as centralized. Perhaps a political crystallization of the princedom type would have been produced if they had had more time to develop, as will be discussed later in this chapter. In the Hunsrück-Eifel, Aisne-Marne, and Berry regions, the density of habitation sites and cemeteries reached an unprecedented level during this period (Demoule 1989). The same conclusion is reached by a study of the settlement pattern in Bohemia (Waldhauser 1981b).

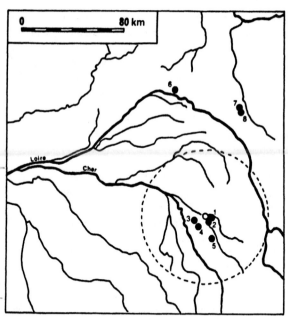

2.2 Distribution of sites containing Greek-Etruscan imports of the second half of the fifth century BC in central France. Empty circle: habitation sites of Bourges (fortified?). Full circles: tombs, 1. Bourges "les Fonds Gaydons," 2. Bourges "la Route de Dun," 3. Morthomiers, 4. Le Subdray, 5. Prunay, 6. Mardié, 7. and 8. Sainte-Geneviève-des-Bois "la Ronce." Large circle: circle of 100 km in diameter corresponding to the average size of principalities belonging to the preceding period.

Celtic expansion

From the beginning of the fourth century, numerous Celtic groups, organized under the authority of aristocratic chiefs, were established in northern Italy. The first, the Senones, probably came from Champagne. Another large contingent, the Boii, arrived later from Bohemia. This movement affected the whole of the Celtic world. Direct sustained contact with Latin and Etruscan civilization led Celtic groups to adapt by adopting not only a new mode of artistic expression, the famous Celtic art style of the La Tène period, but also, apparently quite rapidly, an urban-type territorial organization (Peyre 1979). This evolution toward increasing organizational complexity is observed not only in Italy but also in the south of France. Small fortified cities became common in the fourth and third centuries BC. It does not appear, however, that the Celtic expansion in southern France was massive. Infiltrations here must have produced progressive Celticization without affecting the continued process of increasing social complexity, supported by the presence of Marseilles. Celtic expansion also took place toward the west and the east.

However, these disturbances led to the disintegration of the traditional exchange networks. In effect, prestigious Mediterranean objects only rarely reached central Europe.[1] Rich tombs became rare, and population density fell noticeably. This regression should not be exaggerated, however. Only the highest level of social integration disappeared. Local-level communities probably rediscovered their political autonomy but their internal organization remained stratified. Differences in social rank persisted, as is indicated by the variation in wealth found in tombs. The social range represented by this variation was simply more limited.

The density of cemeteries remained high, one every 4 km on average, but these were small, containing the remains of two or three aristocratic families at the most. The Duchcov votive deposit (Czechoslovakia) shows the development of craft production on a large scale for certain goods, such as ornaments (Kruta *et al.* 1978). Intra-Celtic stylistic homogeneity remained very strong, demonstrating the continuing intensity of exchanges throughout the cultural complex. With the occupation of northern Italy, the south–north exchanges also had a tendency to take an intra-Celtic form.

It appears that Celtic expansion attained its maximum extent in the third century BC. While it is certain that these movements of Celtic people took place, it is unlikely that they were as massive elsewhere as they were in northern Italy. Regions such as Armorica and England, for example, retained a strong individuality and it is difficult to discern the influence of immigration and acculturation there.

Celtic states

Territorial reconstruction

Celtic expansion ended in the second half of the third century BC during the La Tène C1 phase. This is when some additional new elements appeared alongside older characteristics. The three most visible new elements are the adoption of coinage, the reappearance of the rite of cremation, and the creation of new sanctuaries. All three were still only in an incipient phase. Coinage, which remained rare and retained its intrinsic metallic value, did not circulate in a manner any different from the other prestige goods. The gradual nature of the transformation of the funerary rite suggests that the new elements should be explained in some manner other than by recourse to rapid and large-scale population movements. The new communal sanctuaries could signify the need of these sodalities to define their territorial boundaries more clearly and, by association, to strengthen community identity.

This transformation is associated with the La Tène C2 period, which began around 180/170 BC. Money came into general use as currency for the first time – its value a convention guaranteed by the issuing authority. Cremation was practiced almost without exception. The settlement pattern changed. Large boroughs that were centers of craftwork and marketing activity were established. Some of these boroughs erected enclosing ramparts – e.g. those at the site of Amboise (Büchsenschütz 1984) in

France. This recently excavated town seems to invalidate the supposed earlier development of the *oppidum* in the eastern Celtic area, with the sites of Stradonice and Pohanska cited as especially early examples. These hill-forts, however, remained very few. In the present state of knowledge, unenclosed settlement agglomerations of tens of hectares were more numerous in the east as well as in the west – e.g. Mistrin, Střelice, Vienne, Bad Nauheim, Breisach-Hochstetten, Sissach, Basel-Gasfabrik, Feurs, Levroux-les-Arènes (Collis 1984a). Several of these boroughs have produced evidence of coin production. All have yielded evidence of very specialized craft production in gold, bronze, iron, glass, bone, or pottery. Significant quantities of Roman amphorae are often found in them. On the whole, these sites possess most of the features that have been found in more recent *oppida* sites, with the exception of fortifications.

In the course of La Tène D1, some of these larger settlements were surrounded by ramparts. Occasionally these fortifications enclosed an area which exceeded the boundaries of the residential part of the site – i.e. Manching, Berne-Engehalbinsel, and Besançon. In most cases, however, the populations were moved to a nearby fortified prominence. Three examples are now well known – at Breisach, where settlement shifted from Hochstetten to the Münsterberg; at Basel, where the inhabitants moved from the Gasfabrik to the Münsterhügel, and at Levroux, where the Arènes was abandoned in favor of the Colline des Tours. Otherwise, as J. Collis (1984a) has stressed, the majority of *oppida* are new towns, founded *in extenso* on sites devoid of pre-existing fortification. We must, then, assume a transfer of people and functions.

This process appears to have been gradual in spite of the fact that it seems to represent only a shift in topographical preference for settlement location (Fig. 1.3). Large agglomerations were formed little by little by centralizing craft production and commercial functions. Those sites which produced their own money were also centers of a political power capable of ensuring its value. Some settlements had been fortified by the beginning of La Tène C2. Their ramparts already enclosed large areas on prominences – 80 ha at Stradonice and 50 ha at Amboise. Their internal organization is not well understood, which makes their interpretation difficult.

A more numerous class of settlement was the unenclosed lowland borough. These evolved in two ways; either the original town was eventually fortified, or the settlement was moved to a nearby fortified prominence. This phenomenon was particularly prevalent during La Tène D1 and at the beginning of La Tène D2, that is, during the first third of the first century B.C.[2]

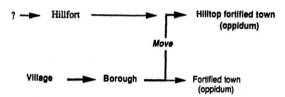

2.3 The development of fortified Celtic towns (oppida).
Bold arrows show most frequent direction of evolution.

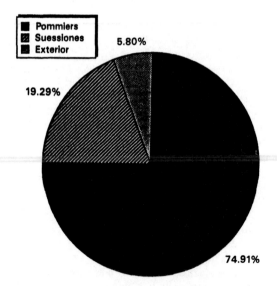

2.4 Relative proportion of coins bearing CRICIRV found
in the central site of Pommiers (principal oppidum of the
Suessiones) and the remainder of the Suessiones territory
(boundaries of the medieval diocese) to those found
outside this territory.

Were these fortifications a response to an insecure climate? It is possible that military conflicts took place between groups undergoing political restructuring, and opening up to Mediterranean trade. The negligible military value of certain ramparts should be noted, however, particularly the most extensive examples which were also the most costly. It is more likely that these were an ostentatious manifestation of power and a symbol of territorial control, a symbol reinforced by a dominating topographical location. The rampart was thus the principal public monument. Its length was a function of the power of the state, proportionate to the surface area of the polarized territory extra muros.

The internal organization of these sites challenges the idea of a gradual process of centralization. The density of structures was actually very low. All oppida are characterized by household units composed of individual houses plus ancillary structures (granary, cellar, pit) centered around a palisaded courtyard. This household cluster evokes, in reduced form, contemporary farms. Thus, the traditional architectural organization was still the structural basis of the later settlements. To this were added open spaces, situated inside the fortification. These could serve as pasturage or for agriculture, which would decrease even more the contrast between rural and urban space.

The oppida of temperate Europe can, however, qualify as towns. We are certain that several of the largest had inhabited areas of 20 to 40 ha, which even with a low settlement density implies a large permanent population. Various service activities were concentrated there and coinage was being produced. The oppidum was, thus, the seat of political and economic power. It tended to be situated in the center of the territory it controlled. This structural link between the urban and rural populace is manifested by the correlation between the surface area of the central site and that of its territory. This relationship is explicitly indicated by Caesar. It is testable archaeologically by the distribution of coin types produced by the center (Figs. 1.4 and 1.5).

Reinforcement of social stratification

During the last two centuries BC, in spite of a limited amount of recoverable data, an uneven distribution of wealth is apparent among the known tombs within several culture areas – particularly in Belgian Gaul from Normandy to the middle Rhine. There, on the north-western periphery of the Celtic world, we know of thirty or so tombs containing parts of wagons, which were exposed, like the deceased, to the flames of the funeral pyre. Some Roman vessels have been recovered from these rich tombs as well. Concentrations of luxurious tombs around oppida are conspicuous (Fig. 1.6). They resemble the configurations of "princely" tombs and settlements from the end of the early Iron Age. The evident hierarchy of fortified sites also expresses marked social stratification.

The archaeological evidence does not contradict the literary sources. These distinguish three social categories: aristocratic warriors, from whose ranks were recruited the sovereigns or supreme magistrates; the druids, some of whom we know were aristocrats; and all the others – the majority of the population. The written sources also suggest that, at least for royalty, social status was inherited through the male line. For the highest social categories, filiation was patrilineal and residence patrilocal, as is suggested by examples of inter-tribal marriages where the

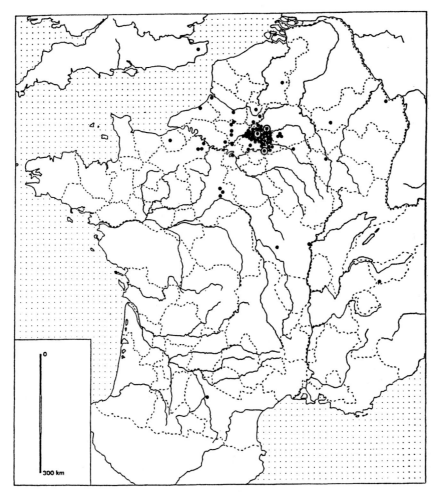

2.5 Distribution of coins bearing inscription CRICIRV on a map of politically autonomous Celtic territories to the extent that they can be reconstructed from the boundaries of medieval dioceses. Dotted circles: coin hoards.

spouse goes to live with the husband (Caesar, *De Bello Gallico [BG]* i. 18,7) (Lewuillon 1990). At the other extreme of the social scale we can assume the existence of a slave category, in spite of the silence of the ancient sources on this subject (*BG* vi. 19,4). We are uninformed as to their numeric importance and their function. In addition, we do not know if the servile class consisted only of domestic slaves, or if it constituted the base of the workforce as it did with the Romans.

Social differentiation was not only vertical. Economic specialization was strongly accentuated, particularly in the towns. Many more individuals practiced craft production and trade full time. But of course, the vast majority remained peasants who produced the necessary surplus to supply the town-dwellers.

The Celtic territories of the first century BC: chiefdoms or states?

At this stage in the description of an evolutionary process, we must ask if the politically autonomous entities which appeared in the final two centuries BC were still at the level of some type of chiefdom, or whether they constituted the first states of temperate Europe. This question brings us back to a more general theoretical problem: does

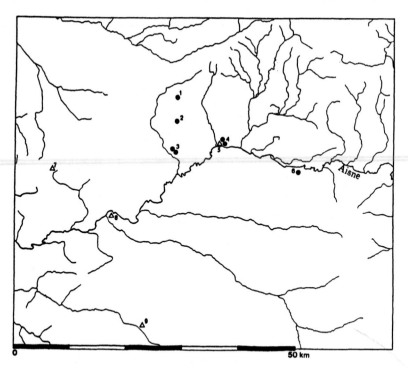

2.6 *Concentration of tombs with imports of La Tène D (circles) around the* oppidum *of Château-Porcien "Le Nandin." 1. Hannogne "le Grand Chemin," 2. Banogne, 3. Saint-Germainmont "le Poteau," 4. Château Porcien "la Briqueterie," 5. Château-Porcien "le Nandin," 6. Thugny-Trugny* oppida *(triangles): 7. Saint-Thomas, 8. Condé-sur-Suippe, 9. Reims.*

the emergence of the state represent only quantitative change, or a real mutation, a qualitative change taking place during the formation of chiefdoms, as proposed by Carneiro (1970)? Our case study suggests that, at least in the Celtic world, state formation represented real qualitative change by comparison with the chiefdom-level entities which preceded this transformation.

The use of coinage as currency implies a political organization which controls the monetary pool in circulation, controls exchange at the borders, and controls the authenticity of legal tender. Without doubt, this constitutes the most decisive argument in favor of calling these political entities states. Another category of evidence proves to be of great importance in this regard – the written records (Goudineau 1989). Around 200 BC a series of Celtic language inscriptions transcribed in the Greek alphabet appear in the south of France. During the first century these records, not surprisingly, follow the Rhône corridor up as far as Bourgogne (Fig. 1.7). So far around 400 inscriptions of more than one letter are attested to. Most are graffiti on pottery. They remind one

of the Helvetian ceramic tablets enumerating the emigrants stopped by Roman troops in Burgundy (*BG* i. 29). According to Caesar, writing was not used for religious purposes although it was reserved for druids; it was used primarily to draw up accounts as well as public and private records. We can thus conceive of a higher administrative entity that managed treaties and contracts and was made up of individuals with religious legitimacy. Such a recording system in conjunction with the use of monetary currency suggests the existence of an influential social group endowed with administrative powers and capable of guaranteeing economic and legal transactions.

Consequently, what we observe in the evolution of the Celtic world is not only an increase in the degree of centralization, of vertical and horizontal differentiation, but, above all, the appearance of a specialized governmental institution, a bureaucracy, in which the principal public powers – judicial, military, and religious – tended to concentrate. A parallel development is the establishment of a monetary economy, an economy based on a unit of value which had to be accepted in exchange for any

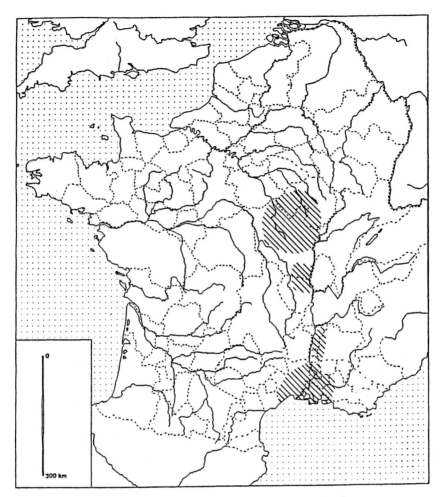

2.7 Distribution of Gallo-Greek inscriptions in Gaul.

commodity; a value system that allowed and facilitated differential consumption. Thus, a qualitative change was achieved. Political and economic organization became changed in character; Celtic society acquired the fundamental criteria of what we call the state.

The principles of evolution

Internal factors
The archaeological record of the Bronze Age, in particular the social correlates of settlement patterns, suggests that for over a millennium the social hierarchy remained founded on long-distance trade and not on the control of land. Chiefs probably exercised control over the

apportionment of land through their role as arbitrators of conflicts such as intra-community border disputes. They did not, however, control the primary products of the land and its surplus, quite simply because these only travelled short distances. For most local chiefs, secondary products with a higher exchange value were exotic – their control of these could only be weak and partial. Thus, they remained deprived of the economic base necessary for the permanent expansion of their territorial power (Harding 1984).

It is apparent that Bronze Age communities displayed expansionist tendencies (Rowlands 1980) involving a significant demographic increase, the cultivation of previously uncultivated lands, and an increasing density of occupation. For reasons difficult to understand, the

North-Alpine Complex spread more than others at the expense of neighboring complexes. Migration of settlers is one possibility. This expansion seems to have come to a halt at the dawn of the last millennium BC. There are several lines of evidence that suggest this. These can be interpreted as the result of a social and economic crisis – of an internal contradiction between a fast-growing population and stagnating modes of production – a situation which generated increasing conflicts.

The profound changes which appeared with the Hallstatt B3/C periods can be interpreted as the solution adopted to resolve the crisis, whereby autonomous communities would be stabilized and consolidated. The new strategy can be deduced from the increase in fortified centers, the development of an iron metallurgy that was less dependent on trade than tin-bronze metallurgy, the economic specialization of certain sites in the exploitation of salt or pig farming, and the adoption of innovative techniques in textile production such as the weaving loom with four warp bars, permitting the fabrication of luxury clothing and tapestries. In other words, communities were endowed with new secondary products produced from raw materials which were more widely distributed. Social stratification could be crystallized, given that the local economic base, which was controllable by the chiefs, was henceforth potentially present everywhere.

Once the necessary local base was in place, contact with the Mediterranean stimulated a considerable enlargement of both the scale and the level of integration, leading to the emergence of the principalities of the West Hallstatt Zone. However, as during the Bronze Age, this dependence on exterior influences left entities of a certain size in a very fragile position. It was not, however, an interruption in the provision of prestige goods which caused the disintegration of these principalities, since Etruscan goods continued to pass beyond the Alps during the whole of the fifth century BC. There is another possible external cause for the collapse of the late Hallstatt polities which will be proposed in the following section.

The ostentatious manifestation of power was eventually transmitted to the north-western periphery of the former principalities of the West Hallstatt Zone. It does not appear that a comparable degree of stratification had the time to develop there. Internal tensions, described by the ancient texts and compatible with the archaeological record, were caused by overpopulation and social conflict. These tensions were not resolved by an increase in social complexity, but rather by the emigration of excess population. This horizontal movement of people resulted in a decentralization of the stratification process during the fourth and third centuries BC. On a scale of social

integration, the early La Tène polities barely surpassed the local level – a situation equivalent to that which existed during Hallstatt B3/C, between 900 and 600 BC.

During the second century BC, local factors made possible the emergence of state formations. Archaeology has produced evidence of significant change in agricultural practices. This phenomenon has not yet been the object of the research it deserves, but it is certain that many tools and agricultural techniques appeared during this period. Agriculture during the second century BC involved methods which, for the first time, permitted production on a scale sufficient to support a relatively large non-agricultural population concentrated in large settlement agglomerations. It seems that in temperate Europe more complex methods of agriculture were necessary in order to produce this surplus than those that have come to light in either the irrigated regions of the Middle East, or in Mediterranean areas of dry polyculture. After the second century BC, temperate European communities were able to maintain the conditions that were necessary to support a level of social differentiation as developed as that of the state. These internal developments, combined with external influence, enabled a breakthrough to a higher level of social complexity.

The dynamic of the Mediterranean world-economy
During the Bronze Age, displays of wealth and power (monumental tombs, rich grave goods) are frequently associated with exotic prestige goods of metal and amber. From this we can deduce that wealth and power were tied to preferential access to prestige goods. But this observation does not inform us as to whether this access was the cause, or only the consequence of social stratification. Another fact – the geographical localization of the most spectacular displays of power – tips the scale in favor of the first proposition. These displays did not occur close to the primary source of the critical material, but instead along the communication routes through which the prestige goods passed.

The Mediterranean world-economy integrated the North-Alpine complex during Hallstatt B2–3/C. The Greek and Etruscan towns experienced an increasing demand for raw materials which led them to enlarge their supply areas until they embraced a large part of the continent. In this vast exchange system, certain well-positioned local chiefs played the role of privileged intermediaries. They were able to monopolize trade and exchange, and controlled the supply of Mediterranean prestige goods, ultimately extending their influence into neighboring territories. They reduced local rulers to vassal status. These "princes" played the part of necessary intermediaries between the Mediterranean cities and the supply communities which they controlled on the one hand, and the more northern communities on the other. The economic system in which the Celtic "princes" played the role of intermediaries corresponds to that which F. Braudel (1979) brought to light for the fifteenth and sixteenth centuries AD, which he called a "Mediterranean world economy." I. Wallerstein (1974–80) developed a model of the same type that covers a much longer time period.

I have recently developed an explanation of the socio-political disintegration of Hallstatt D in terms of a functional breakdown. The late Hallstatt principalities would have been stripped of their preeminent role by competition from emerging exchange routes in the Tessin, the middle Rhine, and the Champagne areas. In intruding into the preexisting exchange system, the negotiators from the Tessin could have looked for intermediaries further to the north. But the chiefs of these regions were no more than links in the chain of a down-the-line trade network, assuring contacts with their social equals and with the more northerly zones in order to assemble indigenous products in the form of metal, salt, meat, skins, furs and slaves. A more elegant explanation can be proposed: it can be argued that the scale of social integration was extended into new zones where ritual feasting apparatus was also present, but that it did not have time to crystallize because the invasion of Italy disrupted the exchange routes. According to this hypothesis, the Golasecca culture which occupied the Tessin (Pauli 1971) is seen as a functional outgrowth of Etruria in the second half of the fifth century BC. It would have corresponded to an expansion of the first sphere of the concentric system of the world economy. This hypothesis requires the existence of towns in the Po plain at the fringe of the Golasecca culture. A representative site is the Etruscan center of Forcello at Bagnolo S. Vito, near Mantua (de Marinis 1988). Consequently, the transfer of the role of intermediary in the exchange network to Berry, Champagne, and the middle Rhine could represent a variation of the second sphere of the world-economy.

The adoption of an expansionist strategy by the northern Celts interrupted this process. It is not known why this solution to internal tensions was favored over reinforcing the existing level of integration. Clearly, this choice had important consequences for the structure of the world-economy. Nevertheless, the latter was not totally destroyed. The evidence suggests that the object of this Celtic expansion was to encircle the power centers of the world-economy – to control the whole of the second sphere, after having attempted to advance upon the cities of the first

sphere in order to profit more directly from the system. This probably would not have been a problem if the Celtic expansion had taken place primarily in the intermediary zone. However, by attempting to gain too much too quickly, the groups which adopted this strategy ended by damaging the integrity of the Celtic world as a whole.

In the course of La Tène C2, from 180/170 to 130/120 BC, the whole of the first sphere of the world-economy fell under Roman control. The future imperial capital at first was the center of a system which was being revived. The second sphere corresponds to the Celtic states zone where *oppida* began to appear gradually. All excavated *oppida* have produced evidence of intensive commercial interaction with Rome. Celtic coinage, inspired by Mediterranean prototypes, is one of the earliest indications of the restructuring of the world-economy. The concentric functional organization consisted of three levels of politico-economic complexity, decreasing from the center to the periphery.

Because of the intensification of exchange with Rome, however, the difference between the levels of development of the first two spheres was reduced. The beginnings of the princely phenomenon appeared in the third sphere. When Roman power extended as far as the Rhine, integrating the whole of the Celtic States zone, true principalities formed in free Germany. This phenomenon is evidenced, above all, in the famous group of Lübsow tombs (Eggers 1951). Roman influences spread from 200 to 600 km beyond the *Limes* in close association with Roman trade. As in the fifth century BC, the growth of the first sphere caused the displacement of the second sphere further from the center.

Theoretical implications

It is of interest to conclude by submitting our case study to further theoretical analysis. First, it appears that the evolution of the Celtic world does not conform to frequently proposed explanations which assume that there was a growing relative scarcity of resources (Boserup 1965). According to this theory, scarcity causes conflicts, the resolution of which leads to a delegation of power by a populace to an arbitrator. Besides, a scarcity of resources does not necessarily give rise to an increase in social stratification. The emergence of the state in the Celtic world was the result of an intensification both of agriculture and of long-distance exchange. This explanation corresponds most closely to the neo-Marxist explanatory framework proposed by J. Friedman and M. Rowlands (1977), which is as appropriate to the evolution of the state in Mesopotamia as it is to similar developments in Peru or China. The intensification of agriculture allows for the support of a rise in non-agricultural production and this entails a cumulative process of centralization/ stratification. Clearly, the more production intensifies, the more frequent are the occasions for dispute and, consequently, the greater the necessity for arbitration (Vullierme 1989).

A solid local economic base is indispensable to the emergence of a more complex, enduring organization. In the case of principalities such as those of the Celtic states, the influences emanating from more complex neighboring societies stimulated the process of social stratification. However, this influence only reinforced and accelerated a phenomenon made possible by internal factors and by technical progress which allowed the intensification of production.

It can be argued that innovations in technology came about in response to the well-known contradiction between population growth and the carrying-capacity of the environment (Boserup 1965). The economic foundations put in place in the ninth and eighth centuries BC were, however, incapable of supporting a political scale of integration greater than tens of square kilometers. They did permit the stabilization of territorial units and social hierarchies, which had been fundamentally unstable up to that point.

During the sixth century BC the considerable increase in the level of integration, due to the functioning of the world-economy, was just as artificial as the unsuccessful attempts of the Bronze Age. The principalities seem to have disintegrated because of a modification in the spatial distribution of economic functions at the heart of the world-economy (concentric, functional tripartition). This occured as a result of external causes. Significantly, the disruption of the south–north trade networks in the fourth-third centuries BC brought about a return to the scale of integration which had existed from the ninth century BC onwards. In order for a superior level of social complexity to develop, a change in agricultural production was necessary. Techniques capable of intensifying production on the heavy and deep soils of temperate Europe were required in order to deliver a surplus sufficient to supply the needs of a greater number of non-agriculturalists.

The evolution of Celtic polities presents another interesting phenomenon relevant to a more general discussion of social stratification. An increase in social complexity is not the only means of remedying internal tensions. Territorial expansion or emigration are others, as is suggested by the aborted processes at the end of the fifth century BC. At that time the level of integration decreased, showing that the process is not irreversible. Thus we can determine

the necessary conditions for the emergence of the state, but we are unable to determine their extent. This difficulty may be due to the fact that there is a certain degree of probabilistic chance involved in the choice of a new type of social organization. The process of evolution acts in the manner of Prigognine dissipative structures, as suggested by van der Leeuw (1981).

Differential access to resources is generally considered a necessary condition for social stratification. In all known cases, this inequality has preceded the formation of the state, but it has always increased with its consequent development. G. Johnson (1982) has proposed that social hierarchies are the result of a differential capacity for processing information. These two points of view are not incompatible. Privileged access to material resources presupposes the processing of information concerning the location of resources, the conditions of their transport and distribution and, above all, the partners and the codes of exchange. It is not so much that the elites are more capable of procuring the material goods, but that they have the means of disposing of these goods. What the elites exchange are agreements which ensure the supply of goods at a precise location and time (Vullierme 1989). The processing of information is first and foremost a service activity. The crucial importance of information processing is sharply delineated in particular in the institutions which characterize the state. In effect, the state is defined as a form of government endowed with a specialized institution for the processing of information: an administration.

Thus it should be possible to see our *problématique* in terms of self-organizing systems theory. Technical innovation, the necessary condition in the subsistence domain, and its corollary, intensification of production, depend upon a series of steps involving the processing of information – innovation, diffusion, exchange of services, etc. This series of prestations makes it possible to overcome in a positive way the imbalance between population and the capacity for production. Population growth, which multiplies the number of potential parties, consequently increases the quantity of information to be processed. It can thus provoke scalar stress which, in the absence of sequential hierarchies, can be resolved either by hierarchization or by the creation of additional hierarchical levels (Johnson 1982). The contradiction can be resolved in a negative fashion by a reduction of population, which can be controlled to a greater or lesser degree by contraception, a rise in marriage age, emigration, war, disease, or famine. These observations and their implications suggest that we should integrate into our approaches methods adopted from the study of chaotic systems, systems in which evolution defies expectations. In spite of their complexity, these systems are not random. They possess structure. Physicists, meteorologists, and biologists have noted the preferential or "attractor" states which a system undergoes in the course of its evolution. In addition, these attractor states frequently possess a similar structure on various scales of observation – a fractal structure.[3] Clearly, this type of approach could be applied to human social systems – the ultimate complex systems.

An examination of the evolution of social stratification in the Celtic world reveals a systole/diastole type of dynamic, a cycle of evolution and devolution. This phenomenon requires us to recognize the significance of agricultural intensification in the process of increasing social complexity and to equivocate the role of long-distance exchange, even in a system of the world-economy type. This statement, for all that, does not leave us in an inextricable knot of internal contradictions.

Notes

1 This term refers to the region between the Mediterranean and northern Europe.
2 There is no solid archaeological argument for making the La Tène D1/D2 transition correspond with the end of the Gallic wars, around 50 BC.
3 Fractal structure refers to seemingly random structures which have been found to have underlying symmetry and to obey certain mathematical laws.

3
Building an historical
ecology of Gaulish polities

CAROLE L. CRUMLEY

Did you ever hear of sweet Betsy from Pike,
Who crossed the wide prairie with her lover Ike,
With two yoke of oxen and one spotted hog,
A tall Shanghai rooster and old yellow dog?
(traditional American folksong)

Introduction

Probably written in the 1850s by songster John Stone, the folksong "Betsy from Pike" encodes the subsistence strategy of many who took part in the American westward expansion; Betsy (from Pike County, Missouri) took animals likely to be useful either along the route or in establishing herself in a new farming community. In this paper I follow Hubert (1934) and suggest that Betsy's strategy is an aphorism for that of later Iron Age Celtic peoples, who also drew on elements of a mature, temperate European subsistence strategy, and for whom migration was also a solution to issues of population, politics, and economy.

By illuminating this strategy, I bring into question two conventional assumptions. The first is that a growing distinction between (urban) center and (rural) periphery characterizes settlement in so-called complex (chiefdoms and states) societies. Indeed, archaeological evidence at continental, regional, and local scales suggests a markedly different pattern in Celtic polities for which literary and archaeological evidence nonetheless supports marked class differences.

The second is that Roman domination of the ancient world was somehow the result of moral and intellectual superiority over less civilized foes. Analysis of environmental conditions that pertained in Europe during the last years of the Celtic Iron Age (La Tène) and the Roman period suggests that a stable Mediterranean climatic regime persisted in those characteristically less balmy latitudes, and contributed to an "ecology of conquest." Contrary to modernist assumptions, the critical elements of Roman economy and settlement that successfully

penetrated temperate Europe are more demonstrably the result of opportunities and losses related to environmental change than any presumed superiority of urban culture.

Finally, I call for a new definition of complexity which uncouples socio-political organization and settlement patterns, admits the variety of settlement characteristic of ranked societies, and urges the spatial analysis of the economy and ecology of particular historical situations.

Elements of Celtic society

The task of characterizing the social structure, ecology, and political economy of Celtic peoples in the half-century before the Roman conquest has long been a central theme in European studies (e.g., Fustel de Coulanges 1908; Childe 1925, 1926; Déchelette 1927; Grenier 1924; Hubert 1934). Literary and archaeological evidence plentifully supports a remarkably rich, albeit uneven, picture of Celtic society on the eve of the conquest.

From Hungary to the Atlantic, and from the British Isles to Spain and northern Italy, there is evidence of the pervasiveness of the Celtic pantheon (Green 1986). While major deities were shared, there are abundant indicators of the considerable importance of regional gods and goddesses as well (Green 1986; Oaks 1987). Successively more magnificent and unifying art styles link the whole area during the Iron Age (Powell 1966; Megaw 1970); certain polities, such as the Aedui with their enamelling *ateliers*, exhibited particular virtuosity in craftsmanship and design (Bulliot and de Fontenay 1875).

Contemporary Greek commentators favorably compared druidic philosophy with Egyptian, Assyrian, Persian, and Indian thought; Diogenes Laertius reports that many considered the study of philosophy to have begun among the Celts. Caesar and Ammianus report that the Druids themselves, while fulfilling governmental, educational, and moral responsibilities to their respective polities, were linked more broadly in a fraternal organization that met yearly to hear inter-polity grievances near Chartres.

Tacitus and Caesar note that polities designated kings (who acceded to the higher authority of the Druids) or elected officers (*vergobrets*) on the basis of explicit criteria for fixed terms (for Classical references see Crumley 1974, 1987c; Hubert 1934:220). Ample evidence exists for political parties based on the patron-client relation which crosscut class and kin lines and whose structure was essentially the same as those found in contemporary Rome (Taylor 1966; Crumley 1974, 1987c). It is clear that at least some of these polities were democratic monarchies and participatory democracies with senates and polity and supra-polity high courts guided by pan-societal law.

Caesar reports on Celtic polities that exhibited class-based social differentiation, including an aristocracy of religious and governmental leaders, a landed equestrian class (*equites*) with explicit military responsibilities resembling a similar formation in the antebellum American south, as well as free and unfree agriculturalists, skilled tradesmen, entrepreneurs, and laborers (Crumley 1987c).

The economies of larger and wealthier polities were based on a monetary system from at least the beginning of the second century BC (La Tène III) (Lengyel 1969). Wealth was generated from four main types of commercial production: 1. stockbreeding (horses, cattle, sheep, pigs); 2. metal mining operations; 3. artisanal activities (especially weapons production); and 4. agricultural production. The other main sources of wealth were taxation, the import and export of raw and finished materials, and, as a service to other wealth-producing operations, protection (Crumley 1987c). It is perverse to insist that such polities were not states.

Henri Hubert, in his book *The Greatness and Decline of the Celts* (1934), advances the theory that some branches of the Celtic peoples were primarily pastoral, others primarily agricultural – depending on both the environment and the length of time the group had occupied their region – and all were rural. His "leapfrogging" theory of Celtic colonization was meant to refute not only the wave theory of population movement then current, but to offer a model of Celtic society that imputed considerable social, political, and ecological sophistication to them.

Briefly, he argues that social and economic practices related to pastoralism were well entrenched among the Celts, although agricultural production was predominant in polities that had occupied their lands for a longer period. He encourages an image of increasing population, resulting not in centralization but in fission, where wealth was divided between group members who stayed on the ancestral lands and others who received their share in animals (horses, cattle, pigs) and other mobile wealth, then moved on. These colonizing groups would have been remarkably flexible, able to adapt to a wide range of environments using agricultural, pastoral, horticultural, and artisanal skills as needed.

While the bulk of Hubert's argument is based on linguistic evidence and Classical accounts of inter-polity relations, he did draw on the pertinent archaeological data available to him. *Oppida* are characterized as fortresses and armories, not fortified cities, with no large resident population except, perhaps, on days when fairs were held. He follows Déchelette in noting that many of

the *oppida* inhabited in La Tène III times had stood abandoned since the Hallstatt period.

Over half a century after Hubert's book was published, considerably augmented archaeological evidence would appear to substantiate many of his assertions. Audouze and Büchsenschütz (1989) support a view of the late Iron Age (La Tène III) Gaulish landscape as essentially rural, characterized by isolated farms, villages, and *oppida*. These latter were not cities, but more like Hubert's fortresses and armories; indeed (as Déchelette had argued) many were abandoned for generations, then reinhabited and transformed in response to the penetration of economic forms and urban styles from the Mediterranean. Audouze and Büchsenschütz argue that this commercial penetration was the first element of the Roman conquest in place; the second was the military action itself, and the third was the abandonment of *oppida* and the establishment of Gallo-Roman cities.

Caesar comments extensively on the Celtic polity called the Aedui and on Bibracte, the major *oppidum* of the Aeduan state. Goudineau and Peyre (1993) report a reassessment of earlier excavations and an extensive current archaeological program at this huge hillfort in Burgundy, the perimeter walls of which enclose 200 ha. They offer several possible reconstructions of the interior (pp. 64–6), and suggest that the area was not densely packed with structures. On the contrary, their rendering of pastures, orchards, and gardens is predicated upon evidence for a variety of subsistence activities, as well as for areas of industrial production and religious veneration, within the impressive walls.

Similarly, our archaeological survey of an upland pass 18 km south of Bibracte (Crumley, Marquardt, and Leatherman 1987:151–3) suggests that the area (today the *bourg* of Cuzy and its environs) was a functional center (Crumley 1976:67): a spot, place, site, or location serving a function or functions not equally available elsewhere. The term is useful in that it does not, *prima facie*, imply any particular residential pattern or population density; it is intended to separate the function of a place from sometimes misleading terms usually associated with an urban/rural population distribution (village, town, city).

The survey data do not suggest a town or village so much as a crossroads, around which activities were slightly more concentrated; this would have been due to topography and the proximity of a considerable volume of trade, moving to and from Bibracte along a north–south crest road and thence descending east to the Saône or west to the Loire. Tradespeople could be expected to congregate at this natural break-in-bulk point, including blacksmiths, wheelwrights, innkeepers, and others.

American examples of this pattern still may be found in the passes of the Appalachian summit, where a few houses and a store in sight of one another remind us that communities are not necessarily incorporated and that density is relative.

Thanks to Caesar's account, we know of the fraternal dispute which divided a prominent Aeduan family and mirrors the politics of the entire polity: the Roman sympathizer and Druid Diviciacus controlled the *oppidum* of Bibracte, his brother Dumnorix the countryside. Despite his promise to Caesar to deliver grain to the Roman army, Diviciacus was powerless to force Aeduan farmers, more likely loyal to Dumnorix, to comply. Diviciacus also worried over his brother's right to collect tolls on the Saône river. Thus, Aeduan centers of wealth and power were scattered about the countryside, and not necessarily within the walls of their chief *oppidum*, Bibracte (Crumley 1987c:404–9). Even after the conquest, when Gaul became a part of the Roman, Frankish, and Carolingian Empires, much of its indigenous economic, political, and social power was still frimly rooted in the countryside (Berry 1987).

In summary, individual and collective wealth was distributed both extensively and intensively across the landscape, and individuals (such as Dumnorix) could exercise considerable power in the absence of control of the chief *oppidum*. In the Celtic landscape, unpopulated or sparsely populated functional centers – highland pass or river ford, sacred grove or spring – were every bit as empowering as hillforts. Implantation of the urban form on this profoundly rural society necessitated twin tactics: forced hillfort abandonment and concomitant urban construction, and the eradication of the Druids (see below). Both were calculated to alienate Celtic society from the practice of democratic, heterarchical power relations and foster acceptance of a centralized, autocratic Mediterranean hierarchy whose emblem was the city. Archaeological, documentary, and environmental evidence for the late Iron Age in Gaul reveals the tableau of an urbanized, hyperhierarchical agrarian society engaged in the military and economic penetration of agropastoral polities (at least some of which were not only states but legislative democracies), which were linked by cultural forms and strategic alliances and spanned a continent.

Environmental and economic change

From approximately 300 BC to AD 300, continental Europe experienced a markedly warmer and drier climate; the period is termed the Roman Empire Climatic Optimum (Denton and Karlen 1973; see also Gunn and Adams 1981; Crumley 1987b). During this period, the relatively narrow overlap zone between temperate Atlantic/Continental and semi-arid Mediterranean climatic and biotic regimes (termed an *ecotone*) moved north of its average twentieth-century position in southern France. Precisely how far north Mediterranean conditions prevailed is not certain, but today the maximum northerly extent of commercial viticulture is in the Champagne region of France (about 49 degrees latitude). MacKendrick (1987) reviews Classical sources that report flourishing vineyards as far north as England (southern England is *c.* 51 degrees latitude), suggesting a shift of the ecotone at least 100 km north of its present position.

This does not, of course, mean that Mediterranean climate dominated as far north as England; the most important effect of the warmer period was that north-west Europe experienced extreme climatic events only rarely. Viticulture and the cultivation of other Mediterranean flora (e.g., olives, figs, dates) are practical when late spring or early fall freezes are rare and rainfall is predominantly in winter (Lamb 1977); these conditions are characteristic of a Mediterranean climatic regime. In contrast, temperate European vegetation is supported by an Atlantic regime, which brings rain in the summer, and a Continental regime which threatens inopportune frosts (Le Roy Ladurie 1971). For hardier northern species, such conditions are not problematic in the long term.

Today the ecotone may be seen most dramatically at the crest of the Montagne Noire in Languedoc, where the vegetation changes in less than a meter from Mediterranean to Temperate flora. More subtle but equally remarkable is the transformation which may be observed by moving along a north–south trajectory in the Rhône-Saône corridor; here cultural indicators such as roof tiles and culinary preferences, while hardly the empirical data of botanical surveys, give the strong sensory impression of moving from central to southern Europe.

What are the implications for the Celtic realms of a marked change in the dominant climatic regime? It is easiest to see if we again turn to Burgundy as an example. Burgundy has long been the locus of this shift, although (as explained above) not the sole region to feel its effect. Guinot (1987) notes that the region's enduring central position between north (*langue d'œil*) and south (*langue d'oc*) is reflected in its dialectical history. Burgundy serves as both historical and contemporary microcosm of the effect of dramatic shifts in the position of the ecotone.

In periods when Atlantic and Continental regimes dominated (as in the first half of the Iron Age) a flexible suite of economic strategies, drawing on diverse species of flora and fauna, would have been superbly suited to those regimes' extremely variable conditions (Crumley and Green 1987). An agropastoral economy, such as that practiced by the Aedui in their highly tessellated landscape, has enormous advantages when climatic regimes marked by extremely variable conditions predominate. Druids, among other members of Aeduan society, would have been repositories of considerable economic and environmental lore, enabling the society to adjust to almost any exigency. Gunn (1994) has termed this detailed, trans-generational transmission of information about a region's environmental variation "capturing".

The advent of warmer, more stable conditions would have created considerable economic pressure to profit from the lucrative Mediterranean wine and olive industries (Clavel-Levêque 1989) and the ready urban grain market. More conservative strategies would have been abandoned, first in the drier valleys, then in rolling uplands. In Burgundy, the only locales in which the old rainfall patterns continued were at high elevations (e.g., Bibracte), which, as much as any other factor, can explain the reflorescence of *oppida* in La Tène III. With the forced abandonment of hillforts such as Bibracte, the establishment of urban centers (Augustodunum, modern Autun), and the removal of the Druids from public life, the Romans were able to complete their economic penetration of Burgundy and much of north-west Europe. A stable climate facilitated urbanization, the homogenization of the landscape through the commoditization of rural produce, and the devaluation of the inter-generational transmission of environmental lore.

Burgundy became a cow tethered at Rome's northern door. As long as climatic conditions were stable, the attenuated economy was viable; when at the end of the warm period conditions again became variable, key elements of Burgundy's successful Iron Age economic and social adaptation had been swept away.

The "unshaven" confront civil society

I have argued elsewhere (Crumley 1976) that at least three categories of settlement are associated with the state, only one of which includes as one of its features the city, defined as follows: a place that has a resident population comprising members of all classes whose subsistence requirements are furnished by the population of the surrounding complementary region. Archaeological evidence for a city as defined above would be (1) the presence of separate areas of the site that quartered the wealthy, artisans, merchants, and various groups of skilled and unskilled laborers, and (2) artifactual and/or textual evidence of the active exchange of urban products for the

agricultural products and raw materials produced by a surrounding population (Crumley 1976:67).

This settlement category I term *synchoritic* (where the population of the center is supported by the surplus produced by a rural population) (p. 68). The medieval states of the Sahel (Gamst 1970) and the early modern period in the British Isles could be considered special cases of synchoritic states, in that peripatetic monarchs commandeered high-ranking clients' domiciles for a time and turned them into *de facto* capitals.

It is important to note that many Greek *poleis*, which often serve as paradigmatic examples of the state, do not fit the synchoritic settlement category (Small n.d.); instead (following Rowe 1963), their settlement systems are termed *achoritic*, where farmers live in town, the hinterland is essentially vacant, and market activities take place elsewhere. A third general category is *epichoritic*, where centers are all but deserted except for a few specialists (priests, civil officials) but the outlying area supports a sizeable rural population (Crumley 1976:68). Epichorism characterizes early state settlement systems in China and Mesopotamia (Uruk), as well as those of dynastic Egypt (Hoffman *et al.* 1986 notwithstanding) and the early classic Maya (Tikal).

The point is that there are a number of solutions to both elite and non-elite residence which can nonetheless support the apparatus of the state. With this observation in mind, it is certainly worth considering whether the appearance of urbanism in Europe is tied to the formation of the state at all. This question reminds us that hierarchical socio-political organization does not necessarily imply a settlement hierarchy. The administrative and economic (e.g. production, marketing, transport) structures necessary to states need not coincide spatially. That they do so on occasion (e.g., Imperial China, medieval Europe) should make us all the more wary of assuming the physical evidence of their coincidence to be a *point culminant* marking state formation.

Cultural-historical and cultural-evolutionary approaches (e.g. Childe 1934, 1951; Steward 1949), which advocate an exclusive link between urbanism and the state, have been particularly popular in Anglophone countries, finding only limited favor in France, Germany, and elsewhere. More specifically, post-World War II and especially post-Sputnik American archaeologists found inspiration in the cultural evolutionism of Leslie White (1949, 1959).[1] White's macro-scale analysis of human history in terms of increasingly efficient energy capture found a ready audience among positivist social scientists who were eager to find historic confirmation that technology is the key to human progress. In like fashion, the assumption of Childe (1951), Adams (1966), and others that complex societies are civil (that is to say urban, from the Latin *civis*, city), and in contrast to barbarian (from the Greek *barbaros*, bearded stranger), has become paradigmatic in the archaeology of the state.

The roots of such assumptions are as deep in Western philosophy as in Western languages. The idea of progress – that is to say, the identity of human evolution and history as gauged by the increasingly complex transformation of materials – is not only the cornerstone of so-called 'modern' thought (Nisbet 1980). The notion may be traced at least from the eighth-century BC Greek philosopher-farmer Hesiod, through medieval Christianity's Great Chain of Being and the Danish museologist Worsaae's Three Age System, to Morgan and Spencer, its best-known nineteenth-century proponents. By disassembling the fabric of societies into autonomous temporal (Stone Age, Bronze Age, Iron Age) and structural/functional units (kinship, government), the theme of increasing complexity became focussed on technology and urbanization as indicators of sophisticated social and political organization. This analytic structure not only harkened back to supposed influences on Europe of the Mediterranean city-states; it also mirrored the preferred interpretation of nineteenth- and twentieth-century industrial capitalists, who saw advances both in technology and in the global penetration of a centralized free-market (*laissez-faire*) economy through urbanization as a cure for social and political backwardness.

Thus high-density population centers supported by rural agriculturists and an intricate technology under the control of elites were adopted as the hallmarks of complex societies, past and present. This reading of the history of society set the agenda for Western colonialism and tied the future of much of the world's peoples to a particular economic, social, and spatial definition of progress.

Contemporary cultural evolutionists have eschewed improved technology and population growth as indicators of increasing complexity, embracing instead the role of finance, control, and ideology in the empowerment of emerging elites (Earle 1989). While this represents a laudable increase in the sophistication of evolutionary models, value continues to be placed on states' stability despite a growing literature to the contrary (Paynter 1989). The underlying assumption remains intact: polities without both spatial and social centralization (that is to say, settlement hierarchies and urban elites) are still widely considered inherently unstable, transitional, and incomplete, and their trajectories unfinished until such time as they become states or their instability leads to collapse. Such polities are termed chiefdoms.

Although there exists a corpus of literature that examines the relation of social differentiation (inequality) to spatial patterning (Paynter 1989; Wenke 1989), most workers continue to assume that the correlation is always positive: societies with rank-size settlement distributions (a relatively smooth curve formed by plotting most-to-least populous agglomerations, i.e. cities–towns–villages) are states. It is, however, quite possible for elites to govern without benefit of nested settlement hierarchies, and for marked class distinctions to be played out without leaving the spore of cities (see Gibson, this volume).

Finally, evidence from every major culture area points to environment as playing a crucial enabling role in the choice of subsistence strategies; and environmental instability is a well-documented factor in the collapse of the administrative structure of complex societies (e.g. Hassan 1994). Our question should be: how do so-called complex societies mitigate the necessity of political and social accommodation to systemic change? A portion of the answer may require the demystification of civil societies.

What constitutes complexity?

I have argued elsewhere (Crumley 1987a:160ff.) that many archaeologists erroneously conflate complexity with order, order with hierarchy, and hierarchy with power (e.g. McGuire 1983:91).[2] Others (Johnson 1982:395ff.) have equated complexity with the increased decision-making effectiveness of leadership hierarchies. This latter definition of complexity has encouraged the importation of mechanical models of social stratification from engineering and business, which effectively obviates other definitions of power as well as the role of individuals. Ironically, such hierarchical models have recently been replaced in management by more flexible and inherently more complex heterarchical structures that link individual responsibility and accomplishment with corporate success.

I define heterarchy as a system in which elements are unranked relative to one another or ranked in a variety of ways depending on conditions (Crumley 1979; 1987a). The term is borrowed from cognitive psychology (McCulloch 1945) through artificial intelligence (Minsky and Papert 1972) and refers explicitly to a heterarchy of *values*; an individual might ignore conflicting personal values (such as simultaneous opposition to abortion and support of the death penalty) or an awareness might precipitate a crisis. This is similar to what Bateson refers to as the "double bind" (1972).

The implication for the values of an entire society is that

an intricate net of power relations – *counterpoised* power – in which negotiating individuals operating in varying contexts play a critical role, can not only support state apparatus but give rise to supra-state confederacies as well. To understand so-called complex societies, we must recognize that hierarchy is invariably a temporary solution to the problem of maintaining order (Paynter 1989:375). Furthermore, generalized heterarchical structures – both cultural and environmental, which are always present (though not necessarily dominant) – lend flexibility in the negotiation of power relations. Perhaps most importantly, the individuals who interpret, explain, and integrate values in a society (religious practitioners, lawgivers, philosophers) always play a pivotal role in maintaining order.

Gamble (1986:29) has argued that complexity must have both diachronous (scheduling) and synchronous (alliances) referents, adding important temporal, cognitive and (potentially) ecological considerations to a definition of complexity.[3] Ecological parameters would seem to be particularly important, since the distribution of resources and the stability of the system as a whole would necessarily add to the complexities of scheduling and alliances for sedentary as well as more mobile populations. It follows that societies with value systems that are more likely to retain more democratic heterarchical institutions would have individuals and groups able to respond effectively to both environmental and cultural change (Crumley and Marquardt 1987; Gunn 1994). Cultural knowledge, which Gunn has termed 'capturing', would be extensive and highly valued in such societies.

Johnson (1982) has struggled with reconciling egalitarian values with evident inequality, distinguishing *simultaneous hierarchies*, where a single group of people rule (states), and *sequential hierarchies*, where power does not always rest with the same people (chiefdoms). Johnson's difficulties would be eased if he abandoned the term egalitarian (implying as it does an equal distribution of resources and power) in favor of the term democratic, which maintains the value of egalitarianism while admitting the inequities of electoral praxis.

A totally value-free meaning for complexity is obviously impossible; however, a minimalist definition would focus on the number of elements in a system and the variety of ways the elements are related to one another. An example is the work of Mann (1986), who traces (albeit with Eurocentric bias) sources and relations of state power. While retaining hierarchies, this definition admits the concept of heterarchy and addresses the need to identify and describe non-hierarchical as well as hierarchical relations in complex systems. I suggest that this is

demonstrably true of Celtic polities, the salient points of which are reviewed above.

Conclusions

To sum up, hierarchical models, such as those routinely employed in the evolutionary sciences, both biological (see Note 2) and social, are inherently no more complex (and may be less so, by the working definition offered above) than non-hierarchical (heterarchical) models; more importantly, they are employed in the service of a progressive cultural evolution. As distinguished from the term 'chiefdom' the term 'state' focuses attention on only one type of complex society: hyperhierarchical, urban, agrarian. Pastoral and agropastoral societies, even when they are legislative democracies, are then, by definition, less complex. The dominant paradigm of cultural evolutionary theory, as it pertains to how the structural elements of society change through time, obscures the dynamic social relations (complex by any definition) among and within many polities for which ethnography, written accounts, and archaeology give us evidence.

Furthermore, the climate of temperate Europe changed dramatically between La Tène I and La Tène III. In that century or so there began the period climatologists call the Roman Climate Optimum, which lasted until about the third century AD. The most notable effect was the movement north of the Mediterranean/Temperate ecotone and stabilization for over five centuries of the characteristically variable climate of northwest Europe. Given the foregoing, it is time carefully to introduce environmental change into a multi-causal explanation of Roman economic triumph and administrative collapse. Implications for the Iron Age, as well as for the time of resurgent rurality and agropastoralism known to us as the Dark Ages or the Migration Period, are enormous.

In an earlier monograph (Crumley 1974) I suggest that Celtic polities had quite distinct economies, based on the particular resources they exploited and the heterogeneity of the landscapes they occupied. I suggest herein that resources and historical circumstance allowed some polities to organize as states, with taxation, conscription, a currency, a class system, and an administrative hierarchy. Caesar reports both polities with elected officials and polities with monarchs; this need not be seen as differentiating more from less "complex" administrative systems, any more than modern France is distinguished on those grounds from modern England.

It is probable that both party- and kin-based patronage were to be found in Celtic polities (Crumley 1987c). Party-based patronage would have appeared more enlightened than kin-based patronage (Weingrod 1968:381) to Roman observers, as it more closely resembled their own. Today we have biases similar to the Romans, but one need only consider modern Saudi Arabia's kin-based patronage and nation-state status to see the logical fallacy.

To test these assertions, it is necessary to undertake an individual assessment of each Celtic polity, utilizing (1) any available literary evidence, (2) extensive regional survey and subsequent excavation to establish sites' functions, and (3) an exhaustive analysis of environmental conditions and natural resources. Although the preceding discussion of literary evidence and the interpretation of settlement data richly deserve further development, I would like to concentrate on the environmental analysis and show how that information might be reintegrated into literary and archaeological contexts to illuminate the whole.

I propose an analytic strategy appropriate to the heterogeneous character of the European landscape and the heterarchical nature of Celtic society, one which recognizes each polity's unique environmental advantages and constraints and relates these to practically available sources of power and wealth. Using both natural scientific and literary evidence, information about the polity's environment, subsistence strategies, and lines of communication and delimitation is collected.

Inasmuch as is possible, I link ecological and economic resources to particular portions of the territory each group was known to control. In our work in Burgundy (Crumley and Marquardt 1987) we have found that the administrative boundaries of the Aeduan polity, while not known with complete certainty, could be generally delineated and it was relatively simple to identify the resources within and at the limits of the polity (Crumley 1987c:404–9). We paid special attention to the political and economic geography of the Aeduan polity's clientelist relations, allowing an added analytic dimension (pp. 421–7).

That continental Celtic polities were distinct from one another in important respects is clear from contemporary classical texts, whatever other interpretive difficulties those sources offer. Accounts such as Caesar's *De Bello Gallico* individually characterize a number of polities in terms of their political and social organization, economic resources and trade relations, language, and customs.

I wish to advocate a more integrated regional environmental and economic analysis of Celtic society on a polity-by-polity basis. Questions of population agglomeration and dispersion (and the appearance of urban centers) turn on natural factors (e.g., climate) which affect the group's ability to sustain a certain density and exploit

particular resources, rather than any imputed sociopolitical sophistication or lack thereof. We must be prepared to find a variety of settlement systems which reflect different economic strategies, and to approach these settlements' interpretation fully cognizant that their size, function, and location offer us primary settlement information. Only in the presence of additional economic and social evidence – not through questionable archaeological inference – might we infer a particular sociopolitical organization.

What do these observations imply for Celtic Europe? First, that the size and function of Celtic settlements are likely to vary in accordance with each polity's distinctive economic and administrative structure. Second, within each polity, settlement function and location will vary with regard to idiosyncratic distributions of environments and resources. Third, in the aggregate, these sites need not conform to any particular statistical configuration to be part of a state system of settlement;[4] the polity's status as a state must be established on other information. Finally, it is likely that urbanism postdates state formation in some Celtic polities.

The means by which anthropologists characterize the organizational structure of human society is ripe for reassessment. By investigating – at global, regional, and local scales, on a case-by-case basis – whether Western philosophical traditions that favor the literate urban victor over the oral rural vanquished have, in the manner outlined above, profoundly twisted our understanding of the historic relation between humans and the environment, and instituted a false measure of human accomplishment.

Notes

1 In geography, Central Place models are used to analyze and plan manufacturing and transport locations (Losch 1954; Christaller 1966, 1972). With little or no modification, archaeologists began to adopt these models in the early 1970s and, based on them, to propose geometric, "ideal type" settlement patterns which both disregard the physical character of the region (e.g. geology, topography, climate) and impose "goodness of fit" rules on excavation and survey evidence. While the explicit use of these models has waned, many of their underlying assumptions remain central to archaeological interpretaton. At best, these models invoke Asiatic information and power hierarchies and idealized Graeco-Roman urban templates which are not only markedly un-European (or at least un-Celtic)

but also the hallmark of thinly veiled cultural evolutionism.

2 This misunderstanding is not confined to archaeologists or even social scientists; many natural scientists make the same error (Pattee 1973; Allen and Starr 1982; O'Neill *et al.* 1986), but see Ricklefs (1987).

3 Gamble also accepts the more general definition of complexity as "elements whose relations are imperfectly known." While lack of understanding might well add to an organism's or a system's apparent complexity, impenetrability should not be the basis upon which social systems are compared.

4 For example, primate (one large center and many very small ones; Ginsburg 1961) or rank-size (lognormal distribution of settlements; Berry 1961) distributions.

4

The early Celts of west central Europe: the semantics of social structure

FRANZ FISCHER
Translation: Bettina Arnold

In European archaeology today the term "early Celts" refers to late Hallstatt culture, part of early La Tène culture, Hallstatt D and La Tène A of Paul Reinecke's nomenclature, or the time of the sixth and fifth centuries BC. The justification for this interpretation is derived from early Greek sources, such as the lost "Geography" of Hecataeus of Miletus, and especially the "Histories" of Herodotus. These sources unanimously employ the term *Keltoi*, whereas later Greek authors – especially in the east – speak of *Galatai*. The Romans in Italy and France refer to *Galli*, although Caesar reports that the Galli of Gaul called themselves *Celtae* (*De Bello Gallico* [BG] i.1,1). Variations of the word *Keltoi* appear after the first of the historic Celtic migrations to Italy and the Balkan peninsula around the end of the fifth century; our term "early Celts" refers to an earlier period.

This discussion focusses on a specific study area: southwestern and southern Germany, eastern France and central Switzerland between Lake Constance and Lake Geneva. It is in this region that we have evidence of *Fürstensitze*, or "princely seats," and *Fürstengräber*, or "princely burials," during the late Hallstatt period, although both are found further to the north-west and east in the early La Tène period. The terms *Fürstensitz* and *Fürstengrab* are creations of modern scholarship. They originated in the discovery of wealthy, gold-appurtenanced graves under burial mounds of impressive size near the Heuneburg on the upper Danube between 1876 and 1877. The term *Fürstengrab* was coined by Eduard Paulus the Younger, the regional conservator of Württemberg at the time; he was likely influenced by Heinrich Schliemann's discovery of the shaft graves in the citadel at Mycenae in 1876.

The term *Fürstensitz* was first introduced by Kurt Bittel and Adolf Rieth in a monograph reporting discoveries at the Heuneburg; the subtitle was "An Early Celtic Princely Seat." The observations which generated this concept were summarized by Bittel as follows: "The location of the Heuneburg, the associated architecture and the wealth of individual finds, some of which are of considerable significance, show that this was no ordinary settlement, but a hillfort continously occupied by an undoubtedly noble lineage" (1951). The large burial mounds in the immediate vicinity of the Heuneburg and clearly associated with it – the *Fürstengräber* referred to above – were interpreted by Paulus, later also Peter Goessler, and Bittel as the burial places of the lords of the hillfort.

The same criteria served as the theoretical and material foundation for Wolfgang Kimmig in 1969 when he attempted to separate the late Hallstatt *Adelssitze*, or "aristocratic seats," as a type from other prehistoric hillfort settlements. As Manfred K.H. Eggert has most recently pointed out in a synthetic overview of this issue, the identification of a *Fürstensitz* is satisfied by three criteria. First, the planned layout of the newly founded settlement manifests itself in the choice of settlement site and the construction of the fortifications already emphasized by natural topographic features. Second, the presence of southern imports, especially of Mediterranean origin, as well as exotica such as amber and coral, characterize the archaeological finds. Third, large tumuli in the immediate vicinity of the settlement and clearly associated with it contain burial chambers outfitted with unusually wealthy grave goods such as metal vessels, gold or gilded objects, and more southern imports that qualify them as *Fürstengräber*.

Kimmig and all later authors, most recently Eggert, have pointed out that this *célèbre modèle* is never completely verifiable. The settlements under discussion here are only rarely accessible to archaeological investigation or preserved as well as is the case for the Heuneburg. Usually the hillforts were repeatedly built up in later times, making archaeological deposits difficult or impossible to recover. The Hohenasperg near Stuttgart, for example, was a fortified town during the Middle Ages, and a fortress in modern times, so that only a handful of ceramic fragments are known from the site to date – fragments which are, however, characteristic of a *Fürstensitz*. A similar situation exists in Breisach although several fortuitous secondary excavations could be carried out there. The Üetliberg near Zurich underwent such extensive alterations in the early Middle Ages and during the nineteenth century that very few traces of the *Fürstensitz* there could be identified. This unsatisfactory state of research is compounded at a number of other sites. At the site of Mont Lassois near Châtillon-sur-Seine, with the *Fürstengrab* of Vix at its base, the two hilltop plateaux have been trench-tested only cautiously to date. It is unclear whether the settlement traces on the upper plateau are actually as extensively eroded as the excavators have claimed. Statements about the fortifications of these hilltop settlements are rarely based on excavated evidence. The location of the settlements on high ground in dominating positions and a few characteristic finds are all that identifies a settlement as a *Fürstensitz*, especially since *Fürstengräber* are not invariably found in the immediate vicinity of such sites (see Arnold, this volume).

Our understanding of the *Fürstengräber* themselves is similarly fragmented. Intensive agricultural exploitation of the terrain surrounding the Hohenasperg has levelled not only smaller burial mounds but clearly also some of the giant tumuli containing *Fürstengräber* either completely or to such an extent that they are only recognizable by means of aerial photography. The *Fürstengrab* of Eberdingen-Hochdorf was so thoroughly levelled that its discovery was due only to the keen observation of a local informant. Comparable burial mounds are known in other areas, but have not been investigated to date. Many of the well-known *Fürstengräber* were excavated as early as the nineteenth century, often in a fashion that was not much better than unsystematic tomb robbery and has left us very few points of reference in reconstructing the spectacular burial inventories that probably once existed. In addition, central burials were often robbed in antiquity or in early modern times. At best the tomb robbers left behind enough objects to allow us to identify what was once an important *Fürstengrab*, as in the case of the Grafenbühl burial at the foot of the Hohenasperg. The large central chamber of the Magdalenenberg tumulus near Villingen was much more extensively robbed, and the central chamber I of the Hohmichele, the largest and oldest of the tumulus group around the Heuneburg, yielded more than 300 glass beads and a gilded belt plate as evidence of the status of the individual buried there.

Under these circumstances we are forced to fall back on extrapolation in the identification and interpretation of individual *Fürstensitze*, which is obviously a constant source of debate. My point here is that we are put in the position of drawing conclusions from very incomplete evidence, without much hope of ever having a truly comprehensive data base at our disposal. While this ought not to be grounds for despair, we should be aware that the significant gaps in the overall "picture" dictate caution in all attempts at interpretation. Occasional surprises like the Eberdingen-Hochdorf burial serve to consolidate

rather than radically alter our understanding. A significant gap is represented by the groups of "normal" burial mounds found in the vicinity of each *Fürstensitz*, in some cases associated with one or more *Fürstengräber*. Systematic investigations of these smaller tumuli are generally rare, and are often impossible due to the extent of their destruction.

It is also clear that each *Fürstensitz* has its own individual history; differentiation by occupation dates and duration is possible at least in rough outline. The Magdalenenberg tumulus, for example, was probably erected around the same time as the Iron Age Heuneburg – in the late seventh century BC – whereas the Hohenasperg is first identifiable as a *Fürstensitz* about a hundred years later, as far as we can judge by its associated *Fürstengräber*. The Hohenasperg, on the other hand, survived the Heuneburg, which was destroyed and abandoned in or shortly after the middle of the fifth century BC, by at least one generation. The Mont Lassois hillfort settlement is identifiable as a *Fürstensitz* around the same time as the Hohenasperg, but comes to an end at the latest around the same time as the Heuneburg. The settlements at the Heuneburg, the Hohenasperg, and Mont Lassois coexisted as *Fürstensitze* only for the period between 530 and 450 BC. Further examples would generate an even more variegated picture. The resulting territorial landscape is one which changes from generation to generation – especially if we also consider the large numbers of early La Tène *Fürstengräber* which appeared west of the Rhine after 450 BC. With regard to these burials we must make the reservation that their *Fürstensitze* are not known to date. The early La Tène burial inventories are simultaneously less elaborate and more strictly regulated than those of the late Hallstatt *Fürstengräber*, and the early La Tène *Fürstensitze* also seem to be smaller in scale than their Hallstatt predecessors.

Kimmig has pointed out the problems with distinguishing the late Hallstatt *Fürstengräber* from less impressivly outfitted contemporary burials in the same area. This can be demonstrated by the example of wagons as grave goods. The female *Fürstengräber* of Esslingen-Sirnau and Schöckingen, for example, do not contain wagons, and in fact the practice of wagon interment extends far beyond the area in which *Fürstengräber* are found, quite apart from the fact that they appear in much earlier contexts as well. A burial from Schlatt in Breisgau contained a chamber tomb and a gold bracelet but no wagon; it is questionable whether this burial can be considered a *Fürstengrab*. These are just a few of many comparable examples. The problem of the differentiation of *Fürstengräber* is not unique to the early Iron Age; Michael

Gebühr has documented a similar phenomenon in the cemeteries of the so-called Lübsow Group in Germania Magna during Roman times.

This brings us to the question of how these observations can be reconciled to the term *Fürstengrab*. First it must be recognized that the designation *Fürst* or "prince, lord" is not intended to be synonymous with the extremely restrictive and socially sharply defined class historically constituted by the medieval term *Fürst* or "lord." Rather the term refers to the class of leading personages which are described by the historical sources of Classical antiquity in peripheral "barbarian" societies. Among the Celts and Germans these individuals are designated by the Latin sources by the terms *principes*, *nobiles*, or *proceres*. These terms, which are derived by Caesar, Livius and Tacitus – to name just three of the most important authors – entirely from Roman terminology and are projected on foreign cultures in the sense of *interpretatio romana* (Tacitus, *Germania* cap. 43,3), are rarely clearly defined but are usually applied *promiscue*, or indiscriminately. Only the less commonly encountered *reges* are particularly emphasized, although their position is described as being constituted by election rather than heredity and characterized primarily by judicial and sacred functions. This does not alter their essentially aristocratic structure, which is documented for the ancient world in proto-urban contexts wherever these are illuminated by the sources. It is assumed, and there is some archaeological evidence for this, that this aristocratic structure, which can be traced back to the second millennium BC with some certainty, is the product of successive generations and never reached the institutionalized final form in pre-urban contexts which became clearly defined in the Middle Ages.

If we consider a certain openness and flexibility to be particularly characteristic of this pre-urban aristocratic structure then the range of variation in terminology which we encounter in the context of our discussion is somehow appropriate. The phenomena which we have been calling *Fürstengräber* and *Fürstensitze* are occasionally referred to as *Adelsgräber*, or "aristocratic graves," and *Adelssitze*, or "aristocratic seats," even *Häuptlingsgräber* or "chieftain's graves." Georg Kossack recently coined the historically neutral term *Prunkgräber* or "ostentatiously outfitted graves," which nevertheless is plagued by the same basic problems of interpretation and differentiation. Of course these phenomena were occasionally equated with wholly legally defined concepts in order to clarify their function, but it should be kept in mind that these are interpretative attempts which cannot be directly derived from the archaeological evidence. The historic analogies which tend to be invoked in this process should be discussed in more detail than is possible here.

If we turn once more to the *Fürstengräber* themselves, it must be reiterated that it is impossible to differentiate the *Fürstengräber* category from contemporaneous "standard" graves in the same region. Of course the diachronic aspects of this phenomenon also must be considered here. Particularly in southern Bavaria we find numerous tumulus cemeteries dating to the seventh century BC which contain wooden burial chambers, frequently also four-wheeled wagons and especially extensive sets of ceramic vessels. As an aside it should be mentioned that the dead themselves, following the tradition transmitted from an earlier period, were cremated on funeral pyres, in contrast to the practice of inhumation which predominated in the sixth and fifth centuries. The ceramic vessel sets referred to above were not governed by strictly defined rules. Nevertheless, it becomes clear in the course of an analysis of these vessels that they were intended to serve as implements in a meal meant for a specific and relatively large number of persons. Similar burial inventories are known from individual contexts as early as the late Bronze Age, in the Urnfield culture. The meal represented by these vessel sets does not necessarily have to be interpreted as a special celebration, as has been asserted by some researchers. One need only recall the significance of the evening *cena*, or repast, which appears everywhere in the world of the Epics and survives in some rural areas to this day. It seems appropriate therefore to interpret these ceramic vessel sets as enabling the interred individual to fulfil what would have been a self-evident social responsibility in life: the provisioning of his extended family even in the life after death. What was at stake was the maintenance of social power.

This fundamental belief undergoes a significant change in the course of the sixth century particularly in connection with the *Fürstengräber*. At this point it is no longer the *familia* – which would have included farm-hands and servants – but a select circle composed of a small number of individuals who are to be sustained by the deceased individual. The vessels used in this repast are no longer made of clay, but of metal, in an ever more elaborate display. We are unable to describe the individual stages of this change because so few relevant burials from the early sixth century were spared tomb robbing or inadequate excavation. The Eberdingen-Hochdorf burial affords us a view of one of these "round tables" from the end of the sixth century. The assembled retinue consisted of the interred individual and eight fellow-diners, each outfitted with a large platter-like plate for the meat portioned out by the leader, as well as one drinking horn apiece. The interred individual himself is particularly singled out by his large iron drinking horn of 5.5 liter capacity; otherwise his utensils are not differentiated from those of his fellow-diners. This seems to imply that drinking practices had a particular importance, and simultaneously explains why it is this part of the dining equipment which is embellished so extravagantly in the later periods. We must keep in mind, however, that our information is derived from a small number of burials which are rarely intact or systematically excavated. This means that any attempt to trace such developments in effect already overtaxes what can be definitely known. We can therefore only cautiously state that in the Vix and Kleinaspergle burials there seems to have been at most one other guest in addition to the lord (or, in the case of Vix, the lady) of the burial. It is also possible that the pairs of drinking vessels in the form of two Attic kylikes in both graves and two additional gilded drinking horns in the Kleinaspergle burial no longer had anything to do with the number of individuals partaking, but rather with the enjoyment of different beverages according to Mediterranean customs. With the exception of the Kleinaspergle, early La Tène *Fürstengräber* never contain more than one drinking horn, if they contain any at all.

If the presence of elaborate drinking equipment seems to be the best criterion for differentiating the *Fürstengräber* as a group, it seems appropriate to view the use of so-called southern imports as another. At this point however a note of caution seems in order. The generalized identification of objects as "southern imports" can easily lead to the neglect of details which must be considered because of sensitive value differences. Ever since Greek imports were first identified in Hallstatt and La Tène burials, Attic ceramic vessels have received considerably more attention than metal vessels of Mediterranean manufacture. We know today that Attic kylikes appear very late in burials, Vix being the earliest example. Metal vessels of Mediterranean manufacture, on the other hand, are known much earlier. This appears to be a natural result of the different value accorded these materials in ancient contexts. Vessels of any metal, especially gold and silver, were regarded as being especially valuable. The household utensils of Alcibiades were immortalized in a stone inscription after they were auctioned off; ceramic vessels, which would have included numerous painted vases, were listed indiscriminately as ἀγγεῖα, whereas the metal vessels were listed according to the different materials of which they were made. In Homer's *Iliad* a two-handled bronze bowl was considered an appropriate prize for a victor (*Il.* 23, 615), and we have already discussed the transition from ceramic to metal vessels as a significant hallmark of the changes in the grave good inventories of high-status burials from the seventh to the sixth centuries. On the other hand, it is important to be aware of differences between individual imported metal vessels as well. The so-called *Rippenschalen*, or ribbed bowls, which

developed out of Greek metal phials, and the trefoil pitchers from burials such as Vilsingen and Kappel on the Rhine can still be considered objects of everyday use, even though their value by the standards of the time was considerable. A different order of magnitude is represented by the ostentatiously magnificent vessels which begin with the Eberdingen-Hochdorf cauldron and the griffin cauldron from La Garenne, and undoubtedly culminate in the Vix krater. It seems significant that such objects have been found only in the vicinity of Mont Lassois and the Hohenasperg, but not at the Heuneburg. This is undoubtedly related to the transfer of power from the Heuneburg to the Hohenasperg which seems to have accompanied the termination of the mudbrick wall horizon at the Heuneburg around the end of the sixth century.

Another consideration is more important in this context. "Southern imports" are, statistically speaking, first and foremost "foreign goods." Explanations of their presence tend to point to "trade" as the operative mechanism, although depending on the circumstances a number of very different transactions could have been responsible. There is no doubt that neither the griffon cauldron from La Garenne nor the Vix krater, possibly not even the Eberdingen-Hochdorf cauldron, can be explained by means of the mechanism "trade." Objects belonging to this category in Classical literature are invariably referred to either as dedicatory offerings in temples or as gifts of state. Since the first of these interpretations is not applicable, it seems likely that these objects are evidence of diplomatic exchanges, even if we can no longer identify the Mediterranean participants. It is of greater significance that the individuals who could claim such objects as grave goods possessed considerable political power, for otherwise they would surely never have been honored with such spectacular gifts of state.

If this explanation is untenable, then we are faced with the question of what could have induced the Mediterranean powers to establish such contacts with those early Celtic potentates of Burgundy, the Hohenasperg and, even earlier, the Heuneburg. There is a temporal connection between the Hohenasperg and the history of the Greek trade emporium at Massalia. This has inspired an interpretation of the spectacular Mediterranean pieces from La Garenne and Vix as part of a strategy involving a trade route to tin deposits in Brittany through the center of Gaul, replacing the sea route cut off by the Carthaginians. The lords of Mont Lassois would indeed have occupied a prime location for the control of such trade. This hypothesis does not explain the *Fürstengräber* which extend further to the north and as far as southern Germany. A wide variety of raw materials, and even slaves, are frequently invoked to explain this phenomenon. I am afraid, however, that the spirit of our own time is reflected in such models more than the reality of that archaic world.

In this connection the mudbrick wall of the Heuneburg manifests itself like an erratic boulder, giving away little that might solve the riddle. There is no doubt that the wall construction had its origins in a foreign, Mediterranean, if not to say Greek, handicraft tradition which contrasts starkly with the contemporary building tradition indigenous to central Europe. In the face of this monument's unique status north of the Alps to date, all explanations like "influence" or "trade" seem inadequate. It seems impossible to deny the role of Mediterranean architects and craftsmen in its construction, whatever their numbers. This is particularly surprising because southern imports do not begin to appear at the Heuneburg until about a generation after the construction of the mudbrick wall. The seemingly logical expectation that these craftsmen and builders would have brought objects with them which might have found their way into the archaeological record is not confirmed by the evidence. Another consideration is even more important. Neither the founding of the Heuneburg itself nor the erection of the mudbrick wall could have taken place without the initiative of the settlement leader. A leader able to order the construction of the mudbrick wall had to have seen something like it before and would have been responsible for importing the craftsmen needed to build it. Under whatever circumstances, such a leader would have had to have spent time in the Mediterranean, and in the circumstances of the times such a trip would hardly have been part of a "European Grand Tour."

Later sources report the use of Celtic, Iberian, and other "barbarian" mercenaries by various powerful personages in the Mediterranean area, and it seems safe to assume that such practices began well before the first recorded incidents. Alpine tribes, Ligurians and Celtic raiding parties from beyond the Alps in search of booty are frequently mentioned in the histories of the later Roman Republic; the cultured and warm lands of the south obviously continued to be an effective lure. In other words, the constantly recurring "contacts" which would have been immediately or indirectly of interest to powerful individuals in the south were probably less of an economic nature and more the result of the sort of ventures described above. Greek and Etruscan metal vessels, as well as other kinds of Mediterranean imports, but especially the spectacular pieces found in the early Celtic *Fürstengräber*, essentially fit within their temporal frameworks and reflect relationships which were typical for the time; they also reflect the existence of powerful individuals of greater and lesser stature in the north. The

significant characteristic features which we identify with the early Celtic Hallstatt and La Tène cultures were the achievements of individual personalities who were able to exploit particular geographic preconditions. These hillforts did not develop "on their own" or automatically. This is an important point because the Hohenasperg, for example, conjures up a vision of the rise of the house of Württemberg based on the toll revenues from the Neckar ford near Cannstatt. The right conditions are undoubtedly important, but there has to be an individual who knows how to make the most of them!

When general terms such as *Fürstengrab* or *Fürstensitz* are applied to these phenomena, it is according to the consensus that they represent only expedient terms and should be viewed in the sense of a *nom de guerre*; this has already been discussed above. The fact that these terms are still used at all is an indication that the theoretical discussion of this subject is still in its infancy. The reasons for this are easily understood. Those familiar with the archaeological data who work with those data on a daily basis are only too aware of their fragmentary, complex, and multi-dimensional nature. In addition, all previous attempts at social historical and historical interpretation have served to increase awareness of the limits of archaeological interpretation. The bitter experiences and disappointments associated with previous bold and seemingly lucid theories, which have on occasion been abused, and which proved to be methodologically unsound even if they could not always be definitively contradicted, have served to reinforce the tendency toward caution and reserve, even to the point of total theoretical abstemiousness. The tendency of archaeological scholarship to hope for ever more sophisticated and exact methods of observation and interpretation has exacerbated this trend. The fact that the limits of archaeological interpretation cannot be overcome even by technological advances has in many cases still to be recognized.

It would be wrong, however, to attempt to overcome this aporie[1] by means of a kind of mental somersault, enthusiastically forcing social historical processual models onto the existing archaeological data base. The resulting debate would lose sight of the essentials while becoming entangled in contradictions of secondary importance. By the essentials I mean the blindness regarding the exceptionally rich scholarly tradition centered on the written sources of the Classical world from the ancient Near East via Greece and Rome to the Middle Ages, in Byzantium as well as the West. This tradition has been concerned with questions of "social organization" – to cite just one very general key term – for almost 200 years. It is a study which has been and continues to be subsumed under very varied aspects and rubrics. The participants are philologists, linguists, theologians, historians, archaeologists, legal and economic historians, to list only a selection of the most important disciplines involved. Inevitably, a high degree of specialization has manifested itself among these disciplines which makes it difficult if not impossible to achieve an overview, and in some cases complete compartmentalization has occurred. In spite of the seemingly confusing variety of perspectives and interpretations, one should not lose sight of the fact that wellfounded conclusions are impossible without knowledge of the original sources, even when this goal appears to represent an impossible task. Although the penetration of these sources and the accompanying scholarly literature on the subject of social organization may be difficult, it makes available an arsenal of potential applications which cannot be dismissed as incidental as a result of language barriers or time constraints.

It seems significant, therefore, that, in spite of the difficulties cited above, so many established and experienced scholars eventually have come to the conclusion that the peoples of prehistoric Europe represent a sort of structural *koine* from prehistoric times until the early and later Middle Ages. The "root" of this *koine* is thought to be a pre-urban, "archaic" society, which is gradually transformed, even occasionally dissolved, by urbanization, but becomes identifiable only with the first written records, which generally develop concomitantly with the urbanization process. N. D. Fustel de Coulanges and Jacob Burckhardt first attempted to describe this process for the Greek and Roman states, but in the interim scholarship in the area of ancient ethnography has advanced to include the *barbariké* represented by the societies on the European fringe of the Classical world, especially the Celtic and Germanic peoples. Anglo-Irish scholarship early focussed attention on the extensive correspondences between the social structure and value systems of early Irish literature and the world of Homeric Greece, and similar observations were repeatedly made regarding certain features of society among the Gauls and the Germanic tribes as described by Caesar and Tacitus. Twenty years ago, Emile Benveniste, scholar of Indo-European studies, attempted to formulate a linguistic interpretation of the prehistoric social order entitled *Le Vocabulaire des institutions indoeuropéennes* (1969). It goes without saying that the emphasis on similarities, which are being stressed here, is not intended to blur the differences in detail or the problems which are frequently encountered in the written record. It is, however, necessary not to allow these detractions to irritate one more than is absolutely necessary.

The fundamental insight that large and small family-based groups evolve into an aristocractic elite which are an intrinsic part of pre-urban, "archaic" societies is largely the product of this protracted discussion, in which theologians and legal historians have also participated. These aristocratic family groups live in constant rivalry with each other. Jacob Burckhardt characterized the early Greek aristocracy, which insitutionalized inter-group rivalry in the supraregional competitions at the big cult festivals, as living an "agonal existence." The majority of the population consists of "little people," mainly small farmers, coexisting with the large aristocratic, family-based conglomerations and frequently drawn into more or less voluntary dependent relationships with the "great lords" wherever urbanization begins to manifest itself. This process eventually gives rise to class conflicts, socalled, with widely diverging outcomes depending on the nature of the context. Those pre-urban societies which even predate class conflicts generally display an economic structure based exclusively on agriculture; subsistence on trade, when it occurs, is initially stigmatized as socially unacceptable. Exclusively agrarian economic structures are also characterized by virtually self-sufficient economic units – represented by the *oikos* of Homer among the early Greeks – laboring exclusively for their own subsistence needs. What little surplus is produced is used to acquire a few luxury goods, as well as metal tools and weapons, when such items cannot be acquired through raiding, war booty or gift exchange. Raiding and feuding are the primary and legitimate preoccupations of the aristocracy. In such circumstances supraregional religious organizations serve as unifying institutions, in addition to loose groupings which we would call tribal confederacies today, without achieving permanent stability. Law and religion are still a single inseparable unit in this type of society.

Why burial monuments of impressive dimensions with grave goods which surpass all previously known burials should appear in some regions and not in others in a society at this level of organization must be interpreted as a fundamentally individual process. We can only observe the fact that such phenomena seem to occur in similar conditions without this serving as an adequate explanation. It is of course worth noting that the oldest Etruscan *Fürstengräber* – at Praeneste – and the Celtic *Fürstengräber* in west central Europe both contain surprising numbers of imported goods. On the other hand, the Classical sources report the existence of *principes* and *nobiles*, for example among the Cherusci around the birth of Christ, in areas where no *Fürstengräber* are known, but relatively poorly equipped cremation graves are found instead. It seems prudent, therefore, to view each burial, even those with above-average grave goods, as testimony of the fortune of one particular individual. Statistically generated groupings of such burials should be treated with corresponding caution. The broad and fine-grained details of pre-urban "archaic" social structure stand out in relief against the backdrop of the Classical sources and the evidence derived from linguistic studies, reflecting a version of reality – if only partial and never in its entirety. As long as we have as our goal the reconstruction of the living reality of that society in all its gradations, even occasionally the identification of the causes which motivated change, we have no choice but to study the record of this early form of social structure intensively and accurately on the basis of the existing archaeological evidence.

Notes

1 This is a term with very specific meaning in Kantian philosophy, and refers to an unbreachable gap in evidence. (Translator's note).

PART II

Recovering Iron Age social systems

5

The material culture of social structure: rank and status in early Iron Age Europe

BETTINA ARNOLD

You think that just because it's already happened, the past is finished and unchangeable? Oh no, the past is cloaked in multi-colored taffeta and every time we look at it we see a different hue.

(Milan Kundera *Life is Elsewhere*)

Introduction

The extensive body of archaeological evidence dating to the late Hallstatt period in west central Europe represents a particularly rich source of data in spite of the chameleon-like nature of past human life. Prehistoric Celtic societies provide an ideal and so far underutilized laboratory in which to generate new approaches to the study of human social evolution. Too often the emphasis in publications like this one is on the limitations of the archaeological record. The discussion below will focus instead on the interpretative potential of a culturally linked group of prehistoric societies which made extensive use of material culture as a way to communicate social messages.

Although there are many aspects of early Iron Age life which remain obscure, several definitive observations can be made regarding late Hallstatt society in the West Hallstatt Zone (Fig. 5.1). On the one hand, social differences do not seem to have been expressed in an obvious way in the settlement record. No structures have been identified to date on early Iron Age settlements which clearly functioned as "palaces" or chiefly residences. On the other hand, mortuary ritual, and the material culture associated with it, was a particularly important modality for the expression of status differences during the late Hallstatt period. The following is a synopsis of the empirical evidence for early Iron Age status differentiation as represented in burial in west central Europe.

1. Late Hallstatt society practiced several different types of mortuary ritual. Archaeologically identifiable disposal of the dead during the period between 600 and 400 BC is represented by both inhumations and cremations either in or between tumuli. A tumulus could either be part of a cemetery or serve as a cemetery in itself. The number of burials in tumuli of this period range from one to over 100. Other forms of mortuary ritual indicate that the majority of the population was disposed of in ways which are not identifiable archaeologically. Such disposal of the dead might have consisted of cremation and dispersion, or of excarnation and dispersion. In either case a distinction was being made between the formal, bounded disposal of one category of persons within the society and the less formal disposal of the remaining population. This distinction does not seem to have been made on the basis of gender or age, since both male and female individuals are found in tumuli, and all age groups except very young infants are represented. Infants under a certain (pre-tooth eruption) age do not seem to have been accorded any kind of formal burial and may have been considered non-persons (Arnold 1991a).

2. Burial in a tumulus was not reserved only for the wealthiest members of early Iron Age society. The grave good assemblages in burials in a single tumulus in the West Hallstatt Zone can range from a complete absence of inorganic grave goods to the full complement of objects associated with high-status elites, including gold and imports. It is important to distinguish between multiple burials (a single burial chamber or pit containing more than one individual)(Oeftiger 1984) and discrete burials (formal, bounded disposal of a single individual). Multiple burials include individuals whose rank and status are

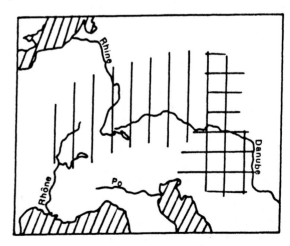

5.1 The West and East Hallstatt Zones. West Hallstatt Zone: vertical hatching. East Hallstatt Zone: cross-hatching.

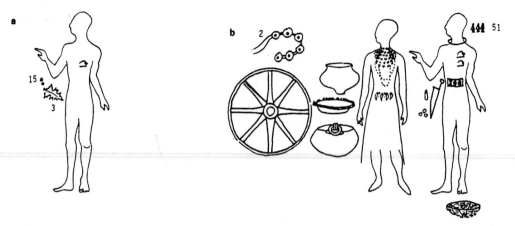

5.2 Schematic representation of grave good inventories from Graves 3 and 6 in the Hohmichele tumulus. a, *Grave 3: one bronze fibula(?), three oak leaves and 15 hazelnuts;* b, *Grave 6: Four-wheeled wagon, horse trappings, bronze vessels, basket. Male individual: knife, whetstone, three iron rings, two bronze fibulae, bronze belt plate, iron neck ring, 51 iron arrow tips. Female individual: multiple necklaces (amber, glass, and coral), finger ring, belt of animal teeth. (Inventory from Grave 6 as depicted here not complete.)*

different from the primary interment (retainers, servants, concubines, entertainers, etc.) Discrete burials, on the other hand, require the effort of a separate burial chamber or pit, and are not necessarily associated with neighboring discrete burials except through kinship ties. Two discrete burials from the Hohmichele tumulus associated with the early Iron Age Heuneburg hillfort illustrate the variation among burials in a single tumulus especially well. Grave 3 from this tumulus contained a single individual buried with the remains of a bronze ornament, probably a fibula, as well as fifteen hazelnuts and three oak leaves (Fig. 5.2a). Grave 6 in the same burial mound contained a multiple burial (one man, one woman) and a large number of grave goods, including metal drinking vessels, a four-wheeled wagon, horse trappings, animal hides, numerous ceramic vessels, bronze and iron weapons and jewelry (one of the necklaces contained over 2000 beads), in addition to evidence for imports (amber and coral) (Fig. 5.2b)(Arnold 1991a). The extreme range in grave good assemblages within individual late Hallstatt tumuli indicates that some form of kinship structure, rather than socioeconomic status alone, was the primary determining factor in tumulus burial. Burials within a single tumulus are linked to one another via the relationship of the deceased to the primary central interment.

3. Sumptuary laws seem to have regulated rank and status representation in mortuary ritual. These rank and status differences are represented in the burial record by drinking and feasting paraphernalia as well as by personal ornament. The distribution of such equipment indicates

that personal ornament and feasting were the aspects of early Iron Age life which primarily differentiated individuals from one another (Dietler 1990b; Arnold 1995 and n.d.). Control over the distribution of food and drink in specific contexts may have been one of the mechanisms by means of which an individual accumulated other forms of material wealth, such as gold objects or imported goods.

4. Women seem to have been able to occupy positions of prestige and possibly power under certain conditions in early Iron Age society, especially during the early La Tène period, which saw a short-lived but dramatic increase in wealthy women's graves containing not just gold ornament but also metal drinking equipment and other exotica (Arnold 1991b).

5. This discussion operates under the assumption that late Hallstatt society was in a liminal phase, on the threshold between a chiefdom and a state. The problem of distinguishing between a (high) chiefdom and an (early) state makes a more exact classification difficult (Smith 1985:97). The situation is not improved by the fact that social structure as reflected in or transformed by burial ritual usually changes more slowly than social organization (Morris 1987:209). This means there may be a lag effect between changes in the social structure of a society and the way it is representing itself in mortuary ritual. Change may not be represented at all until there is some outward sign of upheaval, as in the case of the late Hallstatt/early La Tène transition. The fact that mortuary ritual is not a direct reflection of the social organization of

a society, and that some societies may mask social differences by not expressing them in burial, complicates matters further. Such considerations may complicate an analysis of early Iron Age social organization, but they do not constitute an insurmountable obstacle, as I hope to show below.

Burial and communal representation

The observations listed above all have significant implications for any reconstruction of early Iron Age social organization. The existence of a distinction between formal (generally archaeologically identifiable) and informal (generally not archaeologically identifiable) disposal of the dead during this period is not disputed by most researchers. Social anthropological research has demonstrated the potential of such information. For example, Saxe has hypothesized a link between the organization of cemeteries as formal bounded areas reserved exclusively for the disposal of the dead and the existence within a society of unilineal corporate descent groups, tracing their lines from the buried ancestors and using the cemetery as a symbol to legitimize their control over access to vital resources such as land or livestock (1970:119–21). The fact that many tumulus groups of Iron Age date were laid out in a linear fashion, in some cases along both sides of what were probably prehistoric roadways leading to settlements, implies such a system of social legitimation. The tumulus cemeteries of Rubenheim-Wolfersheim (Reinhard 1988; 1990)(Figure 5.3a), Burrenhof-Grabenstetten (Kurz 1987)(Fig. 5.3b), Grundsheim-Nürtingen (Bittel, Kimmig and Schiek 1981) (Fig. 5.3c), and Emsbüren (Fröhlich 1990), among other examples, were all located along linear features which are no longer visible but were probably roads or cart tracks. Tumuli were intended to function as highly visible communal monuments. They advertised the seniority and importance of the lineages associated with the late Iron Age populations which erected them. Their conspicuous location along major routes of transportation (often on terraces clearly visible from a considerable distance), and their additional demarcation by means of stone rings and stelae, supports this interpretation.

There is also a significant correlation between burial mounds and late La Tène *Viereckschanzen*, which are interpreted as ritual enclosures by most researchers (Arnold 1991a:54). At least twenty-five of the seventy plus *Viereckschanzen* known in Baden-Württemberg (of which only eight had been extensively excavated by 1981) (Bittel, Kimmig and Schiek 1981:514) are associated with groups of tumuli. The close association between *Viereckschanzen*

and tumuli has been noted by a number of researchers (Bittel 1934; Schiek 1977:42–3 and 1982:231; Kurz 1987, among others), but apart from vague speculations about ancestor worship and some sort of continuity, whether genealogical, cultural, or ritual, between the late Hallstatt and late La Tène populations in this area (Bittel, Kimmig and Schiek 1981:445; Fischer 1987:5), the connection has remained unclear. No early Iron Age precursors of the late La Tène structures have been found in the West Hallstatt area that can be unequivocably related to the later Iron Age ritual enclosures, although this may be due to the small number of excavated examples (but see Arnold 1991a:56–8).

Late La Tène *Viereckschanzen* also seem to have served as lineage monuments during a phase of the Iron Age in which such relationships were no longer being represented in the medium of mortuary monuments. There is good evidence to suggest that the rectangular enclosures of the late Iron Age on the continent served a communal function as loci of social discourse in the form of regulated consumption of food and alcoholic beverages (Murray forthcoming). Inauguration and other recurrent (often annual or seasonal) rituals are consistently associated with drinking and feasting in the literature of the British Isles (Arnold 1991a; n.d.). At the site of Sulz am Neckar, a tumulus was actually incorporated into the wall of the enclosure of a late Iron Age *Viereckschanze* (Bittel, Kimmig and Schiek 1981:482–3). This is a concrete example of the continuing significance of lineage-based structures in the landscape of social discourse into the late Iron Age. This interpretation could explain the distribution of *Viereckschanzen* in the landscape, which occasionally number half a dozen or more in the vicinity of a single *oppidum*. As monuments closely associated with inauguration rituals, they may reflect temporal shifts in power from one lineage to another within the local governing elite. As a lineage develops its power base, it constructs a *Viereckschanze* in a new spot, but legitimacy is sought by locating the ritual structure in close proximity with older, Hallstatt-period lineage monuments: burial mounds.

The late Hallstatt tumuli and the late La Tène *Viereckschanzen* demonstrate the continuing preoccupation of Iron Age governing elites in west central Europe with legitimacy and lineage affiliation as reflected in communal monuments. In fact, if transitions of power from one lineage to another were not always seamless, and if *Viereckschanzen* were erected and used by each lineage in turn, then a case could be made for interpreting regions with numerous *Viereckschanzen* as contested, politically unstable polities. Regions or sites with only one or two *Viereckschanzen* might have been more politically stable.

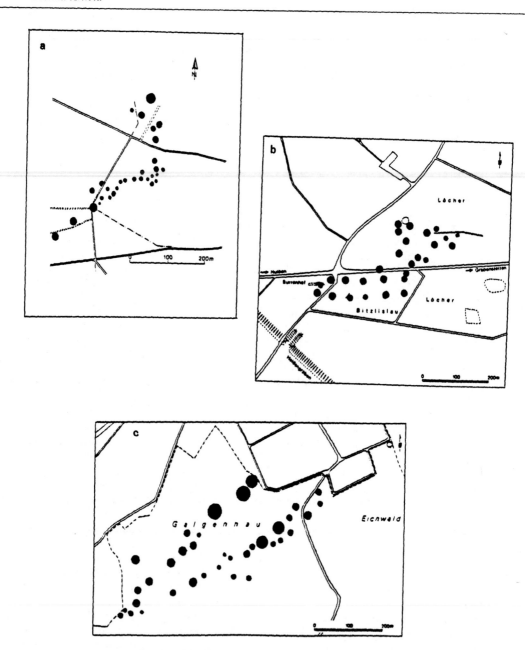

5.3 Linear layout of several Hallstatt tumulus cemeteries in southern Germany. a, *Rubenheim-Wolfersheim;* b, *Burrenhof-Grabenstetten;* c, *Grundsheim-Nürtingen.*

Such hypotheses are testable only if a regional approach to interpreting the Iron Age landscape becomes the focus of archaeological investigation. To date, the approach has been almost exclusively site-specific or chronological (but see Murray forthcoming). This is a potentially fruitful direction for future investigation.

Late Hallstatt centers and the search for "urbanity"

A reexamination of the role of the so-called late Hallstatt *Fürstensitze* is also in order. The hillforts which dominate the landscape and the literature of the West Hallstatt early Iron Age may not have been urban or even proto-urban centers throughout the whole late Hallstatt period, as has been suggested by some researchers (Frankenstein and Rowlands 1978; Härke 1979, 1982; Wells 1980, 1984). A good example is the recent discovery of a hamlet-sized settlement contemporary with the high-status elite burial of Eberdingen-Hochdorf near Stuttgart and in close proximity to the tumulus (Biel 1990, 1991). The Hochdorf burial (Biel 1985) traditionally has been associated with the hillfort center of the Hohenasperg, which is some 10 km away. The discovery of the Eberdingen-Hochdorf farmstead/hamlet suggests that the presence of a high status elite burial in the vicinity of a large apparently central site like the Hohenasperg does not necessarily imply a physical connection between the two. The Eberdingen-Hochdorf discoveries have major implications for the interpretation of the Hohenasperg as a proto-urban central place during the late Hallstatt period. Similar discoveries at the site of Bliesbruck-Reinheim, associated with the early La Tène female elite burial of Reinheim, further support the idea that traditional interpretations of late Hallstatt hillforts need to be revised (Chaume, Olivier, and Reinhard 1994:52).

The relationship between high-status burials and hillforts is more complex than was previously thought. The so-called "*Fürstensitz/Fürstengrab* correlation" may not be valid for all phases of the early Iron Age. There are *Fürstensitze* without associated *Fürstengräber* (the Ipf hillfort, for example) as well as *Fürstengräber* without *Fürstensitze*. Examples of the latter include the *Fürstengräber* of Kappel, Hügelsheim, Söllingen, Baisingen, Dußlingen and Vilsingen. In fact, there are far more *Fürstengräber* without *Fürstensitze* than vice versa. This is to be expected given a settlement pattern in Ha C/D in which high-status elite individuals were dispersed throughout the landscape, not necessarily resident at the regional hillforts.

The territory controlled by governing elites in the early Iron Age might not have outlived them as individuals, especially if territorial control was directly linked to the personal favors owed to and bestowed on lineage members by governing elites. The faunal evidence from late Hallstatt hillforts like the Heuneburg supports the idea that cattle played an important role in the early Iron Age economy (Scabell 1966). Ethnographic studies indi-

cate that wealth based on livestock is subject to fluctuations due to disease, changing birth rates, the availability of pasturage and raiding. If exclusive landownership had not yet developed, and status was based primarily on wealth in cattle and prestige goods, as the archaeological evidence suggests (a pattern also found in the Celtic societies of the British Isles), we need to look to agropastoralist societies, rather than the more traditional agrarian states, when modelling the transition to statehood in the West Hallstatt area.

The emphasis on drinking and feasting equipment as status markers in late Hallstatt burials certainly suggests a system of reciprocity and patronage similar to that documented in later prehistoric and historic times in the British Isles (Arnold 1991a; Dodgshon, this volume). By late Hallstatt times governing elites from lineages with a long history of occupying a particular area seem to have consolidated their social positions. This transition was effected in the West Hallstatt area partly under the influence of an increase in imports from the Mediterranean world. By Hallstatt D2, hillfort "centers" like the Heuneburg became the residences, rather than just the symbolic focus, of late Hallstatt elites (Arnold 1991a).

The late Hallstatt hillforts were probably functionally analogous to early Irish sites, such as Tara or Tailtiu, which hosted the regional "fairs" or *oenachs*. These gatherings served more than the secular purpose of exchanging goods. They were held at times of ritual importance during the agricultural cycle which coincided with lunar and solar festivals, and occasionally included inauguration ceremonies for new leaders (Binchy 1958). Such sites were also seen as the spiritual center of a much larger region composed of loosely affiliated lineages; they were not merely political capitals but acted as symbols of community and continuity. The ideological component of settlement function has been recognized in other time periods, such as the Neolithic. It has been argued that the "text" for the formation of defended settlement enclosures may have initially been "written" in a non-domestic, possibly ritual context (Hodder 1988:70).

Supporting evidence for the hypotheses presented in this section comes from the Heuneburg hillfort, the most extensively documented early Iron Age defended settlement in west central Europe. The large structures found in the unfortified outer settlement of the Heuneburg during Period IV (Ha D1)(Figs. 5.4a, b, and c) support the impression of a dispersed residential pattern during the early phases of the late Hallstatt period, rather than a concentration of elite individuals behind the walls of their fortresses in the feudal mode. The steepest drop of the

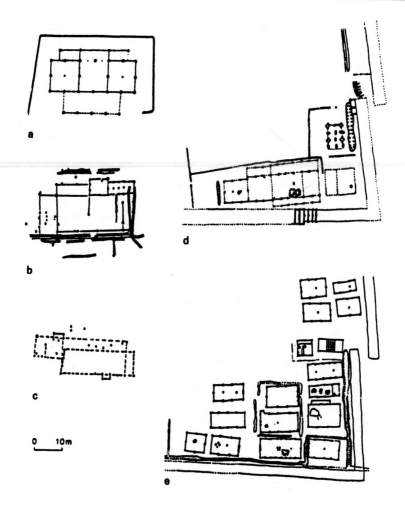

5.4 Comparison to scale of the Period IV outer settlement structures found under the Giessübel-Talhau tumuli with structures on the Heuneburg hillfort plateau in Periods IV and III. a, Structure under Tumulus IV; b, structure under Tumulus I; c, structure under Tumulus II; d, south-east corner plateau structure, Period III; e, South-east corner plateau structures, Period IV.

Heuneburg plateau is also the part of the site which is the most elaborately defended during Period IV (Fig. 5.5), while those parts of the site with the least effective natural defenses are also the most vulnerable. This suggests that the whitewashed mudbrick fortifications were constructed more for their visual impact than for any tactical reason, and were intended primarily to send a social message to those outside the walls.

The outer settlement at the Heuneburg was abandoned after being destroyed in a conflagration which also destroyed the mudbrick wall settlement on the hillfort. The hillfort was subsequently reoccupied; the outer settle-ment, on the other hand, became the burial site for the Period III Heuneburg governing elite. This change in settlement pattern was probably accompanied by a physical move from the extra-mural settlement to the fortified plateau. A consolidation of population is one of the characteristics of early states (Earle 1976:221; Gamble 1981:226). It is significant in this context that the Period III structure (Fig. 5.4d) excavated in the south-east corner of the hillfort resembles the Period IV outer settlement structures in size and layout. They are much larger and more internally complex than the Period IV structures which preceded them on the plateau (Fig. 5.4e). The

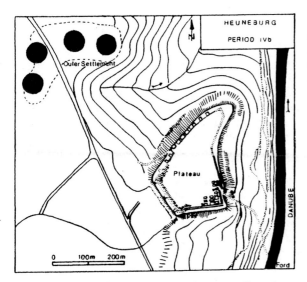

5.5 The Period IVb fortifications and excavated south-eastern portion of the Heuneburg hillfort.

Hochdorf *Herrenhof* discussed earlier is contemporaneous with the Period IV Heuneburg, and also indicates that before Hallstatt D times the settlement pattern was more dispersed, with elites living outside the regional centers.

The closure of the group is an important element in the development of political and economic inequality (Rousseau 1985:41). The factors which restrict the ability of individuals and families to leave one group and join another do not seem to have been operative in early Iron Age society, where *fissioning*, or the budding off of groups from a truncated lineage, may have created the type of dispersed settlement pattern apparently characteristic of Ha C/D1 in the West Hallstatt Zone. This process would also explain the phenomenon of "isolated" *Fürstengräber*, or high-status elite tumuli not associated with a *Fürstensitz*.

The Hallstatt D2 elites related to the individual in the Hochdorf burial may have moved their residence to the Hohenasperg after one or two generations as late Hallstatt society in southern Germany experienced a period of social transformation. The four extremely well-outfitted post-Hallstatt D2 tumuli erected on the abandoned outer settlement at the Heuneburg (they contain most of the gold neckrings and bronze vessels found at the site, and are the only tumuli found in such close proximity to the hillfort) seem to represent a similar physical move onto the plateau, and behind the fortifications.

The consolidation of population which accompanies

the appearance of state-level societies also is often associated with new techniques of production, further underscoring the erosion of household self-sufficiency and the centralization of communal control. Imported ceramics appear on the Heuneburg hillfort for the first time in significant numbers during Period III, the fast potter's wheel is introduced, and more graves containing gold, with more gold objects per grave, appear in the Period III tumuli than in earlier burial mounds at the site (Arnold 1991a). In short, the transition from Heuneburg Period IV to Heuneburg Period III seems to have marked a significant change in social organization; possibly this polity was in the process of developing from a "high" chiefdom to an "early" state. In order to confirm or reject this hypothesis, a similar pattern of population consolidation and small-settlement abandonment during this time would have to be identified at sites other than the Heuneburg. Again, an emphasis on regional archaeology is obviously indicated for the early Iron Age in west central Europe, not least because "spatial structures cannot be theorised without social structure and vice versa" (Tilley 1982:32).

Sumptuary rules, mortuary ritual and status differentiation

The remarkable uniformity of the status object assemblages associated with late Hallstatt high-status elites throughout the West Hallstatt area seems to suggest a *sodality* in Service's definition of the term. Membership in this group appears to have been both non-local and non-residential, two of Service's principal requirements for a sodality. Because of the scattered nature of sodalities, individuals need symbols to signal their membership in the group. Sodalities cross-cut and integrate different residential units and are an important means of integrating residential groups and arranging the configuration of the society (Service 1971:16). The late Hallstatt high-status elite sodality forms a stratum which cuts horizontally across kin groups and territorial boundaries, binding communities together in new ways. This in part explains the relative uniformity of high-status elite material culture in burial throughout the West Hallstatt Zone as compared to the much more heterogeneous material culture associated with non-elite burials through time and space. Such inter-regional connections between elites would have been necessary to facilitate the long-distance trade with the Mediterranean which characterizes this period of the Iron Age.

Hodder describes an analogous phenomenon among the Lozi of western Zambia, where the elite maintain corporateness as administrators and controllers of metal resources by reserving certain artifactual types for their use only, with further differentiation within the elite group. Among non-elites relatively little symbolic differentiation is apparent; there is considerably more individual variablity at the level of secondary elites. For example, all known West Hallstatt high-status elite burials taken together display less variability, despite large sample size, than the Hallstatt cemetery of Rottenburg (Reim 1988), which has a much smaller total number of burials and has yielded no evidence for high-status elite interments. Hodder hypothesizes that because the elite control access to status objects there is no incentive among non-elites to use material culture as a means of internal differentiation (1979:448–9).

The ultimate function of sumptuary rules and of socio-political classes differentiated by such rules is to establish an economic base for power. Groups which begin by differentiating themselves from the rest of the population by means of sumptuary rules may in time establish an economic base which supplants the need for such sodality symbolism. If the transition to economic inequality is successful, the ostentatious funerary display seems to disappear, since it is no longer necessary to legitimize power and prestige. This is a possible explanation for the decline in recognizable mortuary ritual in the course of the late La Tène, accompanied by the rise of the *oppida* and their early state form of social organization, characterized especially by political and economic social classes. Votive deposits seem to replace burials as a means of "destroying" or consuming wealth during this period (Bradley 1985:31).

Ideology as manifested in mortuary practices may mystify, deny or naturalize, rather than reflect, relations of inequality between groups or classes. More importantly, social advertisement in death ritual may be expressly overt where changing relations of domination result in status reordering and consolidation of new social positions (Pearson 1982:110). These observations are especially important in light of the contrast between the burial record of the late Hallstatt period and that of the late Iron Age. The more stable the social conditions, the less overt the mortuary display of social differences (Childe 1945:17; Pauli 1975:199ff) and vice versa. The brief florescence of elaborately outfitted high-status elite burials in the early La Tène period, and the associated looting of most late Hallstatt central tumulus burials, are both characteristic of periods of internal upheaval. The more tenuous the claim to legitimacy, the more important funerary display becomes.

Late Hallstatt/early La Tène internal upheaval: revolution or collapse?

The question of the scale and significance of trade with the Mediterranean world as a source of items involved in display, consumption and gift exchange has been discussed by a number of researchers in different contexts, and poses special problems. Dietler, for example, feels that wear on imported metal and ceramic drinking equipment, as well as the concentration of such objects in burials which are in other respects outfitted above the norm, indicates that such objects were circulated within a very limited group of individuals, and were not involved in a redistributive network (1990b:357–8). It is true that imported drinking vessels of outstanding workmanship, such as the Vix krater, the Grächwil hydria or the griffon cauldron from La Garenne appear only in high-status elite burials. Metal drinking vessels in general, however, are not restricted to this subdivision of the elite stratum, and were mainly of local manufacture during the late Hallstatt period. Early La Tène burials, on the other hand, often contain imported metal vessels without the attendant elite object assemblage characteristic of late Hallstatt high-status elite graves (Arnold 1991a).

While the really rare imports associated with the drinking ritual were probably circulated within a restricted group, indigenously produced drinking and feasting vessels seem to have been part of a redistributive network among elites, as the grave good associations at the Heuneburg and other sites indicate (Arnold 1991a). Bronze vessels are occasionally found in otherwise relatively poorly outfitted graves, indicating that some sort of redistributive system may have existed. Competition for rare exotica may have been the basis of the unrest that is often cited in connection with the abrupt end of many late Hallstatt centers and the thorough looting of most late Hallstatt central burials.

The group which is the most likely candidate for fomenting unrest in late Hallstatt society is not the non-elite majority of the population in the form of a "peasant revolt," as has been suggested by some researchers. It is the non-governing elites who would have had both the resources and the motivation necessary for a disruption of the social order. Fischer has suggested that internal upheaval would probably have been spearheaded by such a group[1] (1982:72). The close relationship between material culture studies and linguistic theory provides a number of working hypotheses which are applicable to an understanding of the dynamic relationship between different elite strata during late Hallstatt times. It is the second highest ranking group that has the most tenuous hold on its social position and also has the most to lose if it is unable to maintain its competitive edge (Labov 1972:244; Miller 1982:89). At the same time, the secondary elites also have the most to gain from a successful challenge of the governing elite. Status objects in the early Iron Age, especially once the regular flow of imports decreased around 400 BC, were manipulated in a struggle for position within the social hierarchy, a so-called "style war" (Morris 1987:42). The suggestion of internal rather than external disruption of the social order is based on the continuity between the late Hallstatt and early La Tène periods, especially with regard to material culture (Schiek 1981:132; Demoule 1989:165). In some areas the two phases seem to be contemporaneous, further supporting the idea that the changes which can be identified were due to a restructuring of society from within.

A possible model for the upheaval of the late Hallstatt/ early La Tène transition is presented in a paper by Björn Qviller (1981), who suggests that the political system of Dark Age Greece collapsed because population growth triggered an escalating spiral of competitive gift exchange. This escalation was caused by *basileis* competing to attract and maintain ever-larger groups of warrior-com- panions through feasting and gift-giving. The struggle created too much stress for the political structure to control, and the *basileis* had to surrender their powers (Morris 1987:203).[2]

Endemic tomb robbery also signals an abdication or loss of social control on the part of the elites in a society; the "second oldest profession in the world" manifests itself in widespread form during such periods of unrest (Steuer 1979:631–2). There were several major incidences of prehistoric tomb robbery in prehistoric Europe – in the early Bronze Age, the late Hallstatt/early La Tène transi- tion, and the early Middle Ages. The late Hallstatt/early La Tène tomb robbery differs from the others in one important respect. Looting was confined almost exclusi- vely to elite burials in the central chambers of tumuli (Pauli 1981:472); secondary burials and graves in flat cemeteries were rarely looted. This is often attributed to the robbers' ignorance of the locations of the secondary burials in the tumulus fill and the expectation of greater gain, but there might have been a socio-symbolic aspect to this systematic desecration as well.

Central burials in tumuli during the late Hallstatt period were literally monuments to lineage legitimacy. The objects associated with the governing elite, such as gold neckrings, drinking vessel sets and other grave furniture, like the Hochdorf couch, or *kline* (which has its counterpart in a number of other looted central burials) were vested with authority. Disturbing such burials and

acquiring such objects had symbolic as well as economic ramifications for the looters, who may very well have either belonged to or been operating under the orders of secondary elites. It is surely not a coincidence that by the end of the late Hallstatt period, at sites like the Heune- burg, burial mounds are located significantly closer to the settlement, and tombs can be shown to have been looted within a very short time after the burial.

A feature all three periods of prehistoric tomb robbing share is the increase of amulets in all burials, also an indication of unrest and troubled times (Pauli 1981:472). An extensive study of late Hallstatt tomb robbing is necessary to clarify its possible social, political, economic and/or ideological motivations. Was there a consistent *modus operandi*? Are there differences in the amount of time which elapsed between burial and looting? What sorts of objects were left behind by the looters, and is there a discernible pattern? What significance do unlooted wealthy central burials in certain regions have for the interpretation of this phenomenon? (Driehaus 1974:154). Who were the tomb robbers? What segment of society did they belong to? Pauli attributes the looting to greedy individuals acting on their own, lured by the promise of particularly wealthy graves (1981:474); this is the most simplistic and least likely interpretation, given the syste- matic and targeted nature of the looting during the late Hallstatt/early La Tène transition.

The disruption of trade with the Mediterranean around 400 BC has often been postulated as one of the causes of the breakdown of the West Hallstatt centers, and it seems probable that the interruption of the redistributive network may have led to an attempt on the part of the non-governing, secondary elites to assert themselves by acquiring status objects through looting. Other factors were certainly operative as well, but are more difficult to identify in the archaeological record as it stands at present.

The period between 600 and 400 BC in west central Europe was characterized by rapid, regionally specific changes in social organization which are documented directly in the burial record and indirectly in the settle- ment evidence, as this discussion has tried to show. The increase in social complexity does not seem to have survived the late Hallstatt/early La Tène transition, although the late La Tène *Viereckschanzen* and relatively rapid appearance of many late La Tène *oppida* from a dispersed settlement base (Murray forthcoming) indicate that continuity was maintained throughout this time. Several directions for future research suggest themselves: 1. an increased emphasis on regional studies focussing on the late Hallstatt period, along the lines of research by

Crumley, Marquardt, Murray and others; 2. a systematic approach to clarifying the temporal relationship between small dispersed settlements and hillfort settlements ("*Fürstensitze*") throughout the early Iron Age; 3. more detailed analysis of burial populations at well-excavated sites like the Heuneburg, including numerous smaller tumuli which have never been systematically investigated. In short, there is good evidence to suggest that the two hundred years which make up the late Hallstatt period in west central Europe represent a society in the process of crossing the threshold from a "developed" chiefdom to an "early" state. If we intend to bring the picture into sharper focus, we will have to formulate more specific research designs which address the question of state formation and social evolution in a European context.

Notes

1 It is this group of individuals also which is responsible for the numerous coup attempts in the early Irish literature discussed in more detail in Arnold (n.d.)

2 Demoule sees the late Hallstatt/early La Tène transition as the result of a "revolution politique," causing the temporary disappearance of the dominant social group, its dependants (including artisan specialists), as well as the disruption of long-distance trade (1989:166). He makes the interesting observation that it may be significant that similar movements against economic and political oppression were in progress in the Mediterranean area around the same time: Tarquinius in Rome and Pisistrades in Athens were both ousted by popular revolts during the sixth century BC.

6
The significance of major settlements in European Iron Age society

OLIVIER BÜCHSENSCHÜTZ

Introduction

The development of "central places" in a number of societies during the European Iron Age is a phenomenon which has often attracted the attention of researchers. As twentieth-century scholars, we associate this phenomenon almost automatically with the expansion of craft industries and trade activities, and also with the development of social hierarchy. In actuality, the components which contributed to the first appearance of real towns appeared separately and at different times in the various countries of Europe. We are not justified to apply the concept of urbanization until the late Iron Age. It was precisely this phenomenon of urbanization which allowed the conquest of all the Celtic countries by the Romans.

I would like to examine the elements which are characteristic of European central places, from the first agglomerations of dwellings to the emergence of *oppida*, and to raise the problem of the social implications of such transformations. I will try to show that these settlements, whether fortified or not, cannot be said to play the role of "central places" in the sense that this expression is normally understood by geographers in spatial analysis. We do not have sufficient data to interpret the nature of these settlement complexes, therefore we cannot define the precise functions which these central places may have had in the societies of Iron Age Europe. I would make distinctions between the different types of major settlements of the last six centuries BC, and propose that these settlements embodied different major functions for the societies of each successive period.

Characteristics of the major settlements in the European Iron Age

Fortified settlements

The Iron Age cultures inherited from the populations that preceded them a long-established tradition, that of the construction of hillforts. Promontory forts and hilltop fortifications first appeared in the Bronze Age and grew steadily in number. At the same time other forms of site planned on a similar pattern underwent development. These settlements were defended by a natural cliff or river system. Further massive fortifications, often of monumental proportions, blocked the natural access.

The widespread preference for settlements possessing these sorts of defenses cannot be explained by the fighting techniques of the period. In many instances these fortified sites occupy exceptional locations, on which one would not be surprised to find a sanctuary instead of a hillfort. Moreover their sometimes very vast enclosed areas would seemingly require a number of defenders in excess of the estimated size of the manpower pool available at that time. Natural defenses are incapable of offering protection from a surprise attack. The ramparts themselves, with their internal wooden framework encased behind an external stone facing, are more impressive than efficient. The point is to show the status of the town and the territorial resources at its command by their monumental construction.

These hillforts exhibit a variable geographical and chronological development. I would like to draw your attention to three characteristic sequences:

1. A tendency to build defenses of increasing complexity, leading eventually to exceptional monuments, particularly in southern Britain.

2. An increase in the areas enclosed, which are, at the end of La Tène times, considerable throughout the Celtic world. The range in size of enclosed surface area increased initially from 1–10 ha to 50 ha, and then rose to 100–500 ha. This change in settlement scale is very important. As a point of fact, we know of farmsteads of early and late Iron Age date which occupy from 1 to 5 ha, but these were inhabited by no more than a few families. When the internal area of a settlement is as small as this, only excavations can give us an estimate of the density of the population. We cannot know without excavation if the settlement consisted of a single farm with surrounding houses, or if it was a village of about ten families. On the other hand, sites that have enclosed areas larger than 50 ha fulfil the functions of central places. They remain exceptional up to the end of the Iron Age.

3. The characteristic feature of settlements of the last

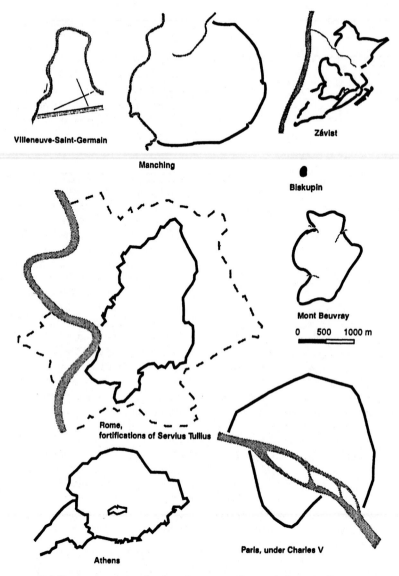

Villeneuve-Saint-Germain

Manching

Závlst

Biskupin

Mont Beuvray

0   500   1000 m

Rome,
fortifications of Servius Tullius

Athens

Paris, under Charles V

6.1 Comparison to scale of surface area of central places in Europe.

phase of the La Tène period is the extension of the artificial defenses. This development was to the detriment of military considerations. *Oppida* were traditionally built on sites which were already occupied during the Bronze and early Iron Ages. But they are surrounded by lines of defense which are continuous, sometimes at the expense of the advantages conferred by relief. It seems that the intention was to separate the internal area completely from the outside. At the same time, the monumental

appearance of the gateway increases. These gates seem better suited to control humans and goods than for defense only.

In settlements such as Manching, Bavaria (Krämer and Maier 1970–89), the enclosing defenses are entirely man-made. The builders have deliberately chosen to fortify 380 ha, as no natural constraint demarcates an area more easily defended. If we are to believe Roman legends, the fortifications that Servius Tullius had build around Rome in the sixth century (or in the fourth century according to archaeological evidence) enclosed approximately 400 ha (Fig. 6.1).

Planned settlements

A second series of settlements might also be described as central places. These are fortified and unfortified settlements which include twenty or more houses, all more or less similar, built in regular lines. Scholars have described such settlement patterns in terms of urbanism, and ascribe them to Greek influence even when their situations in space and time makes such Mediterranean influences totally unlikely (Niesiołowska-Wedzka 1974:227).

The planning of a settlement with an organized layout, which is, after all, an urban feature, may actually appear very early in the long evolution which leads from the first villages to the emergence of towns. This is due to the fact that settlement organization is strongly linked with the problems of defense. Only rigorous planning can shelter as many people as possible behind an efficient fortification. The smaller the site, the more efficiently it can be protected. A smaller defended site allows for more economical use of resources that go into its construction, the most important being wood. It is no wonder then that the first fortified settlements appear beside lakes in the Alps as well as in Poland (e.g. Biskupin). Planning provides the best way to use a limited area.

A basic feature sets these Iron Age settlements apart from Greek towns planned on the Hippodamian model. Ancient Mediterranean towns have streets which intersect at right angles, delimiting square or rectangular blocks. In the Iron Age settlements the streets are parallel. There are no streets which run at right angles to these streets or otherwise intersect them. People could only walk from east to west in Biskupin (Kostrzewski 1950), and from north to south-east in the *oppidum* of Nages in Gard (Languedoc, France; Py 1978). The former settlement in Poland is exclusively constructed of wood, whereas Nages, located not far from the Mediterranean coast, is entirely stone-built. Despite these differences their rigid layout is very similar, if not very convenient for everyday life. The Iron Age settlement recently excavated in Martigues, Bouches-du-Rhône (Chausserie-Laprée 1985), on the isle between the Etang de Berre and the sea, is laid out on the same pattern.

The collective lay-out

The laying-out of areas or buildings for public purposes is also a typical feature of towns. The presence of both a sanctuary and a square, where political business or trade can be transacted, underlines the difference between the town and the rural settlement. The curious thing is that the settlements which I have just mentioned lack such squares. Their internal area is entirely taken up by identical houses. No building evokes a specific function from its ground plan, nor is there any space available for meetings, even in the open air. Examples of collective lay-outs are scarce in Iron Age settlements. For example, no traces of this kind have been noticed at the Heuneburg (Württemberg, Germany; Kimmig 1983a).

Závist in Bohemia is an exception (Motyková *et al.* 1982). On the acropolis of a settlement which was to become the biggest *oppidum* in the country at the end of the La Tène period, a big sanctuary was built in the early La Tène. Excavations revealed several foundations of stone buildings, probably temples and porticos, displaying several construction phases, as did the surrounding enclosure, occupying about 1 ha.

The buildings which B. Cunliffe has rightly identified as temples in the center of the hillfort of Danebury (Hampshire) seem very late (Cunliffe 1984). The building of a "*fanum*" on an *oppidum* immediately after the Gallic War suggests that an area was selected for religious activities on the *oppidum* at the end of the Iron Age. At Bibracte on Mount Beuvray in Burgundy, for example, there was an unoccupied area in the vicinity of the later Roman temple. Recent excavations, directed by K. Gruel, have indicated that this area was always kept free of any buildings or occupation debris. Its enclosure consisted of earthen banks and several ditches and palisades. The archaeological layers, which otherwise cover the whole *oppidum*, do not continue across this enclosed area (Büchsenschütz 1989). Recent research on the *oppidum* of Alesia, also in Burgundy, proves that the central square was to be built only after the conquest.

The covered ditches of Villeneuve-Saint-Germain in the Aisne valley were also built in the decades following the Gallic War (Debord *et al.* 1989; Figs. 6.2 and 6.3). Some 300 m long, these ditches divide the settlement into quarters. Even though the houses at this settlement consist of wood and daub, the layout is already urban. At the junction of the four covered ditches the interpenetration of the roofs was probably very monumental and impressive. This is the only known example of such a feature in the Celtic world.

Specialized activities

We can at least distinguish central places from the other settlements of the Iron Age through the specialized activities that took place inside them. The Celtic world is

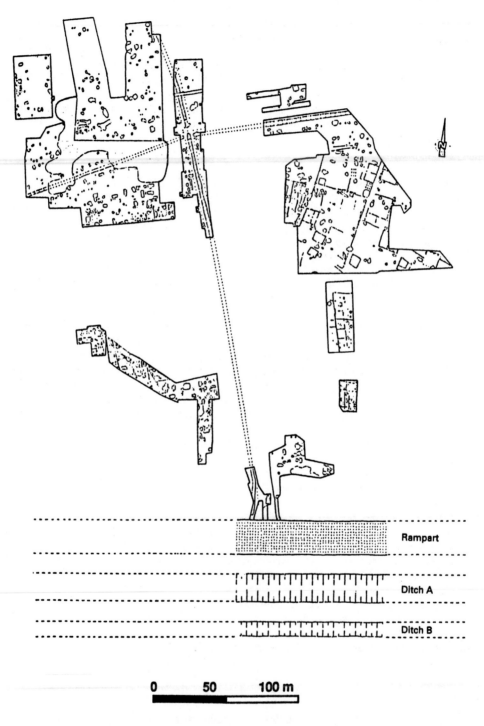

Rampart

Ditch A

Ditch B

0   50   100 m

6.2 The excavated areas in the oppidum of Villeneuve-Saint-Germain and the junction of the four covered ditches.

6.3 A reconstruction drawing of the four covered ditches (drawing by B. Lambot).

characterized overall by its agricultural basis, and the isolated farmsteads and hamlets, as well as the bigger settlements, were primarily farms. As early as the Hallstatt period, some traces of craft industry appear here and there, but they amount to no more than one or two workshops; their activity can be assessed by the quantity of scrap left over from manufacturing that has been recovered.

These traces indicate that craft production remained on a very small scale until the second century BC. It is not on the hillforts but on open lowland settlements that the first concentrations of iron and bronze slags, and refuse from bone artifact production, come to light. In the same settlements the numerous discoveries of gold, silver, and bronze coins, as well as the substantial quantity of amphora sherds that have been found, prove the increasing development of trade activities. We cannot spot a break in the archaeological record with the third and fourth centuries at these sites – the products of the earlier craft industries and of commerce remain more or less the same. But the quantities change so much that we may imagine that the activity of part of the population in these settlements was devoted to trade or craft production.

The evolution of major settlements during the Iron Age

The early Iron Age

From the earliest period the settlements of the Iron Age are characterized by great variation in size and form: isolated farmsteads, hamlets, and villages can be found in regions such as Bavaria. Two kinds of major settlements are found during the early Iron Age in Europe north of the Alps: hillforts and lakeside forts. The latter were planned settlements, but their rigorous plans are the only feature they share with urban centers. They were limited in surface area. They involved communities which were still agricultural. Traces of craft production are diffuse and scarce. To judge from the site plan, no space in the settlement was allocated for activities of a collective nature. Commerce was reduced to a minimum.

Our knowledge of these hillforts is nearly always limited to the fortifications. Traces of dwellings are often discovered in concentration behind the ramparts. On the Wittnauer Horn, Switzerland (Bersu 1946) or on the Heuneburg (Kimmig 1983a), the houses occupied the periphery of the settlement – we do not know if the center was free of buildings, or if it has been destroyed by erosion. Much has already been written on the Heuneburg, even though full publication is not yet available. The artifacts found in the houses suggest the existence of craft production and food storage. It should be noted that the only structure that stands out from the others by virtue of its size and by the number of rooms it had is not located within the fortifications, but lies outside these at the foot of the hill. It would be bold to jump to the conclusion that the chief lived outside his citadel, and that his troops and his court were resident inside the hillfort. Yet we may suppose that a prince lived there with his court, his soldiers, and a few craftsmen. The Heuneburg looks more like a castle than a town. It is a place that was completely dependent upon an aristocrat with absolute power.

The area of the settlement at the Heuneburg covers only 3 ha. We know of bigger late Hallstatt hillforts in the same region such as the Große Heuneburg and the Ipf; however, the excavations at these sites were still too limited to draw conclusions as to the nature of these settlements (Fig. 6.4).

The excavated central places of the first Iron Age are few in number, the settlement areas were small, but their purposes were well defined: the defense of the peasant community in the case of Biskupin, or the service of the prince in the heart of the Hallstatt area. Their function was limited and they played a small role in the settlement system. However, we should not forget that in most regions at this time people remained scattered in the countryside.

Early La Tène and the Celts of Italy

In the early La Tène the use of hillforts seems to have ceased. The available data show that during this period isolated farms or hamlets were scattered across the landscape. At these settlements agricultural activities predominated. The biggest cemeteries correspond to communities of just a few families. Only in southern England were some hillforts still to be found, and these were used largely for storage.

Data on central places are available for Cisapline Gaul as early as the third century, thanks to Roman authors. Ch. Peyre has demonstrated that there were different kinds of settlements that corresponded to the various tribes, and which were also in keeping with the previous level of urbanization that had been attained in the regions where these tribes had settled (Peyre 1979). For the Senones, for example, neither historical records nor archaeological traces of their *oppida* can be found. Contrastingly, in Cis- and Transpadana, Livy talks about *oppida* and also about smaller settlements, the *castella*.

In the case of the Insubri, the capture of the central places by the Romans produced the surrender of the entire population. However the resistance of the Boii continued even after their *oppidum* fell. The Romans were always surprised when the Gauls vanished into the countryside,

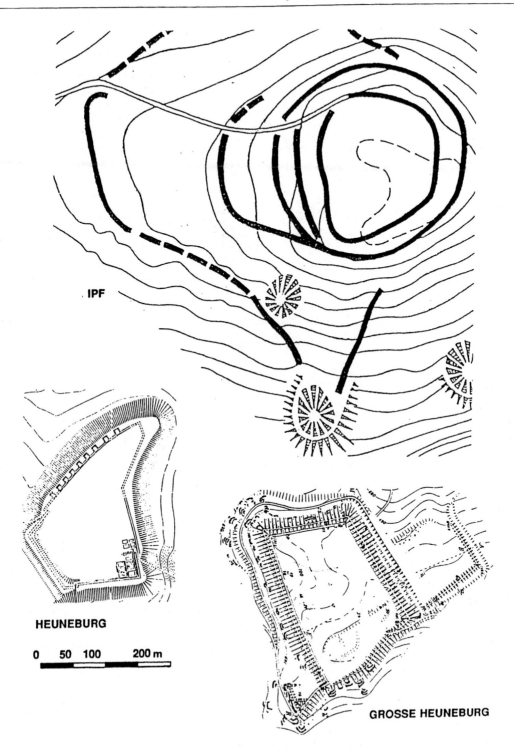

6.4 Hallstatt period fortified settlements in Württemberg.

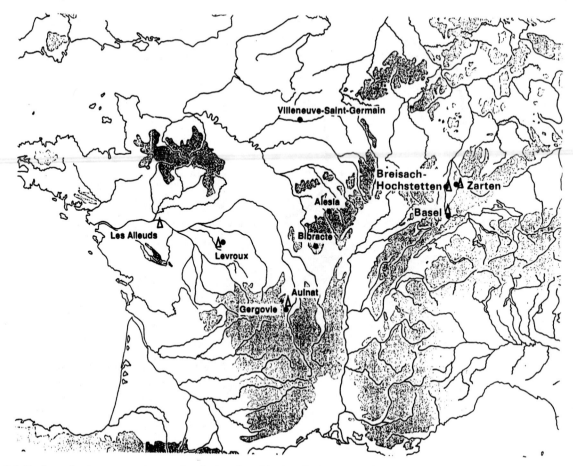

6.5 Craft production centres (open triangles) and oppida *(circles) mentioned in the text.*

where craft production as well as governing authorities were scattered. Livy talks of a Roman embassy sent to the Cenomani, which was compelled to travel throughout the countryside to consult the scattered chieftains.

The Celts of Italy really did come into contact with the towns of the peninsula, and even occupied some of them, but this did not modify their economic and social organization. These towns were not centers of power, nor did they offer protection from attack to their inhabitants. Like their northern counterparts, the Celtic tribes of Italy remained basically rural in their activities as well as in their social organization.

Middle La Tène

In *Gallia comata* a new group of central places appeared during the middle La Tène, probably in the second century BC. These settlements are not well preserved from an architectural point of view, because their houses leave only faint traces of post holes and gullies. Remains of negative features such as storage pits, workshops, and wells frequently extend over an area as large as ten hectares. Excavations at these centers have also produced abundant artifacts which were deposited in pits. These enable us to distinguish the middle La Tène central places from the agricultural settlements of the preceding period.

For the first time crafts and trade come to play an important role alongside agricultural activities in the middle La Tène. As early as the end of the second century BC Hochstetten and Basel in the Rhine valley, Levroux in Indre, Aulnat near Gergovia display their roles as craft making and trading centers. This evidence contradicts the traditional view that these activities first appeared at *oppida* (Fig. 6.5).

*The end of the La Tène period and the "*oppida *culture"*
In the late La Tène the lowland villages of the middle La Tène were deserted, sometimes in favor of a neighboring hill as at Levroux, where the *oppidum* lies about 1500 m from the open settlement. With its continuous fortifications, which enclosed 20 ha from the start, this *oppidum* seems to have been established as a deliberate foundation. The village was moved to a nearby place, which had been prepared to receive the population. We can imagine in this act of foundation the creation of a new town.

I will not describe the characteristic features of *oppida* sites, which have already been well established. Instead, I would like to insist only on identifying those features displayed by *oppida* which are typical of central places. When this has been accomplished, I think that one would have to agree that *oppida*-type settlements can be said to have been towns in the full sense of the word.

Those attributes of *oppida* which justify their identification as central places are:

1. Continuous fortifications with monumental gates. These act to define an area separated from the surrounding country. We imagine that there were tolls at the gates for goods, and that the behavior of the people who lived within the *oppida* was regulated by laws (Büchsenschütz and Ralston 1987).

2. An habitation area much larger than the space enclosed in previous periods. Other considerations could now come into play concerning the selection of locations for these *oppida* settlements, since they were no longer restricted by the relief of their surroundings. Their placement suggests the intention to draw a great number of people behind the fortifications. It calls to mind the policy of the French kings, Charles V for example, who in 1317 extended the fortified area of Paris from 250 to 414 ha in order to attract craftsmen and tradesmen (Fig. 6.1).

3. Strangely enough, many *oppida* were built on hilltops, whilst the villages of middle La Tène lay directly on the trade networks. How can we account for this choice, other than by the return to an ancient tradition, perhaps linked with religious conceptions, which legitimated or helped to introduce many new things in these places?

4. The street network, the planning of sanctuaries, the appearance of districts with specialized activities are suggested more than they are demonstrated by excavations. In Gaul, these features indicative of town planning are most obvious in the post-conquest decades. The buildings of this period may have destroyed older structures. Urban features slowly increase at these centers, which Caesar sometimes referred to as *urbes*. The testimonies of the classical writers insist either upon the still

barbarian or already civilized aspects of these settlements, depending on the context of their remarks.

Urbanization appears in the Celtic world only shortly before the conquest, and before the end of the first century BC nearly all the *oppida* had been deserted by their inhabitants for the new Gallo-Roman lowland towns. The urbanization of the *oppida* is quickly aborted, but undoubtedly merits this description, since *oppida* display all of the functions of central places.

Major settlements and Iron Age society

Major settlements and central places

The nature of the European Iron Age settlements leads researchers to develop spatial hierarchical models. We know in fact of three types of settlements which coexisted from the Bronze Age north of the Alps: hillforts, open villages or lake villages, and isolated farmsteads. This configuration facilitates the development of spatial analysis and the use of central place theory. Many scholars have suggested models of territorial organization, and even of the society, based on the hillforts. The distribution of hillforts would allow the reconstruction of their territories, and their relative sizes made a hierarchical classification possible. D. Clarke, one of the most famous to use these theories, built around Glastonbury a model which integrated open settlements and hillforts. This method is very exciting and helps us to question the data. However it is useless when we come to consider the chronology and the cultural parameters. J. Collis has already demonstrated that if the hillforts utilized in a model are not contemporaneous, such an interpretation is impossible (Collis 1981). Thus it is very dangerous to build a model based on hillforts when their dating is uncertain. The temptation to do so is, however, very great.

The second difficulty has been less often mentioned. It deals with the function of central places. According to writers upon this subject, central places seem to have played the role of markets, and places to exchange goods and information (Smith 1976:6). Authors most often present the relationships between central places and isolated settlements in terms of trade relations. Spatial organization would depend at first on the nature of the exchanges, on the management of surplus, on the means of transport, on the relationships between consumers and producers. Endo- or exogamic strategies and administrative pressures, which do not always have the same purposes as the market, are more rarely mentioned.

In fact, the theory of central places is based on the idea that societies progress irremediably toward urbanization, and that as central places have arisen, they have condensed all the power to the detriment of the rest of the territory. Considering the fact that this general trend is illustrated by the present evolution of nearly all the world's countries, the model is not absurd. But if the historian's aim consists of reconstructing a past period on its own, without seeing in it the origins of his own culture, we have to consider the Iron Age from another point of view.

We have already underlined the fact that Celtic society was not urban in essence. Political power was in the hands of the aristocracy, which were dispersed in the country-side. The function of the hillforts – refuge, storage, feast places, sanctuary – is not obvious for us. Anyway, we know that their distribution, their number, their area, evolved with time. These were permanent monuments which were used, depending upon the regions and the times, for various purposes by different actors of the society.

Typical elements of central places appear very late in the Iron Age. The hillforts and the ancient nucleated settlements have not provided measures which enable us to attribute to them the functions of a pre-urban center. Central place models can be used to study that period, and particularly in evaluating the level of centralization in each *civitas* (Ralston 1992).

Major settlements, central places and Iron Age society

Schematically, we can offer a social interpretation of the evolution of major settlements into central places or pre-urban centers from Hallstatt to late La Tène by consider-ing the other archaeological data (burials and artifacts) and historical data.

The coexistence of hillforts and isolated farmsteads is typical of the late Hallstatt period. In the regions that were in contact with the Mediterranean world, an elite took control of the distribution of prestige goods. It showed its power by erecting rich family burials and hillforts that were small, but had spectacular fortifications. Apparently the elite controlled these hillforts – we do not know if the chiefs stayed in them – where they kept goods and employed the craftsmen who made luxury artifacts for their courts. We propose that hillforts of this type, and this social organization, disappeared at the beginning of the fifth century.

In the early La Tène, wealth and political power were once again spread throughout the country. Cemeteries were situated in the vicinity of a hamlet or of a farm, where a chief, his customers, and their families were assembled. The presence of weapons in the men's burials, and of a chariot in the chief's grave, demonstrates that we are dealing with a society of free farmers. Individual political

status is reflected in the armaments, as it is in many societies of antiquity. Hillforts at that time were for the most part neglected.

The villages of the middle and late La Tène were the first central places, in so far as they constituted a dynamic market place in a diversified economy. Artisanal produc-tion tended then to develop the manufacturing of tools, ornaments, objects for everyday life and for the benefit of everybody. Trade, with the growing use of money, con-cerned a bigger part of the population. These villages of course were set at the intersections of roads. We do not know the origin and the social situation of these craftsmen and tradesmen, but it is obvious that they now constituted a group that was different from the farmers.

The development of the *oppida* seems to have attracted participants from all social levels, the new as well as the traditional ones. The old hillfort tradition was linked with the newest economic activities. The area of the new hillfort was 10 or 20 times as large as it used to be, obviously aiming at attracting the living strength of the country to a central place, to a town.

Was Celtic society deeply modified by this phenome-non? According to Caesar, *oppida* played a role in the destabilization of Gallic society. Traditional chiefs still lived in the *aedificia*. Vercingetorix, born of a royal family, found it difficult to compel recognition in Gergovia. The political control of the major settlements seems to have been fundamental to the domination of a *civitas*; but these places had not yet succeeded in gathering there the whole elite. The *oppida* were the places where the different social classes came into conflict, they were places where the clients of the powerful whom Caesar mentions appeared and disappeared.

A late and quickly abandoned experience, the move-ment to the *oppida* was both the outcome and the end of the Celtic world. As soon as a class of craftsmen and traders, urban settlements, and the organization of the *civitas* developed, nothing prevented the fusion of the Celtic and the Roman worlds. The northern limits of the Roman empire matched approximately the distribution of the *oppida*, leaving outside rural cultures too difficult to be controlled by the Roman state.

Conclusions

The concepts of "major settlement," "hillfort," and "central place" correspond to different types of reality. The "central places," as they have been defined by the modern geographers, do not appear before the late La Tène.

The essential distinction, seen from a contemporary

perspective, between southern and temperate Europe in the late Iron Age is between the societies where the countryside was organized for the benefit of cities and those in which the rise of urban centers met opposition from rural, land-based groups which held on to their power. The Gallo-Roman towns must have taken some time to establish their domination: it is an open question whether the *villae* of Gaul (where they were the successors of the *aedificia*) played a more significant role in this process than in Italy (Lewuillon 1990). Should we view the political organization of medieval Europe, marked by the eclipse of cities in favor of aristocratic, ecclesiastical, or even royal estates, in terms of – *mutatis mutandis* - the resurgence of a Celtic form of social organization? Should we employ "chiefdoms" in our discussions of medieval Europe? It is self-evident that such a practice would add nothing to our understanding.

The use of broad-brush models, such as "central place" or "chiefdom" or "archaic state" intended to subdivide the general, broad-scale evolutionary patterns of primitive communities, is inappropriate for the delineation of European societies between 500 BC and 1000 AD. To apply the latest sociological theory to societies which are known not only from archaeology, but also from textual sources, their coinage and so on, may in the end allow that theory to be evaluated; but it does not help us in our knowledge of the period. The solution will rather be provided by juxtaposing the evidence obtained from different kinds of sources (archaeological, literary, and numismatic); and by more effective means (both statistical and cartographic) of treating the available data. There is no use in asking questions which are too wide ranging. There is no use in producing solely ever more refined chronological and typological studies either. More ambitious questions need to be tailored to take account of the nature and quantity of data available, and of the complexity of the problems that require to be dealt with.

In particular, from the second century BC on, the rapid development of artisanal production differing from the domestic mode is apparent; long-distance commerce in bulk goods expanded rapidly too. The latter has little to do with the exchange of high-status goods which characterized earlier periods. Commerce of the former kind was able to develop because of innovations in industrial technologies and developments in transport systems; moreover, the increasing use of coined money was a significant factor. These changes help to account for the increase of state-level organizations, which no longer restricted their role to the military sector, but from then on took control of part of the commercial activity. Traditional Celtic societies nonetheless continued to flourish alongside the new elites and the new power structures, such as the *civitates*. We may compare Louvernius throwing coins to his clients (Strabo, *Geographia*, 4, 2,3), with Dumnorix living from his revenues as a tax collector on the Saône (*De Bello Gallico*, i.18).

Not only were Celtic societies complex, they were also being split by opposing pressures in the years before the conquest. Fitting supermodels around the fragmentary archaeological data for this period hardly seems an effective way of advancing research. It would be preferable, in our opinion, to read the Classical sources afresh and to compare and contrast the information they contain with the results of new excavations: these have produced a wealth of information on settlement structures, on artisanal production and on the development of coinage.

Recent American anthropological output has had the benefit of displacing European work – undoubtedly too heavily based on archaeological perspectives – on the nature of social structures. In France such a wide-ranging discussion has not been under way since the days of Fustel de Coulanges, Hubert, and Jullian. But any new dialogue should take into account the progress of research, and should not simply reheat issues that were under discussion almost a century ago.

Acknowledgments

I should like to express my gratitude to Bettina Arnold and Blair Gibson, who helped me to find bibliographic references to central place theory, to temper my critiques of some Anglo-Saxon models, and my thanks to C. Goldenstein, who helped me to correct my English.

7

Early "Celtic" socio-political relations: ideological representation and social competition in dynamic comparative perspective

MICHAEL DIETLER

Socio-political transformations

An understanding of the social dynamics of European Iron Age societies has been hindered by typological approaches employing static models of socio-political structure that are focussed on stages or levels of "complexity." Such approaches obscure the historical processes through which political and economic goals are pursued and contested and which are ultimately responsible for structural change. Although rooted in an older functionalist perspective, Aiden Southall's (1968) discussion of stateless societies provides a convenient and useful working vocabulary for approaching and characterizing several fundamental transformative processes in the development of the complex social and political relations which are generally taken to underlie mature states. Several of these processes are potentially identifiable in the archaeological record of Iron Age Europe. However, their investigation requires a critical appreciation of the role of ideological representation and social competition in the enactment of these processes and in the production of the material record by which we know these societies. The processes in question include: 1. the institutionalization of informal leadership into formal political roles; 2. the shift from "distributive legitimacy" to hierarchical authority; 3. the merging of multipolities; and 4. the institutionalization of social inequality.

The first process involves the naturalization or reification of durable authority roles out of fluid, informally negotiated, individual concentrations of social power. By "distributive legitimacy" is meant a situation in which "legitimate political action belongs to multiple points and levels, without any overriding monopoly or delegation from above" (Southall 1968:161). This is a political manifestation of Carole Crumley's (1987a) more general concept of "heterarchy." A shift from this condition toward hierarchy involves a reduction in the number and a ranking of the points of legitimate political action, as well as a concentration and rigidification of the channels of control. As Crumley rightly points out, not all states exhibit a decidedly hierarchical structure. But many do, or did; and where such a process can be detected it merits study. By "multipolities" Southall meant the existence within a single society of plural and highly flexible coadunations of political activity, or what may be called "political communities" (1968:158). The merging of multipolities within a region or a society reduces the number of political communities and increases the size of the territories and populations of those which emerge. These larger clusters of political relationships are, in the phrase of Benedict Anderson (1991), "imagined communities" on a new scale, and for the reproduction of their existence they require the construction of emotionally charged traditions of identity with evocative symbols marshalled to invoke authenticity (see also Hobsbawm 1983). Finally, the institutionalization of social inequality is a process whereby disparities in relations of economic and political power among social groups or categories produced through manipulation of social, economic, and cultural resources are reproduced in ways that naturalize and formalize their existence.

A dynamic comparative analysis of Iron Age socio-political systems offers particularly promising potential for addressing these issues and for assessing the plausibility of social interpretation. Such analysis should focus on diachronic patterns of contrast among interacting societies, and may be especially effective when exploring contrasting reactions to a common phenomenon, in this case the colonial encounter with Mediterranean states. Given the interconnected historical development of Iron Age societies, only such comparative analysis which views local histories at the juncture with larger regional structures of power is capable of revealing the nature of socio-political processes and structures in any given society (Dietler 1989, 1990a).

Early Iron Age western Europe: regional focus

This discussion will center around societies occupying two interconnected regions in western Europe during the early part of the Iron Age, from roughly the late seventh to the mid fifth century BC. These regions include the lower Rhône basin of southern France and the West Hallstatt region of eastern France, south-western Germany, and western Switzerland. The article will emphasize an exploration of the divergent responses by indigenous societies in these two regions to the "encounter" with the same Mediterranean colonial states during this period. This process of colonial interaction has frequently been implicated in the development of social and political relations among the native societies of both areas (although not without dissent and caveats in the case of the Hallstatt region: cf. Bintliff 1984a, Gosden 1985, Dietler 1989, 1990b; Pare 1991). Theoretical frameworks for exploring this issue have ranged from more or less explicitly articulated concepts of "Hellenization" and "acculturation" (cf. Benoit 1965; Py 1968; Wells 1980; Kimmig 1983a), to Wallersteinian, Braudelian, and other, more ambiguous versions of "world-systems" theory (cf. Frankenstein and Rowlands 1978; Brun 1987; Cunliffe 1988), to historical political economy and related perspectives (Dietler 1990a; Py 1990). Responses to contact were, in fact, far from uniform; and a comparative regional examination of the patterns of settlement, funerary treatment, and consumption associated with colonial interaction may reveal a great deal about socio-political relations and processes among these societies.

The initial region to be considered is constituted by an area extending over eastern France, south-western Germany, and western Switzerland. For the early Iron Age, this area is commonly considered as a kind of "core" of what is called the West Hallstatt Region. This discussion will center around what, for convenience, may be called the Hallstatt *Fürstensitze* zone within this larger West Hallstatt Region. This zone is characterized by certain stylistic commonalities in material culture and, more importantly, during the final phase of the early Iron Age (Hallstatt D 2–3 or Hallstatt final), it evinces what may arguably be interpreted as a consistently replicated settlement pattern of micro-regions with central defended hilltop settlements surrounded by wealthy tumulus burials (see Kimmig 1969, 1983b; Härke 1979; Fischer 1987; Pare 1991; and the prudent caveat of Eggert 1989).

The second major region, which I refer to as the "lower Rhône basin," is situated several hundred km to the south. It is a roughly triangular area that abuts the Mediterranean on its southern edge and lies at the base of the valley formed by the Rhône as it cuts between the Alps and the Massif Central. It is in the lower Rhône basin that significant contacts with the Mediterranean states first occurred. These contacts began during the late seventh century BC with the expeditions of Etruscan traders to the shores of southern France. At about 600 BC, Greek colonists from Phocaea founded the first permanent col-

onial outpost in the region, the city of Massalia (modern Marseilles), and gradually eclipsed the Etruscans as the main agents of trade in the region (see Villard 1960; Benoit 1965; Morel 1981; Py 1985, 1990; Bouloumié 1985, 1987; Dietler 1990a; Arcelin 1992; Bats 1992).

At a superficial level, there are several cultural similarities between the societies inhabiting the two main regions selected for discussion, including a mixed agropastoral subsistence base (employing essentially the same range of crops and animals, but in different proportions), hilltop settlements, tumulus burials, and the adoption of exotic goods from the Greek and Etruscan states (particularly objects centering around the practice of drinking wine). However, a closer comparative analysis shows important differences in all these features and in the socio-political organization of these societies and associated processes of social change.

The West Hallstatt Zone

The societies of the Hallstatt *Fürstensitze* region have for a long time been identified as possessing a markedly hierarchical social and political structure. Initially this attribution of hierarchical structure was simply an assumption based upon the impressive wealth collected in certain large tumulus burials, such as the famous Vix tumulus in Burgundy with, among many other luxury goods, its wagon, gold torc, imported Attic pottery, Etruscan bronze pitcher and basins, and 1.6 m high Greek bronze krater (Joffroy 1979). More recently, this inference of hierarchical structure has been reinforced through more sophisticated analyses of both settlement and burial patterns using different measures of hierarchy (cf. Frankenstein and Rowlands 1978; Härke 1979; Wells 1980; Büchsenschütz 1984, 1988; Brun 1987, 1988a; Olivier 1988; Pare 1991).

What these analyses from various micro-regions of the Hallstatt *Fürstensitze* zone show is that by the final phase of the Hallstatt period (D2–3) a consistent spatial pattern had developed with wealthy tumulus burials clustered around a fortified hilltop settlement (the so-called *Fürstengräber* and *Fürstensitze* in the German terminology proposed by Kimmig 1969). Kimmig's original formulation has been justly criticized for its anachronistic medieval social terminology, for its Hellenocentric fixation on an "acropolis/suburbium" concept, and for overstating the temporal and spatial homogeneity of the *Fürstensitze* pattern (Eggert 1989). The archaeological record of many areas remains too poorly known to evaluate properly their conformity to the model. However, employing the more general sense of the term noted earlier, there are relatively well-documented cases in Burgundy (Joffroy 1979), Baden-Württemberg (Kimmig 1983b), the Swiss Plateau (Schwab 1983), and the Hagenau area in the Alsace (Legendre 1989), as well as a greater number of suggestive instances in other areas. Significantly, as Pare's (1991) recent summary of the evidence convincingly demonstrates, outside of south-western Germany (where it appears earlier) the *Fürstensitze* pattern is almost entirely confined to the Hallstatt D2–3 period (roughly 530–450 BC).

Within each micro-region the tombs which are wealthiest also tend to be the largest monuments with the most complex internal structures. In the wealthier burials, the specific configurations of objects and features which compose the grave furniture (such as wagons, weapons, drinking and feasting gear, wooden chambers, gold torcs and bracelets, and Mediterranean imports) also tend to be limited, consistent, and hierarchically patterned in terms of association over a wide region (see Frankenstein and Rowlands 1978; Wells 1980; Pare 1991, 1992). Hence, a consistent hierarchical spatial structuring of settlements and burials developed within each of the various micro-regions of the Hallstatt *Fürstensitze* zone, and a specific iconography for representing status distinctions came to be shared for a certain set of wealthy burials in a very consistent way across many different micro-regions. The striking lack of a similar inter-regional homogeneity in the less elaborate Hallstatt burials (cf. Wamser 1975; Zürn 1987; Reim 1988) serves to emphasize the extraordinary consistency of the wealthier tombs.

As Pare (1992) has recently documented in detail, this consistently associated set of funerary status markers (four-wheeled wagons, weapons, drinking and feasting gear) in elaborate Hallstatt tumulus burials shows several correlated diachronic trends. From the early to the late Hallstatt period such burials become at the same time: 1. increasingly exclusive (i.e. found in ever smaller numbers); 2. increasingly widespread (i.e. found over a much wider region); and 3. increasingly more richly endowed. Although initially characteristic only of south-western Germany, by the Hallstatt D2–3 period they are found throughout eastern France and western Switzerland as well (see Pare 1991, 1992). Moreover, by this late period Mediterranean imports began to appear in the most elaborate of these graves and on the fortified hillforts associated with them.

The lower Rhône Basin

In the lower Rhône basin the situation is quite different. Throughout the early Iron Age there is no demonstrable

hierarchy of settlements in terms of size, location, or specialized functions. Most appear to have been small, unfortified, relatively undifferentiated villages or hamlets with a mixed agropastoral subsistence economy. Only three sites had fortifications before 550 BC, and only ten scattered sites have evidence of possible fortifications dating to the period from 550 to 450 BC, as compared to the hundreds of fortified sites in this same region dating to the late Iron Age (Arcelin and Dedet 1985:31). Of these, only Saint-Blaise and Lattes, both of which are within a few kilometers of the Mediterranean coast, show possible evidence of unusual size or other extraordinary characteristics (Bouloumié 1992; Py 1988). Although burial evidence is abundant, there are no clear spatial configurations of settlements and wealthy graves pointing toward privileged patterns of association. Mediterranean imports are not restricted to a few central settlements and wealthy graves as they are in the Hallstatt area, but are found in large numbers on virtually all settlements along a coastal band that extends further into the interior over time (see Dietler 1990a).

There is no identifiable consistent hierarchical patterning (as one finds in the Hallstatt tumuli) in terms of permutations of grave inclusions, funerary structure, mode of corpse treatment, spatial organization, or energy expenditure. At least three modes of corpse treatment are found. Central burials are usually single, but may be collective, and include men, women, and children. Tomb types include tumuli (the most common type, but with extremely variable internal structure and size), flat pit graves, reused megalithic graves, and cave burials. Although very few objects were included in individual graves, the range of items used as grave goods is quite large. Neither wagons nor the kind of large bronze feasting vessels found in Hallstatt graves (e.g. cauldrons, situlae, ribbed buckets) played a role in the burials of this region (see Dietler 1990a; Gasco 1984; Dedet 1992). Mediterranean imports are relatively rare in graves and unspectacular in comparison to the items found in the Hallstatt tombs. They are not consistently associated with any particular type of burial or set of grave furniture, nor is there any clear correlation with richness of the grave inventory or size and complexity of the funerary structure (see Dietler 1990a).

At least 500 burials or burial mounds of probable early Iron Age date are known from the region, and these are often found grouped together in large cemeteries sometimes containing up to a hundred or more small tumuli. In comparison to the tumuli of the Hallstatt area and the Alps (where mounds of 50 to 100 m diameter are frequent), those of the lower Rhône basin are all rather small. They range in diameter from about 2 to 24 m with examples larger than 15 m being uncommon. Gasco's (1984:128) analysis of Languedocian tumuli has revealed a degree of chronological spread in several tumulus groups, indicating that the cemeteries were built up over a period of time. However, most tumulus burials date to the earlier part of the early Iron Age; and after about 550 BC the number of recognizable burials in general declined sharply. During the latter phase of the early Iron Age, there were both far fewer total burials in the region and fewer burials in almost all individual cemeteries, marking a clear shift in the mode of funerary treatment (see Dietler 1990a).

Dynamic comparative analysis

Mediterranean imports in both the lower Rhône basin and the Hallstatt *Fürstensitze* zone are largely confined to items centered around drinking wine. However, there are some significant differences, and the contrast in both the nature and find-contexts of imported Mediterranean goods consumed in the two regions provides a key to understanding socio-political differences.

In the Hallstatt zone the imports are relatively few in comparison to those in southern France; but those in late Hallstatt funerary contexts are often of a rare or even spectacular nature, such as the large and elaborate bronze vessels from the tumuli of Vix, La Garenne, Hochdorf, Conliège, and Grächwil (Joffroy 1979; Biel 1985; Lerat 1958; Jucker 1973). All Mediterranean imports found on settlements of the early Iron Age come from late Hallstatt (D2–3) contexts, as do most of the grave finds (including especially the large spectacular bronze vessels). Among the overall range of Mediterranean goods found in the Hallstatt region, the burials contain impressive bronze mixing vessels, other smaller bronze vessels (such as Etruscan wine flagons and basins), a very few drinking ceramics and amphorae, and a handful of singular assorted exotica. On settlements are found wine-drinking ceramics (largely Attic cups and kraters, with a few examples of Grey Monochrome and Pseudo-Ionian pottery from southern France) and a much smaller quantity of wine transport amphorae (mostly Massaliote, except at the Heuneburg). During the final Hallstatt period these Mediterranean imports are concentrated almost entirely on the central *Fürstensitze* settlements and in a few surrounding tumulus burials where they are associated in a highly consistent pattern with the largest and most elaborately and exclusively endowed tumuli.

In the lower Rhône basin Mediterranean imports are both vastly more numerous and much less spectacular,

consisting overwhelmingly of simple wine transport amphorae (Etruscan, Massaliote, and a few other types) and smaller but significant quantities of ceramic drinking vessels (Etruscan, Massaliote, and small numbers of Attic and other Greek types). Moreover, they are found in copious amounts on a wide variety of settlements. In fact, by the late sixth century BC they are found on virtually every settlement in the region (see Dietler 1990a). In contrast to the settlements, Mediterranean goods are relatively rare in graves of the lower Rhône basin. There is nothing in particular in terms of association and context which distinguishes graves with Mediterranean imports as a class. The objects themselves are far from impressive when compared with the large wine-mixing vessels found in the Hallstatt area, a significant feature given that vessels such as the Vix krater very probably first arrived in France through the port of Massalia. For the late seventh and early sixth centuries BC they consist predominantly of small Etruscan bronze basins (Bouloumié and Lagrand 1977), a single "Rhodian" type bronze wine flagon (Bouloumié 1978; Shefton 1979), and a few ceramic drinking cups (Bouloumié 1987); and after the mid sixth century BC they consist of a small and heterogeneous collection of ceramic sherds (Dietler 1990a). They are found in both tumuli and flat graves, and with both inhumations and cremations. They are not systematically associated with larger or more elaborately endowed graves or with any class of indigenous objects, or characteristic set of such objects, which is exclusive to graves with such imports. Whatever the original social significance of their inclusion in graves in the lower Rhône basin, Mediterranean imports clearly do not constitute part of a widely accepted iconography of status differentiation in funerary ritual as they did in the Hallstatt region.

This pattern also indicates a selective focus on impressive durable paraphernalia used in drinking events rather than on a regular supply of an exotic form of drink (wine) in the Hallstatt area; whereas in the lower Rhône basin the focus was largely on the importation of wine itself. A glance at the Attic ceramics found in both regions provides further support for this contrast. Those on the Hallstatt sites show a high proportion of kraters (large wine-mixing vessels), while this type is relatively rare in the lower Rhône basin (where drinking-cups are the norm), thus indicating a relatively greater emphasis on impressive drinking paraphernalia in the Hallstatt area. In fact, the entire Hallstatt region combined has produced fewer amphorae sherds (cf. Ramseyer 1990; Flouest 1990; van den Boom 1990) than various individual settlements in the lower Rhône basin. Attic pottery (almost exclusively wine-drinking and service vessels) is generally more abundant on the *Fürstensitze* than are transport amphorae; and the relative representation of Attic pottery is certainly much higher than on lower Rhône basin sites, indicating that the paucity of amphorae is not due to recovery problems.

If this regional contrast in relative quantities of classes of ceramics can be accepted as broadly valid, then it would tend to indicate the absence of a real trade in imported wine into the Hallstatt region. It has been suggested that large amounts of wine may have been transported into the region in perishable hide containers (e.g. Bouloumié 1985). Tchernia has pointed out, however, that such leather containers were too costly to have been disposable. While frequently employed for very local repetitive transport, their use in such long-distance trade (a suggestion based upon a single Classical text) would be a unique event in the history of wine (Tchernia 1992:475). Moreover, if skins had been used to transport wine toward the interior, it seems difficult to explain the presence of some amphorae on Hallstatt sites and large numbers of amphorae at sites well north into the lower and middle Rhône basin (Dietler 1992).

In the Hallstatt region items of drinking paraphernalia served a diacritical symbolic function in differentiating elite (or, perhaps more accurately, "court") feasting practices as exotic and rare additions to a long-established repertoire of symbolically important feasting gear. They were apical "luxury goods" in the sense of Appadurai (1986:38): that is goods which have primarily a "rhetorical" role as "incarnated signs" within the social and political domain. They served to imbue elite drinking practice with diacritical significance even though elite drinkers were most often consuming the same drinks (barley beer and mead) as everyone else. In the lower Rhône basin, on the other hand, wine was incorporated as a more generalized and regular addition to native feasting institutions as a means of engaging in locally appropriate forms of "commensal politics" (see Dietler 1994a). It was used by a wide range of individuals and groups for labor mobilization and manipulation of informal political power through competitive hospitality.

Imports in the Hallstatt region were "singular commodities" (Appadurai 1986:16) valued for their uniqueness within a certain class of goods, whereas those in the lower Rhône basin were "homogeneous commodities" valued because of their class characteristics. The divergent patterns of selection of exotic imports and their find contexts in the two regions are highly consistent with the different models of socio-political relations that can be inferred from comparative analysis of the settlement and funerary data.

For the lower Rhône basin, the absence of any widespread consistent hierarchical patterning in the complex heterogeneous mixture of modes of funerary treatment corresponds not to an absence of all status differentiation, but rather to a complex polythetic overlapping of roles, statuses, and affiliations encapsulated in Crumley's (1987a) concept of heterarchy. In political terms this corresponds to Southall's (1968) "distributive legitimacy": that is, a non-convergent plurality of points from which legitimate political action may be initiated and contested. On a broad regional level this pattern also points to the related characteristic phenomenon of "multipolities": the existence of multiple political communities (Southall 1968).

For the Hallstatt region, the continuation of locally heterogeneous patterns for the set of poorer graves of the different micro-regions serves to emphasize through contrast the striking homogeneity, over an increasingly wide area, of the wealthy burials and to suggest that regionally shared status iconography was restricted to an upper level of the society. These features, when viewed both against earlier patterns in the region and against the diverse contemporary patterns exhibited in neighboring regions (cf. Freidin 1982; Willaume 1985; Bocquet 1991), may very plausibly be interpreted as indicating the merging of multipolities into a larger political community with a shared iconography of status and authority, and the concentration of political functions into a more hierarchical distribution of legitimacy of action. As Olivier (1988) and Pare (1991, 1992) have both shown, the general iconography of elite status differentiation remained consistent in the Hallstatt domain from the early through the late Hallstatt period, but the degree of differentiation among graves (measured in terms of energy expenditure in funerary ritual, monument construction, and grave furniture) increased dramatically over time.

In the lower Rhône basin nearly the inverse occurred. In addition to cave burials, reutilized megalithic tombs, and flat graves, the late seventh and early sixth centuries BC in this region were especially characterized by large tumulus cemeteries. Beginning in the late sixth century BC, however, formal burial of all types became increasingly less well represented in the lower Rhône basin. This trend occurred at the same time that Mediterranean trade (particularly Massaliote) was expanding in the region and Hallstatt burials were evincing increasing elaboration and differentiation. By the early fifth century BC formal burial virtually disappeared in the lower Rhône basin in favor of some less durably conspicuous, less energy intensive, and consequently less archaeologically visible method of corpse disposal such as simple exposure or uninterred cremation. This decline in formal burial is marked by both a dramatic reduction in the total number of burials for the region as a whole and a corresponding reduction in the number of burials in each of the erstwhile cemeteries (Dietler 1990a).

These changes may be related to regional differences in the process of ideological representation of social relations. As several scholars (e.g. Cohen 1974; Bourdieu 1977; Giddens 1979) have pointed out, ideology may serve to obviate the conflict inherent in relations of social inequality through either symbolic denial of their existence or the naturalization and objectification of such relations. In order for personal political power to be converted into legitimate authority and for informal leadership to be transformed into institutionalized political roles, there must be an effective ideological naturalization of the new order. These roles and power must be transformed to the degree that they are perceived to take on the durability and materiality of things which are independent of the personal relations between individuals that they entail. This mediation of power relations through objectified institutions and structures frees those in dominant positions from the work of continuously maintaining their power through the perpetual creation and manipulation of direct personal relationships, and increases the potential for expansion of domination (see Bourdieu 1977:183–97). Alternatively, in the absence of such institutionalization, a stimulation of competition among those wielding informal power, or an escalation in differences in wealth and power in the face of an egalitarian political ethos, may provoke an attempt symbolically to deny the existence of inequalities in social and political relations. Unless camouflaged by such ideological alchemy, these disparities in power, by their exacerbation, threaten to expose the arbitrary nature of the perception of self-evident harmony between the structure of the natural and social world which Bourdieu (1977:164) calls "doxa."

Admittedly, archaeological funerary data are notoriously difficult to interpret, and they have generated a tremendous literature of contentious theoretical discussion (cf. Binford 1971; Tainter 1978; Pader 1982; O'Shea 1984; Morris 1987; Cannon 1989). However, funerary contexts, because of their intentional construction as part of public ritual activity, are a prime example of what Cohen (1974) has called "politico-symbolic drama" operating simultaneously at two levels. They are an obvious theater for the kind of ideological manipulation discussed above through the representation of idealized or "euphemized" (rather than necessarily real) social relations. At the same time, within the structured iconography of

representation of the perceived social order there is a potential in active performance for symbolic statements by social groups or individuals competing for the definition of their relative status.

The ultimate success of this ideological strategy of legitimation and its relationship to the real course of social relations is uncertain. Forms of expansionary domination often contain the seeds of their own destruction. Moreover, it is a mistake to assume that people are completely duped by hegemonic ideological representations even when they act as if they were in carrying out the performances which recapitulate an idealized or euphemized model of social relations. The archaeological evidence, particularly that concerned with ritual, is predominantly a reflection of these acquiescent performances that Scott (1990) calls the "public transcript." However, there exist many subtle forms of everyday resistance which at times give rise to overt opposition once the "hidden transcript" of dissent is publicly voiced and people suddenly refuse to comply with hegemonic performances (see Scott 1985, 1990).

Given these considerations, it is not clear whether the dramatically increasing hierarchization noted in late Hallstatt funerary treatment was a genuine reflection of effectively increasing stratification and political control or whether it was the result of an increasingly desperate and elaborate attempt by a regional elite to bolster the legitimacy of its authority in the face of diminishing control, popular resistance, and strife. The Hallstatt centers disappeared fairly rapidly some time near the mid fifth century BC, just after the period of greatest escalation in elaboration of elite burials and the greatest territorial expansion of their distribution. This process is commonly explained as a sudden collapse due to changes in trade patterns with the Mediterranean states (e.g. Villard 1960; Frankenstein and Rowlands 1978; Brun 1987). However, this popular explanation is based on the assumption that the development of the Hallstatt political structure was driven by Mediterranean trade and that it had become dependent upon sources of Mediterranean goods for its reproduction. As several dissenting scholars (Bintliff 1984b; Gosden 1985; Dietler 1989; 1990a; Pare 1991) have argued recently, there is good reason to doubt the validity of this dependency model and to look for other factors which may explain the genesis and reproduction of sociopolitical formations in the region. Evidence of the repeated destruction of the Heuneburg walls (Kimmig 1983b) and of the frequent looting of elite tumuli near the end of the Hallstatt period and the beginning of the succeeding La Tène period (Wells 1980:31–2; Spindler 1983:195–200) suggests that the collapse was due to a failure of the mode of ideological hegemony in legitimating the expansionary domination involved in the processes outlined at the beginning of this chapter and to the consequent process of resistance noted above.

The geographical expansion of the *Fürstensitze* and *Fürstengräber* pattern during the final Hallstatt phase does suggest the merging of multi-polities into a larger political community dominated by an elite class with increasingly closer regional links. To be stable, this new "imagined community" would need to forge emotionally charged symbols of communal identity which would both consolidate loyalties among the general population and at the same time reify the structural position of the dominant group. These symbols of identity seem to have been articulated through an elite class with a new regionally shared status iconography. This iconography played upon an association of long-established motifs in several fields of "symbolic capital" (drinking and feasting paraphernalia, wagons, weapons) to evoke the naturalizing authenticity of "tradition." At the same time, it pushed the diacritical symbolism within these fields as a means of objectifying and institutionalizing the hierarchy of social and political relations. This latter process can be traced in the increasing differentiation of burials, including particularly an increasing elaboration of the upper range of burials that involved the incorporation of more spectacular exotic elements (from the Mediterranean states) used in the performance of feasting ritual. These rare and impressive implements of consumption would have helped to mark elite feasting practice as "tournaments of value" (Appadurai 1986:21), which restrict competition and the privilege of participation to a certain group of peers, solidifying the common identity of a regional elite at the same time that they served to distinguish this group from those below on the social hierarchy.

In the case of the lower Rhône basin, the evidence suggests a rather different process of evolving ideological representation and social competition. One can discern a shift in the arenas of social competition accompanied by a movement in the funerary domain toward the symbolic denial of inequalities in economic and political power through, perhaps, a more stringent representation of equality in death. The funerary evidence for the earlier part of the early Iron Age certainly indicates that funerals provided a venue for making public and durable statements about identity, status, and relative wealth within very local traditions of representation; but, contrary to the Hallstatt case, not in a manner that suggests an institutionalized hierarchy of social relations or extreme differences. By the end of the early Iron Age, this theater of politico-symbolic drama was effectively closed to competition while another, that of feasting, was in the process of escalation.

In characterizing early Iron Age societies in the lower Rhône basin, one might focus upon either, for example, forms of social organization (e.g. the age-set based, segmentary lineage based, or amorphous network type classification of Colson 1969), or upon modes of leadership (e.g. the big man, great man, "leader" scheme of Lemonnier 1990). However, such distinctions are generally very difficult to make for archaeological cases, and one should expect a variety of permutations of such features which must be investigated in local contexts where possible. What is common to the range of such societies is that institutionalized structures of domination much beyond those based upon age and gender are poorly developed. Consequently, the exercise of power must rely upon what Bourdieu (1977:190) has called the "elementary forms of domination." Power is embodied and reproduced not in relations between institutions, but in the strategic manipulation of direct relations between individuals. These must be continually renewed through the creation and deployment of "symbolic capital" in a number of social fields and cultural contexts of variable and shifting importance (pp. 171–83).

We do not know exactly what the funerary rites of the early fifth century BC in the lower Rhône basin entailed. However, we do know that, in contrast to the earlier situation, virtually no individuals were covered with a conspicuous permanent marker and interred with personal possessions. This might be interpreted as a particular manifestation of a more general phenomenon identified by Cannon (1989) of cyclical shifts in the style of funerary display from ostentation to restraint as a result of an historical process of contrast and emulation in the course of social competition.

However, funerary ritual is not an isolated domain, it is merely one of many arenas in which competition may be played out; and one should expect shifts in the principal theaters of politico-symbolic competition as well as transformations of mortuary style (e.g. see Bradley 1990). In this case, the evidence points to a correlated shift in emphasis toward feasting as a central arena of social competition and a transformation of funerary ritual as an attempted means of symbolic denial of growing differences in wealth and power (or of increasing competition over these things) which had begun to threaten the "doxic" perception of the social order. These changes were triggered by the encounter with Massalia and the Etruscans, a process which was articulated in large part through the arena of feasting (Dietler 1990b, 1994a).

This change in funerary rites occurred in conjunction

with a steady increase in the volume of Mediterranean trade in the region. Throughout the course of this trade a very selective and consistent range of items was imported from all of the various Mediterranean sources: almost exclusively wine and drinking vessels. These were consumed on a wide range of settlements. Though quantitatively impressive in comparison to the Hallstatt zone, the wine imported into this region did not completely replace native drinks in indigenous contexts; for example, early Iron Age amphorae are significantly less numerous than later Roman amphorae found in the region from a period when wine was reported by Greek and Roman observers to be still a minority drink in comparison to beer (see Tchernia 1983). However, this imported wine very probably had a significant disruptive impact on social relations similar in many ways to the colonial introduction of large quantities of shell valuables in New Guinea (Strathern 1971), or money and wage labor in many small-scale societies around the world (cf. Dalton 1978; Robbins 1973). In effect, it opened a new channel of access to obtaining the means necessary to operate in one of the important traditional arenas for status competition: that is, the "commensal politics" of feasting (Dietler 1994a). This new access was dependent upon trade with, or labor services for, the Mediterranean states rather than upon the established system of building up a subsistence surplus base capable of sustaining lavish hospitality. An escalation of competition played out in feasting activities was likely to have occurred between those with privileged access to the traditional forms of drink (e.g. lineage elders, village headmen, big men) and those with newly advantageous access to the exotic form (Dietler 1990b). Feasting is an important arena for social competition for several reasons. In the first place, because it operates through the idiom of generous hospitality, it very effectively "euphemizes" the self-interested manipulation of social indebtedness which is involved. Moreover, because it serves as one of the primary means of mobilizing labor in small-scale, pre-monetary societies, it operates as a pivotal link in reciprocal conversions between economic and symbolic capital (see Dietler 1994a).

Corroborating evidence for the stimulation of feasting activities is found in the two new series of ceramic wares called "Pseudo-Ionian" and "Grey Monochrome" which were produced in indigenous territory using borrowed Greek techniques beginning in the sixth century BC.

These wares, which became highly popular on native sites all over the lower Rhône basin, are table service wares which feature particularly Greek-style drinking cups and wine-pitchers (Lagrand 1963; Py 1979–80; Arcelin-Pradelle 1984; Dietler 1990a). Their production involved a reorganization of part of the indigenous ceramic industry in a way which indicates a significant increase in demand that is linked to the influx of imported wine (Dietler 1990a, 1994a).

The disruptive effects of heightened social competition stimulated by the encounter with the Mediterranean states and increasingly played out in the realm of feasting may have been ritually mitigated in the funerary realm by a strategy of ideological representation that artificially emphasized equality of the dead. The conflict inherent in various inequalities of wealth and informal power which a sudden surge in intensity of competition had exposed to public consciousness was thereby symbolically denied at the same time that competition became more focussed within an arena with greater potential for euphemizing the struggle for power.

Viewed in synchronic and geographical isolation, none of the archaeological patterns presented above would be very revealing. However, examined in both spatial and temporal comparative perspective, they offer a basis for some very plausible inferences about the socio-political processes discussed. They also present an argument for the viability and utility of studying processes of ideological representation and social competition as an alternative (or prerequisite) to typological classification of socio-political structure. The institutionalization of both social inequality and political roles and authority within fields of social competition is a subject of particular promise. It is not, after all, the origin of these features but rather the process of their institutionalization which is socially significant and archaeologically visible. Because this process involves attempts at ideological legitimation, and because material symbols and ritual are often an important aspect of such legitimation, it is precisely this critical process which is likely to be the most accessible to archaeological analysis. However, the crucial importance of a dynamic comparative approach to the analysis of socio-political systems must be emphatically reiterated, as the effectiveness of strategies of ideological manipulation and modes of domination can only be discerned from a critical historical perspective.

PART III

The question of statehood in La Tène Europe

8

States without centers? *the middle La Tène period in temperate Europe*

JOHN COLLIS

Introduction

The general trend in European prehistory is toward increasing complexity both of social organization and settlement structure, linked with more specialized production. However, this overall picture does mask both regional variations and periods when there seems to be a reversion in the trends, as well as periods of very rapid change. For the Iron Age of central and western Europe, the major periods can be characterized in the following way (Collis 1981):

Hallstatt C, 700–600 BC. Generally decentralized settlement pattern, but with the burial record implying marked social differentiation within undefended village communities, evidenced by burials of individuals interred with vehicles in wooden chambers under mounds. There was some trade with the Mediterranean world.

Hallstatt D, 600–475 BC. Locally, in south-western Germany and eastern France, extreme social differentiation with ostentatious burial under huge mounds, with gold and imported Mediterranean goods, associated with defended hillforts in which specialist production seems to be concentrated.

La Tène A–B1, 475–350 BC. A shift in the areas which display the greatest wealth (e.g. central Germany, northern France), though other areas such as western France produce occasional rich objects, implying that our knowledge is biased by the distribution of a recognizable burial rite. This period is also characterized by marked social differentiation, though less than previously, and dispersed settlement pattern with no obvious centres of production.

La Tène B2–C1, 350–150 BC. Dispersed settlement (known mostly from cemeteries), lack of exceptionally rich burials, limited trade with the Mediterranean. Settlements, where these are known, are small and unspecialized.

La Tène C2–D, 150–20 BC. Increasingly centralized settlement pattern with the appearance of large defended sites, the so-called *oppida*. Increasing trade with the Mediterranean world with an explosion in contacts in the first century BC, and indications of marked social differentiation (for a general summary, see Collis 1984a).

During this last period the evidence points toward some sort of state organization with urban settlements. The evidence we have comes mainly from Caesar at the time of his conquest of Gaul in 58 to 51 BC. He talks of an oligarchy, though on occasion we encounter kings, and there seems to be an unstable situation in which individuals were attempting to obtain absolute power. The tribe Caesar describes in greatest detail, the Aedui of central Gaul, had an annually elected chief magistrate, the Vergobret, but with rules surrounding his election which included the exclusion from election of any close relative of a living ex-Vergobret, suggesting an attempt to limit personal power, or the power of individual families. We also hear of meetings of a "senate," though we are not told who the senators were, and that the state had its own revenues, in part, at least, raised from auctioning the right to collect tolls from traders. In other contexts Caesar mentions the use of the Greek alphabet for writing records, and we also have inscribed coinage implying literacy was common among certain classes.

If we are looking for characteristics which might differentiate a complex chiefdom from a state, we find some of those characteristics present. First, the state is capable of holding funds in its own right rather than these being invested in the person of an individual, such as a chief. Officials exist which are appointed independently of the control of any one individual, and there are hints of a bureaucracy in the form of written records. On the other hand, there is no hint of a permanent standing army, but this is usually a later development (cf. the relatively late date in the Roman state for the appearance of full-time soldiers). The appearance of coinage too suggests a central authority with powers to act on behalf of the state in the minting of coins. Finally, we see that urban settlements are well established.

From both the written and archaeological sources, we know the Aedui had a number of major sites, including the *oppidum* of Bibracte, now the deserted hilltop of Mont Beuvray near Autun. They had a developed coinage of silver and cast bronze coins, extensive trade contacts with the Mediterranean world, and specialist industries producing, among other things, pottery, glass, bronze, and iron objects. These industries were concentrated on the major settlements (though we know little of other settlements).

This pattern of large defended sites and centralized production with coinage is found over an extensive area of central and western Europe, and it is reasonable to infer a similar level of social organization over this area, that is one of tribal states. In some areas where the archaeological record for the *oppida* is better than among the Aedui, there are hints of artisans grouping according to their trade, for instance in the distribution of industrial debris at the site of Manching in Bavaria. This is a pattern reminiscent of the specialist quarters for guilds in medieval towns.

The question that I wish to consider in this chapter is how an apparently decentralized society with limited social differentiation can suddenly transform itself into a highly centralized society with urban centers, marked social differentiation, and developed political and economic institutions (Collis 1982). Is it a process which is disguised in the archaeological record, or can we pick up signs of an evolution happening, and is there really a sudden transformation of the society?

Methods of study

In societies from which we have little or no documentary evidence, we can only rely on the archaeological evidence to give us clues about what held groupings larger than a single settlement together, evidence, in other words, of regional or super-regional organization. Thus, in the late La Tène, we have the *oppida*, which in archaeological terms stand out by their large size, concentration of population, and the expenditure of energy on a massive scale, perhaps most clearly exemplified in the construction of their defenses. Their important role is confirmed by the literary sources where they are also mentioned as centers of political power, storage of provisions, and nodes of trade. These demographic, political, economic, and social characteristics are those which geographers would ascribe to "central places," if not genuine urban centers.

What we are seeing on these sites is a conjuncture of several elements – centralized defense, and a nucleated population. In the European Iron Age we can see other types of centralization even more clearly than on the *oppida*. At the Heuneburg in Hallstatt D we have a concentration of exceptionally rich burials, imported luxury goods, and the production of prestige goods in and

around a central defended site. Cult, religious, and ceremonial centers form another category – the Navan fort with its prestigious but non-defensive earthworks, its massive timber building and stone mound, the imported barbary ape, and a literary tradition that it was a royal center (Raftery pers. comm.); or the massive stone structures on the 'acropolis' at Závist in Bohemia, dating to Hallstatt D – La Tène A (Motyková *et al.* 1988; Drda *et al.* 1991).

However, these are the clear cases. What do we make of the rich burials of La Tène A–B which are widely dispersed across the landscape, with no obvious marked concentration as at the Heuneburg? Even the occurrence of imported Mediterranean goods is not exclusive in this period to the richest burials, and the burials wealthiest in goldwork such as Reinheim and Waldalgesheim, from the nature of their grave goods, are likely to have been female. What do we make of sumptuous isolated finds such as the helmets from Agris and Amfreville (Duval and Gomez 1986), or the circular monument of the Goloring which resembles the Irish sites in its earthworks, and a single standing timber post, but which lacks any other indication of special status (Röder 1948; Collis 1977)? In these cases we are not dealing with a conjuncture of different elements, but a single isolated element – a rich burial or luxury item, which is not backed up by other indicators of "importance."

From the documentary evidence we can identify situations where we would have no inkling of what was happening from the archaeology alone – e.g. the development of kingship among the Arverni in the second century BC, or the gathering of the Druids in the territory of the Carnutes. Too often we take the archaeology, or rather the lack of it, simply at face value. Thus, we assume that because the Champagne and the Hunsrück-Eifel regions produce the richest burials in La Tène A, they are therefore of necessity the wealthiest areas in the Iron Age, and the origin, for instance, of La Tène art.

In the past there has also been too much made of something called "Celtic Society," which was everywhere passing through defined stages of development, from tribe, to kingship, and on to a tribal state governed by an oligarchy. Because we know of one or two societies where such a transition was taking place does not mean it can be automatically inferred elsewhere (e.g. Roymans 1990:33–8). Celtic society as depicted by authors such as Powell (1958) merely represents a mishmash of information from different times and different places which is often of little value for understanding the societies being described. Descriptions, or rather caricatures, of societies cannot be transposed in time and space under an invented concept of the "Celts"; indeed, the whole use of the terms Celt and Celtic is something which should be avoided as it distorts our understanding of the archaeological record (Collis 1986b, and forthcoming). With all its flaws, we are largely drawn back to the archaeological record, and to attempting to correlate this with anthropological concepts.

Chiefdom and state

In using such terms, we are implicitly trying to identify centralizing elements of the sort I described above. In the case of a chiefdom, we are looking for individuals in whom power and wealth were invested. In the case of the state it is rather institutions, such as the appointment or election of magistrates and officials, which we seek to identify, with evidence of greater stability and more complex social and economic organization than in a chiefdom.

We have two problems in studying societies for which documentary evidence is limited or lacking. First, there is understanding the scale of the political systems which may have existed, and how we may be able to identify this from archaeology alone. To give concrete examples, in the first and second millennia AD we can easily identify London as the peak of a settlement hierarchy in England. But in the early Roman period it was a provincial capital in an empire of which Rome was the center. In the eighth century it was a major trading settlement in one of a number of competing kingdoms. In the seventeenth century it was the capital of a kingdom comprising England, Scotland, and Wales. In the nineteenth century it was the capital of a world-wide empire. One way may be to look at the relative ranking of sites in terms of size. In a kingdom, the major city will not be that much larger than other neighboring cities in the same kingdom, whereas the capital of an empire will far outrank all its nearest neighbors, as second-rank cities will lie at some distance in the provinces. However, there is also conservatism in the system, with settlements continuing to reflect a previous stage of development, as Renfrew and Level (1979) encountered when trying to apply the X-tent model to the capitals of Europe (Grant 1986). To take a prehistoric example, because Stonehenge is a unique monument in its elaborate structure and the concentration of rich burials around it, do we interpret it as a monument of significance to Britain as a whole, or for southern Britain, or only for part of Wessex? The latter might seem the most likely alternative, given what we know of the technology and social organization that probably prevailed in the European early Bronze Age, but can we be sure?

Translated into Iron Age examples, how do we envisage

the Hallstatt D societies of south-western Germany? Are the Hohenasperg and Heuneburg part of the same political entity, centers competing with one another within a single political entity, or are they centers of independent political entities, complex chiefdoms in competition with one another? What of the *oppida* of Bohemia? Are they all centers within a tribal grouping of the Boii, competing with one another at an economic level (as centers of trade and production), but all part of a settlement hierarchy under centralized political control; or are they the centers of independent and competing tribal groups?

The second problem is to identify the nature of the links which bind society together – kingship, clientship, religious belief, military hierarchy, or an economic organization – and how these are likely to be expressed archaeologically. Usually there is a combination of these different elements, producing the conjunctures which I described earlier in this article, the recognition of settlement hierarchies, concentrations of wealth, and presumably power. We can also add a dimension of scale, the relative "wealth" of graves between one period and another, or the size of major settlements and the distance between centers. Thus we normally envisage that *oppida*, such as Manching, with areas of dense concentration measured in hundreds of hectares were part of a larger and more complex entity than was the Heuneburg in which the occupied area is measured in hectares, or at most tens of hectares. In a similar way we might envisage the enormously wealthy burials of Hallstatt D (e.g. Hochdorf) as symbolizing a more complex society than the wealthy, but less rich burials of La Tène A (Reinheim). On such evidence as this we can suggest, but perhaps not prove, a differing complexity of social organization to which we can attach terms like "chiefdom," "complex chiefdom," and "state."

The *oppida*

In the case of *oppida* such as Manching or Mont Beuvray we encounter a conjuncture of different elements which picks them out as central places, and as foci for political and economic activities within their respective societies. However, in La Tène C–D there are many exceptions to this "*Oppidazivilisation*" suggesting it was not as typical as is often assumed:

1. There are societies which, to judge from aspects of the material culture such as inscribed coinage, had a similar level of social and political development, but which lacked the central places or any other evidence of centralization. This is especially a feature of western France (Boudet 1987).

2. There are societies in which *oppida* were established, but where they never developed into major centers of production or population. Generally in these cases there are other aspects which are not developed, such as the use of coinage or industrial production. This is characteristic of northwestern France and central Germany.

3. There are areas surrounded by regions which possess coinage, *oppida*, etc., but in which coins and *oppida* are not found (for instance in the southern part of the Massif Central in France).

4. Some areas have densely occupied *oppida*, but the sites are ephemeral, and were abandoned or replaced after a generation or so – a feature of the Auvergne and the Aisne valley (Guichard *et al.* 1993).

This does not represent the full range of variation – there are differences in the amount of coinage, the development and centralization of industry, etc., as well as *oppida* which seem to have been purely emporia with no political function (e.g. Hengistbury Head, Cunliffe 1987). It is clear that some of these areas, for instance western France, have all the trappings of what we have above identified as tribal states, but which lack the central nuclear site.

This phenomenon does also have a chronological dimension. The *oppida* are deliberate foundations, established by societies with adequate political, social, and economic organization to support urban development. So even in areas where the fully developed *oppida* occur, there is a period immediately preceding their foundation when we are faced with the phenomenon of a highly developed society which lacks a central focus. Are there any hints of the nature of social integration in the middle La Tène before the establishment of the *oppida*?

Before the *oppida*

First let us consider the settlement evidence. From the *oppida* themselves we have limited information about the situation at the moment in time when they were founded. As most of the *oppida* are on pristine sites, especially in defensive situations, their foundation would seem to have been a deliberate and planned act. This might be claimed for the defenses, and the occupation could be a secondary process growing up haphazardly within the defenses, but what little evidence we have, from sites such as Guignicourt in the Aisne valley of northern France (Audouze and Büchsenschütz 1989; Roymans 1990), suggests that the layout of the settlement was itself also planned, perhaps at the same time as the defenses were built.

An analogy can be found in the Saxon burhs of southern England in the tenth century AD, when the Wessex kings such as Alfred established defensive sites against the Danish invasions, but at the same time a grid of streets was laid out. Several of these sites quickly evolved into thriving urban centers. In this case the Saxon kings had a model, both in the remains of Roman towns, and also in the trading entrepôts of the eighth and ninth centuries. For the Iron Age it is not clear to what extent such pre-existing models may have existed, and whether there was an awareness of what Mediterranean towns were like.

So far only in one case can we identify a major urban complex which was gradually evolving from a village settlement into one of urban proportions, the site of Manching on the Danube. This site starts in La Tène B1, and by the beginning of La Tène C it may have been as much as 50 ha in size. What its role was – an administrative center or an independent entrepôt, we cannot answer on the archaeological evidence. It does, however, indicate that in one area at least an evolution was taking place.

However, Manching stands alone. Elsewhere where we have nucleated settlements preceding the *oppida*, they are small, of late date, perhaps preceding the *oppida* only by a generation or two, and may themselves be deliberate foundations – sites such as Levroux in western France (Büchsenschütz et al. 1992), or Basel and Breisach on the Rhine. These sites are in any case little or no earlier than the foundation of the first *oppida* in central Europe, specifically in the Czech Republic, where the earliest sites date to La Tène C2.

A third situation is suggested by the area around Clermont Ferrand in central France (Malacher and Collis 1992; Guichard *et al.* 1993). Here there is a sequence of defended sites, Corent, Gondole, Gergovie, that are in turn preceded by a series of sites in the fertile plain of the Grand Limagne. Here we see a concentration of small sites, the largest only a few hectares in area. Much of the information has unfortunately been destroyed in the urban expansion of Clermont since the war, but in the best researched area, a concentration of five or six sites is known within a square kilometre or so. A couple of these at least were engaged in the range of industrial activities normally associated with the *oppida*. Only two sites have been excavated on any scale; Aulnat-La Grande Borne lies in the main concentration of sites, and was engaged in the working of iron, bronze, silver, gold, and bone, as well as the production of coins and textiles; and Le Pâtural, located 2 km to the north, specialized in iron smelting. Aulnat at least starts in the La Tène C1 phase.

What we seem to see here is a complex of sites in which the industrial aspects of an urban site are already concentrated, but where formal structures of urbanism such as a nucleated population, town planning, etc., are still lacking. Though these sites were progressively abandoned during La Tène D, when the earliest of the defended sites on Corent was founded, the precise chronological relationships have yet to be established. At present, like Manching, this is also a unique situation.

The interpretation of La Tène B1–C1 as being essentially decentralized, with less social differentiation than in previous and subsequent periods, rests largely on the burial evidence. Little fieldwalking has been done to investigate settlement patterns, but in northern Bohemia, where work has been done in advance of lignite quarrying, the settlements seem to be small villages with a small amount of industrial activity for local needs (Waldhauser 1981a). The burial evidence both here and elsewhere consists of small cemeteries, with the richest burials containing nothing richer than bronze jewelry in female graves, and swords and other weapons in male burials. It could be argued that the differences in social rank were being disguised. The last of the early La Tène rich burials is Waldalgesheim, which dates to the first half of the fourth century BC, and contemporary rich objects are known from other, perhaps votive contexts, such as the helmets from Amfreville and Agris in western France (Duval and Gomez de Soto 1986). After this, gold is rare in any context until the arrival of coinage in the late third–early second century BC. Metal analysis of such small gold objects as are found, such as finger rings, suggests a much more limited production and trade in gold than in preceding periods, supporting the interpretation of relative poverty for this period.

In some areas such as the Mosel area of western Germany, there are hints of greater social differentiation in terms of wealthier grave goods during La Tène C2, when some individuals were again buried with vehicles, and especially in burials of the first century BC imported bronze vessels, wine amphorae and other prestige goods reappear (Metzler *et al.* 1991). However, over most of temperate Europe the more normal trend is for formal burial to disappear. In one case the change in emphasis can be documented. At Münsingen in Switzerland the graves become increasingly poor in grave goods, burials with swords disappear, and by the time the cemetery was abandoned in La Tène C2, few of the burials had any grave goods at all (Hodson 1968). What was apparently happening was a shift in the locus of destruction, especially of weapons, from the burial context to religious contexts. It is precisely at the time when the weapons disappear from burials that the deposition of swords at the eponymous site of La Tène itself, on Lake Neuchâtel, began. The interpretation of this site as one of deliberate votive deposition in the river and lake is now widely, but not universally accepted (e.g. Schwab 1990).

For many years La Tène has been unique as a formal ritual and deposition site dating as early as La Tène B. Such sites become common in La Tène C and especially D, notably the *Viereckschanzen* of southern Germany. But even these sites, such as Holzhausen, seem from their dense distribution to have only a local significance, whereas the wealth of material at La Tène – over 200 swords, for instance – appears to be of more regional significance (de Navarro 1972).

In the last decade two sites with deposition of material on a scale similar to La Tène have been identified, both in northern France. The first is the sanctuary of Gournay-sur-Aronde, which starts during La Tène B, and continues to evolve, with the final stage having a Roman temple (Brunaux *et al.* 1985; Brunaux and Rapin 1988). Deposition here also concentrates on weapons, mainly deliberately broken before burial, and deposited in the ditch surrounding the sanctuary. This site, too, has produced over a hundred swords.

Even more spectacular is the site of Ribemont-sur-Ancre near Amiens (Cadoux 1986; 1991). By the Roman period, this site had become one of the great rural sanctuaries of northern France, boasting a fine temple, a theatre, and numerous ancillary buildings. It too starts in La Tène B or C, with the deposition of weapons, though not at present on the scale of Gournay and La Tène. What is unusual is the deposition of human bones, including some disarticulated or partial skeletons, though skulls seem to be absent. In what may be two corners of a religious enclosure have been found two heaps of human bones, in one case consisting of nearly 500 femurs, the other unfortunately largely destroyed by World War I trenches.

The scale of deposition at all three sites suggests that they were served by more than the immediately local communities, and more such sites have started to appear in northern France. We thus have at least three major cult sites which were in existence by the end of La Tène I, about 300–250 BC. They are primarily concerned with martial equipment, though animal bones and other items are present, but female objects such as bronze brooches and bracelets do not seem to appear on sanctuaries until La Tène D. Similar sites are also beginning to appear in central France, as at Mirebeau (Guillaumet and Barral 1991) or Nuits-Saint-Georges (Pommeret 1992).

Generally these ritual sites are not associated with the major *oppida* – there are exceptions, as at the Titelberg, Otzenhausen (Metzler 1992), Gournay, and Corent – but more commonly they are associated with what subsequently became rural sanctuaries in the Roman period. In one or two examples they became the focus of small towns, or major sanctuaries of urban character, for instance Ribemont and Nuits-Saint-Georges. Generally the development of religious centers and urban centers was independent. These sanctuaries do, however, give us a focus of regional importance; Roymans (1990) has suggested that for northern France they represent organization at the level of the *pagus* rather than the *civitas*. However, at present few of them go back much before the late La Tène.

Conclusions

Returning to the question which I have posed, there does seem to be some evidence that society was not totally fragmented during the period La Tène B2–C1. The evidence of the burials does seem to reflect the genuine situation, that extreme wealth, perhaps based on trade with the Mediterranean, had disappeared, and that a less marked hierarchy had appeared, but one in which the military aspect was dominant, as exemplified both in terms of the grave goods in male burials and the deposition on sanctuaries. But locally other trends were making themselves felt, such as the development of specialist production centers, either nucleated as at Manching, or more dispersed as around Clermont Ferrand. But it is not clear to what extent these two situations may be more widespread than the archaeology at present betrays. My feeling is that comparable situations may emerge, with respect both to specialist settlements and to sanctuary sites, but they are perhaps not the norm or more examples would have emerged by now.

I have, on a number of occasions, stated the opinion that for the later Iron Age excavation should at present be concentrating on rural settlements. In the case of Aulnat and Le Pâtural, this has given us vital information about the organization of industrial production in the period preceding the *oppida*, but we also desperately need to know about the development of the palisade enclosures and larger timber houses which appear on the *oppida*. It is always assumed that these represent the residences of a land-owning elite, and therefore that they should have a counterpart on the preceding richer rural settlements. Le Pâtural certainly had a massive timber house and palisade enclosures probably dating to La Tène D, and this contrasts with the simpler La Tène B–C houses at Radovesice in Bohemia (Waldhauser 1981b). In so far as the burial evidence cannot tell us about the social processes going on prior to the *oppida*, house types represent one of the few possibilities of discerning change.

In summary then, we can at least define where the major gaps in the archaeological evidence lie, and we have the means to fill them, but it will involve a reorientation of research away from the prestigious excavation of major sites, to the less spectacular rural settlements. The evidence so far suggests that the processes of social change, for instance the appearance of a social elite, that the foundation of the *oppida* implies had already commenced before their foundation. The necessary political organization of a primitive state may equally have been developed. If so, these were primitive states which lacked what for many archaeologists is a prerequisite of state organization – urban centers – though this was to follow quickly and suddenly. La Tène C2–D2 in central Europe was indeed a period of sudden and revolutionary change.

9

Late Iron Age society in Britain and north-west Europe: structural transformation or superficial change?

COLIN HASELGROVE

Introduction

The later pre-Roman Iron Age in temperate Europe was a period of major and rapid changes, well documented in both the archaeological and historical record. The most striking of these developments include the widespread appearance of a new class of large, often strongly fortified, sites, usually known as "*oppida*" after the Latin word for towns; innovations such as coinage and literacy; and a marked increase in long-distance trade, particularly with the Mediterranean world. Many of the *oppida* seem to be major nucleated settlements, with significant productive and distributive functions and most recent opinion would regard them as truly urban sites, at the apex of a well-developed settlement hierarchy (e.g. Collis 1984a; Wells 1984; Audouze and Büchsenschütz 1989).

Many authors too, see the *oppida* as the physical expression of a deeper transformation of society, involving increased political centralization and stratification, and the replacement of kinship by a mode of integration and information-processing based on commercial exchange (e.g. van der Leeuw n.d.), in effect a move from complex chiefdom organization to a form of political statehood (e.g. Gibson and Geselowitz 1988b). This view derives further support from the way in which classical authors like Julius Caesar describe later Iron Age societies, especially the Aedui in central France (e.g. Crumley 1987c), although we should note that by mentioning indigenous roles and institutions in terms familiar to their Mediterranean readers, these writers may be greatly exaggerating their sophistication and prominence. Iron Age interaction with the more developed Mediterranean civilizations and Roman imperialism are themselves widely canvassed as key factors in the developments of the period from *c.* 200 BC to AD 50 (e.g. Haselgrove 1987; Nash 1987), during which Roman political control expanded from a single overseas colonial foothold in Spain to embrace north-west Europe as far as lowland Britain and the river Rhine.

Problems with the current paradigm

The preceding view of the later Iron Age as a period of urbanization and state-formation is not without its difficulties. There is, for example, growing awareness that such perspectives mask significant spatial and temporal variation among the *oppida* (e.g. Büchsenschütz and Ralston n.d.). Thus, in central France, few sites show any significant development until the early Roman period, and describing even the leading Iron Age settlements as urban seriously overstates what we can demonstrate by archaeological means alone (Ralston 1984). Indeed, while many *oppida* or their near-neighbors in France and Britain subsequently became Roman administrative centers, this is often the only indication we have of their pre-conquest status and certainly does not prove them urbanized. Recently, too, Fletcher (n.d.) has suggested that even the indisputably pre-Roman settlement at Manching in southern Germany, far from being densely occupied, had only a small residential population and was perhaps the location of a seasonal fair (cf. Wells 1984). He bases this argument on a general model of the communication and interaction constraints on the growth of settlements. Manching was only used for one or two centuries and held its maximum size for no more than fifty years.

The level of later Iron Age political development – general as well as in specific areas – can also be questioned. Both archaeology and the historical sources suggest that the socio-political complexity of the peoples of northern France around 50 BC lagged well behind their southern neighbors, and a similar distinction can be drawn in Britain 100 years later, between south-east England and the peripheral areas to the north and west (e.g. Haselgrove 1989). However, Woolf (n.d.) has argued that even in central France – supposedly the classic example of later Iron Age state formation – the level of differentiation, organizational capacity, and the integrating institutions achieved by the indigenous political groupings stops well short of statehood. The coinage supports this conclusion, with the major monetary developments not occurring until after the Roman conquest (Haselgrove 1988). Even where a higher degree of political centralization is implied, as in the kingdom which dominated eastern England on the eve of the conquest, the pattern of inheritance was evidently inherently unstable and the overall configuration has more the characteristics of a paramount chiefdom than a primitive state (Haselgrove 1988; 1989). Again, we have quite possibly read more into classical authors' references to Iron Age institutions and subsequent Roman administrative practices than either the coherence or the stability of pre-conquest socio-political groupings actually warrants.

These points will be developed further below in two short case studies dealing with northern France and lowland Britain respectively. First, there are some other central issues which also need to be considered. As we have already seen, the current interpretation of the archaeological changes of late pre-Roman Iron Age Europe can be doubted, at least in specific instances. However, simply reopening the evidence to question in terms of such dichotomies as non-urban/urban or chiefdom/ state serves little purpose; the taxonomic approach itself is too restrictive (cf. Woolf n.d.). Gibson and Geselowitz's (1988b) observation that there are few material correlates of primitive states that differ predictably from those of complex chiefdoms makes exactly the same point. What we need instead is an analytical framework which allows the debate to be opened up. This, I believe, means recognizing and giving due weight to the very different roles played by long-term evolutionary developments, cyclical patterns of growth and decline (cf. Bradley 1984) and contingent historical processes in shaping both the observed form of the archaeological record, and the actual changes experienced by particular societies which lie behind these material configurations.

In short, failure to isolate the individual processes at work in late Iron Age Europe – and to specify their particular causation – may be leading us both to confuse what may be relatively superficial and reversible changes with underlying structural transformation, and to unjustified generalization. There are two aspects to this problem. First, chiefdoms (Earle 1987), including those of Iron Age date, show an undoubted propensity for undergoing fairly regular cycles of expansion followed by crisis and contraction – processes of rehierarchization-dehierarchization or demilitarization-remilitarization as Moberg (1977) calls them – as part of their normal longer-term pattern of development. If arrested in mid-cycle, for example by the Roman conquest, there is a danger that such developments will give an unjustified impression of permanent structural change.

This leads to the second problem. Few would doubt that Roman political imperialism was a significant factor for change in later Iron Age Europe, as various studies invoking a 'core–periphery' perspective have argued (e.g.

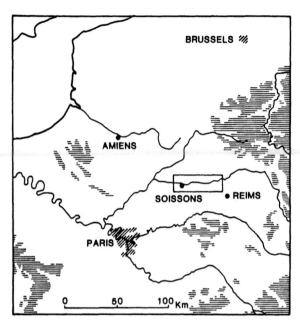

9.1 Northern France, showing the location of the Aisne Valley study area.

Haselgrove 1987; Nash 1987). However, what is much less certain is whether the resultant changes in Iron Age societies are really a matter of kind rather than degree. Arguably, highly visible Roman imports (and indeed the historical sources) open up to more detailed archaeological scrutiny the workings of Iron Age societies – which otherwise continued to function much as before. Undeniably, such trading with a more developed economy can also bring about permanent political changes (e.g. Kipp and Schortman 1989), but here this will be mentioned merely as the springboard to an alternative hypothesis: that over much of Europe, the pattern of later Iron Age change may reflect little more than the kind of cycle of expansion and contraction which occurs frequently in warrior societies, onto which the historical process of Roman imperialism has grafted a false degree of coherence – and additional impetus.

The Aisne Valley, Northern France, in the first century BC

In recent years, the river gravels of the Aisne Valley region in northern France (Fig. 9.1) have seen an intensive program of archaeological investigation (e.g. Demoule and Ilett 1985), including large-scale rescue excavations on the remarkable first-century BC fortified nucleated

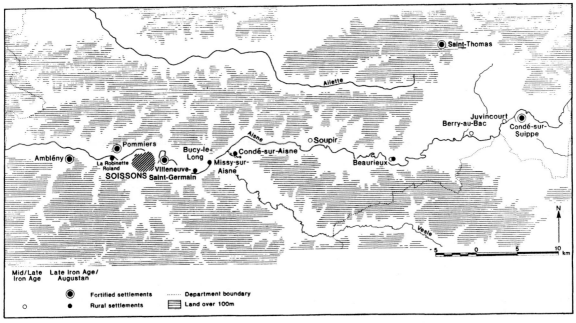

9.2 Principal Iron Age sites in the Aisne Valley.

settlements at Condé-sur-Suippe and Villeneuve-Saint-Germain, which are now among the best studied *oppida* in western Europe (e.g. Audouze and Büchsenschütz 1989). There has also been considerable work on the contemporary rural settlements (Haselgrove 1990), enabling detailed chronological, functional, and locational comparisons to be made between these different components of the late Iron Age settlement pattern. The principal Iron Age sites are shown on Fig. 9.2.

The large valley-bottom settlements are widely seen as indicative of a fully developed settlement hierarchy and thus as precursors of Reims and Soissons, the Roman central places of the two local peoples, the *Remi* and the *Suessiones* (e.g. Pion n.d.). Their strict orthogonal layout (Fig. 9.3) and functional subdivision into living areas, workshops, and agricultural zones reflect an impressive level of organization. Both sites show evidence of extensive industrial activity and were importing Italian wine, albeit in relatively modest quantities (cf. Demoule and Ilett 1985; Haselgrove 1990).

Chronologically, two points emerge. The main occupation of the two valley-bottom fortifications is virtually mutually exclusive not only of each other (Condé is earlier), but also probably of the neighboring late Iron Age plateau-edge fortified sites at Saint-Thomas and Pommiers respectively (Haselgrove 1990). Second, the

rarity of intercutting features and the homogeneity of their respective assemblages show that the occupation of both Condé and Villeneuve was short lived; probably a generation at the outside. Like the planned layout, this implies that neither site grew up gradually over a period of time. Both must in some sense be planted settlements, an Iron Age equivalent of the fortified new towns of the Middle Ages. And while the late Iron Age plateau-edge fortifications in the Aisne Valley lack extensive modern investigations, they too were certainly nucleated settlements, and Pommiers, at least, probably had an orthogonal internal layout (Haselgrove 1990). The same is true of Reims in its earliest phases. In short, the late Iron Age nucleated settlement record is one of brief occupation and could also suggest changes in location between valley bottom and plateau edge.

However, discontinuity is just as much a feature of the rural settlement record at this time. Most sites occupied in the mid to late Iron Age – such as Beaurieux, Les Grèves, Berry-au Bac, Le Chemin de la Pêcherie, and Juvincourt, Le Gué de Mauchamp – were small, open farmsteads and were all apparently abandoned in the late second or early first centuries BC, just as the major fortified nucleations appear. Moreover, while some of them were later reoccupied, as at Beaurieux, most of the minor sites dating to the mid to late first century BC seem to be new foundations

Condé-sur-Suippe

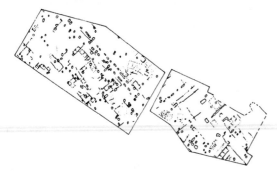

Villeneuve-Saint-Germain

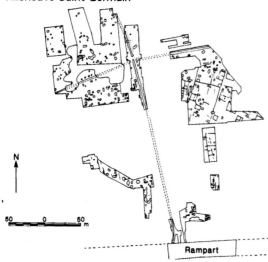

9.3 Plans of the late Iron Age settlements at Condé-sur-Suippe and Villeneuve-Saint-Germain.

and their character differs markedly from before. Excavated examples include Condé-sur-Aisne, La Maisonette, Missy-sur-Aisne, Les Gardots, Pommiers, La Robinette Roland and, most recently, Bucy-le-Long, Le Fond du Petit Marais. Compared to the small open sites found at the beginning of the period, they are generally enclosed and appear larger and more organized, probably comprising several social units, reinforcing the impression of a major interruption in rural settlement development (Haselgrove 1990).

Since this gap appears to coincide chronologically with the occupation of the major nucleated sites, we must be correspondingly cautious in interpreting these as the apex of a developing settlement hierarchy. At present, the crisis model elaborated by Collis (1984a) seems to offer a more

convincing fit to the data. This model directly links the establishment of these fortified sites with the abandonment of the rural sites during a major crisis, the rural population subsequently returning to their farms when the emergency had passed.

As Fleury (1986) notes, the residential compounds at Condé and Villeneuve have many of the characteristics of rural farmsteads with cattle yards transposed into a relatively confined area, and neither site has conclusive evidence for major public buildings or religious structures. Arguably, too, their industrial quarters represent no more than the centralization in one place of activities which were previously dispersed across the landscape. Indeed, almost all of these are also represented on the region's rural sites, implying that the difference is one of scale, not function. The one major exception on current evidence – coin production – would probably be at its most intensive during a major emergency anyway.

In the Aisne Valley, the Roman invasion cannot have been the crisis that sparked off the period of extreme nucleation, as Condé and probably other sites were founded well before this date. Instead, we may perhaps envisage a prolonged period of stress going back to the start of the late Iron Age, whether in origin military-political or (less likely) socio-economic. However, the central point is that while these nucleated settlements argue for a certain level of organization in the indigenous population, they need not signify any underlying change in their capacity for centralized decision-making or degree of integration, nor must long-term social or political change necessarily have occurred; once the crisis had receded, life might have reverted to almost exactly as before. Other outcomes are possible too, and might under certain conditions have led toward true urbanization, if, for example, the elite and artisans opted to stay on in these new centers with only the farmers returning to their land (Collis 1984a). In fact, the Roman conquest intervened, prolonging the period of crisis so that, in the end, Roman administrative and military needs were the decisive factors assuring the continued development of Reims, for example, but the abandonment of other less conveniently sited native settlements for new foundations nearby, as in the case of Pommiers, which was apparently still intensively occupied in the Augustan period, and its Roman successor in the valley below Soissons.

The late Iron Age *oppida* of lowland Britain

My second example, concerning lowland Britain, will pursue the theme of Roman impact, without going into any great detail. Roman imperialism is frequently

9.4 The distribution of late Iron Age linear dyke complexes and related sites in lowland Britain.

accorded the paramount role in the development of British *oppida* (e.g. Bradley 1984; Haselgrove 1987). The argument is a familiar one. After the conquest of France in 50 BC, Roman commercial penetration and diplomatic contacts (and also possibly the threat of military intervention) provided a stimulus which enabled British elites to consolidate their power and position over much larger territories, achieving a previously unknown level of political integration and social hierarchy. The process is most marked in south-east England, where the major settlements like Colchester, Silchester, and St Albans can be identified from the inscribed coinages as the seats of particular rulers who were probably Roman client kings (Fig. 9.4). The same process probably occurs between AD 43–70, but to a lesser extent, in the outer parts of the lowland zone when these were still on the frontiers of the Roman province. The massive earthwork complex at Stanwick in northern England, for example, has its *floruit*

at precisely this time, and was probably the seat of the known Roman client ruler, Cartimandua. Other sites which fall into this latter group are Bagendon and possibly Redcliff.

Although this model is now seen as having overstated Roman commercial exploitation (Haselgrove 1989; Millett 1990), that particular aspect will not be pursued here. Rather, my question is once more the particular emphasis on the *oppida* as the physical expression of underlying changes. This is partly because our perception has been heavily colored by the Roman administrative centers established on or near many of these sites. In some cases, like Colchester, a genuine transfer of authority does appear likely. However, at several others, like Leicester and Winchester, the Roman town is virtually our only evidence for the status of its Iron Age predecessor, while many important Iron Age centers such as Braughing or Stanwick had only minor Roman successors, implying that the configuration of political power and territorial integration was still relatively unstable.

All this underlines the diversity of the British sites which have been grouped together as *oppida*, largely due to our not properly separating out the different processes which were at work. In one sense, these sites continue a process of nucleation which began in the third century BC (Bradley 1984), but we must avoid automatically equating this with urbanization. At Silchester, for instance, an orthogonal street plan was imposed over earlier occupation in the later first century BC, which the excavator specifically compares to Villeneuve-Saint-Germain in northern France (Fulford 1987). However, rather than suggesting a link between the two, might we not ask whether this is similar cause and effect – a planned settlement established in response to crisis conditions? Canterbury may yet turn out to exhibit a similar sequence of development. Equally, the internal organization of linear dyke complexes such as Colchester or St Albans (or at a slightly later date, Bagendon and Stanwick), suggests not urbanization, but rather a spatially extensive version of existing settlement types, albeit with more pronounced functional zoning. The sites comprise elite and lower-status residential compounds, separated by their fields, with other discrete areas reserved for industry and for activities such as burial, ritual, and exchange (Fig. 9.5; Haselgrove 1989).

Another problem is our continuing emphasis on the linear dykes associated with these sites. Whatever such earthworks tell us about the capacity of communities for mobilizing the required labor, these dyke complexes are neither as uncommon as was once thought, nor exclusive to the largest settlements. Several other probable late Iron Age complexes exist, such as Grim's Ditch, which lack only a known core settlement (Bradley 1984), while several new examples have recently been identified in Wessex and the south Midlands (Corney 1989; Hingley 1989). Yet other sites such as Baldock have almost all the attributes of the *oppida* except the linear dykes.

The settlements classed as *oppida*, then, may be no more than the most conspicuous in a continuum of broadly similar sites, which all seem likely to be associated with the higher-ranking members of society. The linear dykes could easily delimit the boundaries of particular private territorial estates. The reason that these sites stand out in the late Iron Age may be less that they express entirely new social and political developments, but rather because the other changes at this time – especially contact with the Roman world and the adoption of inscribed coinage – makes these aspects of Iron Age societies much more archaeologically obvious than before.

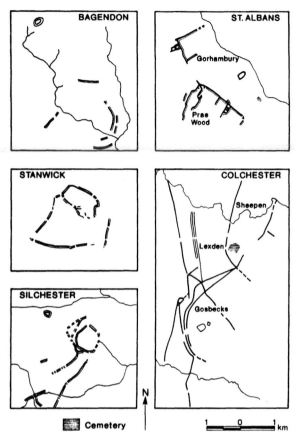

9.5 *Comparative plans of the oppida at Bagendon, Colchester, St Albans, Silchester, and Stanwick.*

The essentially personal nature of power in these societies (cf. Millett 1990) could go far toward explaining the observed variability of the British sites. As the centers from which the elite exercised their social and political authority over a wider population (which would act to concentrate people and activities there), their fortunes would wax and wane with that of their owners. On this model, the particular complexes which came to prominence in the late Iron Age are simply those associated with the most successful rulers of the day in what was still essentially a politically unstable society. The only difference is that on this occasion, this happened as these individuals were themselves being drawn into the wider orbit of the Roman world, and history distorts our perceptions of the process by naming them.

Conclusions

The apparent changes of the later Iron Age may represent less of a decisive break with earlier patterns than many believe, while the role of Roman imperialism is almost certainly overstated. Quite apart from artificially arresting whatever developments were underway at the time, whether or not these were cyclical, Roman expansion puts an artificial focus on the period by increasing the archaeological visibility of socio-political processes which otherwise remained well embedded in existing structures of rank and power. We need, in other words, to disentangle the Roman impact from other processes operating on Iron Age societies at this time, both short and longer term.

Often, it seems, the more prominent cycles of growth – and decline – in prehistoric Europe were preceded by longer periods of more gradual agrarian growth (Bradley 1984). This would fit well with conditions during the first millennium BC, where we can see several processes at work which may have combined to have their main impact during the closing centuries, including agricultural intensification and the growth of population and productive power (e.g. Wells 1984; Gosden 1985). Warfare, too, has a more overt role than at an earlier period of European prehistory (Bradley 1984). Against this background, the eventual crisis periods which brought fortified *oppida* into being in areas as widely separated as parts of the Czech Republic and France, and the regional differences in the actual timing, are both readily explicable – if not the particular combination of internal pressures and external events which caused these crises to occur.

Providing we can free ourselves of its narrow evolutionary confines, the concept of chiefdom offers a useful alternative to the familiar and increasingly discredited stereotype of a generalized Celtic society (e.g. Hill 1989). However, in focussing on Iron Age social dynamics in this way, we need to avoid simply substituting a "social package" type of approach which essentially reduces change to something which occurs only between taxonomic categories. A more productive procedure is to break down social complexity to its essentials – in the case of chiefdoms, their capacity for centralized decision-making and control, the degree of stratification and the effective scale of integration (cf. Earle 1987) – and then to seek to examine how these vary over time.

An important start has already been made in various studies identifying archaeological and settlement correlates of chiefdoms (e.g. Peebles and Kus 1977; Steponaitis 1978). Much of this work, however, has been cast in a static framework, and more methodological attention should be directed to the internal dynamics of chiefdom societies, such as the kind of diachronic developments which are touched on here. This is essential if we are fully to exploit the rich archaeological data of later European prehistory for the broader study of human social evolution, while at the same time, employing approaches founded in wider comparative studies can only enrich our understanding of the particular subtleties which characterize developments in Iron Age Europe.

10
Settlement and social systems at the end of the Iron Age

PETER S. WELLS

Introduction

During the final two centuries of the prehistoric Iron Age, changes took place that profoundly altered economic and social systems in temperate Europe. The most apparent change was the establishment of the walled settlements known as *oppida*. They were much larger than earlier settlements in Europe, with often well over 100 ha of enclosed land (Collis 1984a). Most of the *oppidum* settlements that have been investigated through excavation have yielded evidence for substantial manufacturing activity, particularly in iron implements. The role of these centers in the cultural landscape of Iron Age Europe is a critical issue for our understanding of the social evolution of the Celts (Fig. 10.1).

Social systems and archaeology

Archaeology cannot recover social systems, but only the material remains left behind, intentionally or unintentionally, by persons who belonged to them. In order to assess the potential contribution of *oppidum* studies for our understanding of social and political change in late Iron Age Celtic Europe, we need to think about the relation between archaeological evidence and social and political realities. Since the late 1960s, American and British archaeologists have been much concerned with the concept of "socio-political complexity," and they have developed numerous models for linking archaeological data with social and political forms (Frankenstein and Rowlands 1978; Renfrew 1984; Renfrew and Bahn 1991:153–94). Much of this work depends upon burial evidence, where individuals are distinguished from one

another by differences in grave structure and outfittings (Chapman, Kinnes, and Randsborg 1981).

In the case of the *oppida*, we have little good burial evidence. During the second century BC in most regions where the *oppida* occur, the predominant burial practice changed from inhumation with grave goods to cremation with few or no goods (Krämer 1985). Only in the northwestern region of *oppidum* distribution do sizeable cemeteries occur in the final century before Christ, as, for example, at Bad Nauheim (Schönberger 1952) and Wederath (Haffner 1989). For the most part, we are dependent upon evidence from the settlements and other categories of sites, such as hoards, in our attempts to understand social and political change at the time of the *oppida*.

The *oppida* and social evolution of the late Iron Age Celts

The principal categories of archaeological information from the excavated *oppida* that pertain to social and political change concern the size of the social unit and the scale and degree of specialization in manufacturing activity. Population estimates are difficult to make, particularly since burial evidence is sparse, but also because even at the most extensively excavated *oppida*, only a small portion of the settlements have been explored. Evidence gleaned from the density and character of settlement features, from the quantities of cultural material recovered, and from the amounts of meat represented by animal bones has been interpreted by most investigators to represent populations in the thousands, at least for the larger *oppidum* settlements (Wells 1984:164–6).

Labor expended in the construction of boundary walls and buildings also indicates a substantial investment of human energy and resources. For the wall system at Kelheim, Kluge (1987) estimates that roughly 1.5 million person-days of labor were devoted to the construction. We do not know whether only residents of the *oppidum* worked on the wall, or whether members of neighboring communities participated as well. In any case, this amount of labor invested shows that a sizeable economic surplus was produced at and around Kelheim to support such an expenditure in construction activity. The *oppidum* walls were probably built as much to serve as visual expressions of communities' power as for military defense.

Industrial evidence at the major *oppida* reflects the efforts of substantial numbers of craft workers who processed a range of materials. Represented among the production debris are iron, bronze, stone, wood, leather, glass, and pottery. For iron-working, glass manufacture,

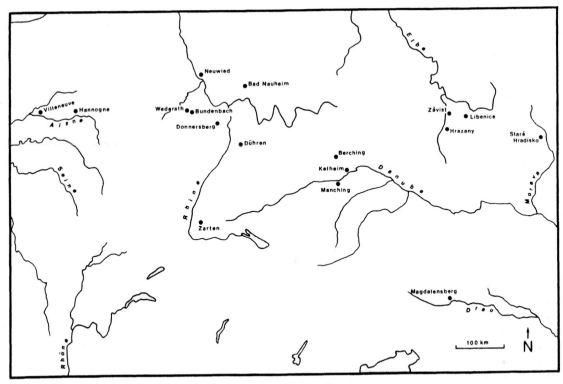

10.1 Principal sites mentioned in the text.

and making of some categories of pottery, specialized craft workers are likely (Pleiner 1982; Gebhard 1989).

Spatial organization in the *oppidum* settlements

Recent excavations in the interiors of *oppidum* settlements throughout temperate Europe show that many included within the enclosing walls both a densely occupied industrial center and a much less densely inhabited non-industrial periphery. Excavations at Manching make this pattern clear (Maier 1985, 1986), and recent results from Kelheim (Wells 1991, 1993), Villeneuve-Saint-Germain (Demoule and Ilett 1985: 215 Figure 10.18), Závist (Motyková, Drda, and Rybová 1990), and Staré Hradisko (Meduna 1970, plan 5; Čižmář 1989) suggest similar situations.

Extensive excavations at Staré Hradisko in Moravia have revealed settlement units resembling complex farmsteads, referred to in the German-language literature as *Gehöfte*, arranged close together and sharing the protection of the enclosing wall system. These units consisted of groupings of buildings, enclosed by foundation ditches, palisades, and streets. A range of different productive activities is evident in many of these units (Meduna 1970; Čižmář 1989). The *Gehöfte* at Staré Hradisko seem to have been equivalent economic and social units, engaged in a similar range of activities. The excavations at Staré Hradisko were not extensive enough to reveal entire *Gehöfte*, but the most completely exposed one indicated on Meduna's plan (1970, plan 5) is about 27 m wide and at least 33 m long. Among the common economic features of the units are pits, fireplaces, quernstones, and pottery kilns.

The excavators at Závist describe similar units there. They identify a range of different settlement units distinguished from one another by their size and complexity, and by the character of the material recovered in them (Motyková, Drda, and Rybová 1990). In addition to the complete *Gehöfte* units, they distinguish other, individual buildings, unaccompanied by a range of ancillary structures. At Villeneuve-Saint-Germain, the plans show the same kinds of divisions in the settlement, defined by foundation ditches, that are apparent at Staré Hradisko. Perhaps a detailed plan for Villeneuve would show economic activities comparable to those carried out in the *Gehöfte* at Staré Hradisko.

The center of Manching shows much larger divisions defined by foundation ditches and streets, often extending some 30 m long and sometimes as long as 60 or 70 m. Smaller subdivisions within these large precincts are not clear from the published plans. More detailed information would provide material for comparison with Staré Hradisko. In the northern parts of Manching, the units are smaller, and foundation ditches enclose some of the buildings there. Many of the buildings in this part of the Manching settlement resemble, in their size, shape, and arrangement, those at small open settlements such as that at Berching-Pollanten (Fischer, Rieckhoff-Pauli, and Spindler 1984), 40 km to the north.

The principal difficulty in comparing the structures on the *oppidum* settlements is in the lack of extensive surface exposure at more than a handful of sites, and the lack of detailed plans such as those for Staré Hradisko. This situation will surely change as more excavation results are published. Some sites classified as *oppida* on the basis of their wall systems and topographical situations, including the Donnersberg (Collis 1984a:219) in the Rhineland and Zarten-Tarodunum in south-west Germany (Weber 1989), have yielded only sparse traces of occupation and may have served principally as refuges for surrounding communities in times of danger.

Evidence for the presence of persons of different social statuses at the *oppida* can be derived from the artifactual materials recovered on the settlements, and especially from their differential distributions. Objects that required high levels of skill to manufacture are well represented, including fine painted pottery, bronze ornaments, and ornate rings. Items of precious metal are present, particularly gold and silver coins. Other categories of objects that appear from the burial evidence (Haffner 1989) to be associated with persons of high status include keys. Imported goods at the *oppida* also reflect status and wealth. They include wine and wine-drinking paraphernalia in the form of amphorae, pottery, and bronze vessels (Fitzpatrick 1985; Werner 1978; Svobodová 1985). At the same time, the *oppidum* settlements yield an abundance of plain material that is not characteristic of high status, such as undecorated pottery, iron tools, and mass-produced iron fibulae.

At most of the *oppida*, the living surface does not survive – it was plowed away long ago. Hence we do not generally find objects *in situ* on the floors of buildings. It is possible, however, to study locational patterning in different categories of objects on a coarser scale, to test whether we can distinguish parts of the settlement where persons of high status and those of lower status resided. This kind of analysis has not, to my knowledge, been carried out for

the *oppida*, but it could provide important information about places associated with population groups of different status at these sites, as preliminary evidence from the distribution of coins at Kelheim suggests (Overbeck and Wells 1991).

Spatial and social organization of the landscape

The communities resident at the major *oppida* were much larger social units than those at other settlements, but there is no unambiguous evidence that individuals of higher status more frequently resided at the *oppida* than lived outside. Motyková, Drda, and Rybová's (1990) arguments regarding the "typicalness" of the remains at Závist, with respect to social and economic patterns of late Iron Age Celtic society as a whole, seem to apply to other excavated *oppida* as well, as far as we can judge from research published to date. All of the industrial activities of the late Iron Age are represented on the *oppidum* settlements. These include the finest craft products, such as glass bracelets, iron longswords, and bronze cauldrons, but also the plainer material culture that is associated with the majority of people. Wightman suggested (1978) that the *oppida* might not have been the exclusive residences of high-status persons; such individuals may have resided in smaller communities as well, for example at Bundenbach near Trier (Schindler 1975). The recent evidence of manufacturing and coin minting at the smaller settlements supports her idea.

The cemetery evidence, where we have it, also suggests a dispersion of social status, not a concentration of high status at the *oppida*. The cemetery at Wederath (Haffner 1989), for example, contains graves that can be interpreted as those of elite individuals, as well as burials of modest character. Many of the richest graves of the period, such as Hannogne in eastern France (Flouest and Stead 1977), Dühren in Baden (Fischer 1981c), and Neuwied in the Rhineland (Joachim 1973), are not clearly associated with *oppidum* settlements.

The circumstances that Caesar describes for Gaul are unusual – the Gallic tribes were at war, with or against the Romans. This situation may have strongly affected the character of the Gallic *oppida*. We cannot transfer Caesar's statements to the sites east of the Rhine, and must rely on the results of excavations to try to understand the character of the *oppida* there. The recovery of evidence for the minting of coins at many small settlements warns against the idea that the *oppidum* communities had a monopoly on the expanding commercial economy (Steuer 1987). The widespread distribution of Roman bronze vessels (Werner 1978; Feugère and Rolley

1991) similarly argues against viewing the *oppida* as the exclusive centers of elite economic activity. None of the *oppida* east of the Rhine has yielded archaeological evidence for what might have been a political center within the enclosed area. Such evidence might consist of the stone foundations of public buildings, or unusually large and sturdy post-built structures, or even an open area near the center of a settlement that was kept clear of habitation and industrial materials. Only in the concentration of population and of manufacturing activity, and in the great enclosing walls, were the *oppida* substantially different from the other settlements of the period. We might even ask, consistent with Wightman's (1978) suggestion, whether some of the *oppida* might have been primarily communities that produced goods for trade, while persons of wealth, status, and power lived separate from these bustling settlements. Only further excavation research at *oppida* and at smaller sites will clarify the issue.

Manufacturing at the *oppida*.

Most of the *oppida* have yielded evidence for on-site production; in some instances the evidence is so extensive as to suggest that manufacturing was a primary reason for the establishment of the community. It is likely that the *oppidum* at Kelheim was founded to take advantage of the rich iron ore available and of the convenient transport afforded by the Danube and Altmühl rivers (Reinecke 1935). Much of the production at the *oppida* was of "utilitarian" goods, such as iron tools and pottery, but "expressive" goods, such as personal ornaments and status objects, were also made.

Nearly every *oppidum* that has been excavated has yielded remains of on-site iron-working (Pleiner 1982). During the third and second centuries BC, the quantities of iron that were being produced from ore and forged into implements increased greatly, and a whole range of new kinds of tools were made for doing different kinds of work (Jacobi 1974; Pleiner 1982). Among the new implements that became common in this period were those used in agriculture, particularly plowshares, colters, and scythes. It is likely that these tools for plowing the soil and harvesting hay helped to increase the efficiency of food production. The development of the rotary quern, which Waldhauser (1981a) thinks increased efficiency of grinding grain by several hundred percent, similarly contributed to more effective food production.

Iron tools also were important for the processing of wood, leather, textiles, and other materials. Construction of wheeled vehicles, boats, and buildings was made easier with the new cutting tools. For the first time, metal was widely employed architecturally. At Manching (Jacobi 1974), Kelheim (Geselowitz 1993), Hrazany (Jansová 1986), and other sites, iron nails and clamps are among the most abundant iron implements. They made the construction of houses and other buildings easier and made the structures sturdier. Although we do not know much about the above-ground character of buildings on the *oppidum* settlements (but see reconstructions in Krämer 1975; Lorenz 1986:38–44; Motyková, Drda, Rybová 1990), this new use of iron must have revolutionized architecture. Large iron spikes were employed in the construction of some *oppidum* walls to hold together wooden beams (Jacobi 1974:237).

Craft workers at the *oppida* also produced objects that had expressive purposes – goods whose use was not principally to serve a physical need or to do work, but rather to communicate information. Our best data about the use of such objects come from the burial evidence (see e.g. Pauli 1972), where particular kinds of personal ornaments are associated with specific categories of persons (men/women, children/adults). Bronze casting was done at the *oppida* for personal ornaments. Scrap from bronze manufacturing is plentiful, though the finished products are found more often in graves than in settlement deposits.

Glass was formed into jewelry such as bracelets, rings, and beads. Amber, bone, antler, lignite, sapropelite, and other materials were carved into beads and rings. Ornate polychrome pottery was made, as well as more common domestic wares. Gold, silver, and bronze coins were minted.

Iron working, bronze casting, and coin minting are well represented on smaller, open sites as well. But the large scale of manufacturing and the diversity of craft production at the *oppida* distinguish them from smaller settlements. The labor devoted to the procurement of large quantities of raw materials, to the manufacturing process, and to distribution of final products all required organization and administration. This scale of organization at the *oppida* reflects a new kind of social unit that emerged at these large communities.

Social change and origins of the *oppida*: *the context of change*

Much of the manufacturing at the *oppida* was intended to produce goods for trade (Gebhard 1989). The trade is represented archaeologically by imported materials such as graphite, amber, sapropelite, and bronze, and by finished objects such as coins and luxury imports. Commerce with the Roman world began by the beginning of the second century BC (Svobodová 1985; Will 1987), and both silver and bronze coinages were started in the course of that century (Polenz 1982). Evidence pertaining to the organization of the trade at the *oppida* is scanty and for the most part indirect. On the basis of an analysis of the Classical sources, Timpe (1985) thinks that local trade was in the hands of indigenous elites who controlled the trade for their own benefit, but that external trade was managed by merchants who did not belong to the elite groups. There is textual evidence for Greek and Roman merchants active at the *oppida* in Gaul, and in Caesar's time some Romans apparently resided at Gallic *oppida*, overseeing trade. Indigenous traders are unfortunately not mentioned in the texts. At the Magdalensberg in Carinthia, we have good information about Roman traders in the second and final centuries BC (Egger 1961). Based on the extensive evidence of Roman imports at the *oppida*, as well as at smaller sites, it is likely that Roman merchants visited and perhaps resided at *oppida* in different parts of Europe, but direct evidence for them has not yet been identified.

The archaeological evidence suggests that social changes during the third and second centuries BC played an important role in the development of the *oppida*. Bujna (1982) has demonstrated the substantial differentiation in burial treatment observable in the flat-grave cemeteries of the fourth and third centuries BC, expressed by differences in grave outfittings. He argues that these distinctions are signs of differences in social status. During the fourth and third centuries BC, many persons from the Celtic lands north of the Alps participated in raids and migrations into southern and south-eastern Europe (Duval and Kruta 1979). In the course of these expeditions, some individuals are likely to have distinguished themselves as successful war-leaders and won both wealth through booty and followers through their leadership skills. As Bujna argues, some such persons are likely to have retained their newly won power upon their return to their homelands in temperate Europe, and came to constitute members of a new power-elite, or aristocracy, in the Celtic lands. The rise of successful war-leaders to positions of political authority, as well as social status, is well documented in other contexts, for example in the early medieval period (James 1988). The strong emphasis on weaponry in the graves of the fourth and third centuries BC would be consistent with this idea. The social units that emerged around such newly established leaders and their followers may have formed the basis of the communities that established the *oppida*.

Bujna (1982) suggests that the great expansion in iron production and in forging during this period occurred in large measure as a result of the need for more and better weapons for the migrating and raiding Celts, an argument that could be supported by developments observed in sword technology (Pleiner 1993). If he is right, then the proliferation of iron in agricultural implements and architectural elements at the *oppida* could be viewed as spin-offs from the expanding military technology. Through his study of the chronological and spatial patterns at Manching, Gebhard (1989:185) suggests that the rapid expansion of that site at the beginning of the second century BC can be attributed to the arrival of Celtic mercenaries returning to their homelands from service in the Mediterranean world. Textual sources indicate that Celtic mercenary activity in Mediterranean armies declined sharply at this time (Szabó 1991), and it is reasonable to suppose that most returned to their homelands.

Rome's increasing economic, military, and political influence in northern Italy and southern Gaul at the end of the third and beginning of the second century BC was a factor in the social and economic changes that took place north of the Alps. The Battle of Telamon in 225 BC was a major event in bringing to an end effective Celtic power in peninsular Italy, and by 180 BC. Roman merchants had established themselves at commercial sites in northern Italy. Will's (1987) recent study of the amphorae from Manching shows that trade between communities north of the Alps and the Roman world began by early in the second century BC.

The movements of peoples in Europe during the second and final centuries BC were important for the growth of the *oppida*. In the year 113 BC the Cimbri appear in the historical sources as a sizeable group moving southward from northern parts of the continent into central Europe; three years later the Teutoni are mentioned. According to our sources (Peschel 1988; Seyer 1988; Todd 1992), the traveling Cimbri, Teutoni, and others were large groups, including women and children and wagons, and engaged in plundering the landscapes through which they passed. A major reason for the establishment and rapid growth of *oppida* is likely to have been to serve as protection for people, supplies, livestock, raw materials, and other goods, from the marauding bands that were a persistent feature of the central European landscape during much of the second and final centuries BC (Fischer 1988).

Names for the different Celtic peoples ("tribes") of temperate Europe first appear in the written sources in this context of growing interaction with the Mediterranean world and of large-scale migrations (Wenskus 1961; Hachmann 1970). By the end of the final century BC, these names occur frequently in the works of writers such as Caesar, Livy, and Strabo. Caesar informs us that the

Gallic *oppida* were capitals of tribal entities and that some were centers for storage of commodities and for trade (Timpe 1985:267–8). The Gallic *oppida* can thus be viewed as serving the need on the part of newly emerging political units for centers of administration, economy, and ritual (Dehn 1951). It is important to distinguish between the *oppida* of Gaul, and those east of the Rhine, for which we have no written descriptions. By the time Caesar became familiar with the Gallic *oppida*, they had been involved actively in trade with Roman southern Gaul for a century, some had Romans living among the indigenous populations, and many were engaged with the Romans as allies or as enemies.

Changes at the *oppida*

A number of investigators interpret the evidence to show that a different kind of economy developed in temperate Europe during the second century BC, one characterized by greater specialization in crafts and with some manufacturing aimed at export trade (Steuer 1987; Gebhard 1989; Kellner 1990). Evidence to support this model is in the form of the great increase in industrial production, particularly but not exclusively at the *oppida*, and in the manufacture of many kinds of goods, such as wheel-turned pottery and glass bracelets, that suggest mass-production strategies executed by specialists. The fact that the products from these industries have been found at places away from the *oppida* (e.g. Waldhauser 1992; Lappe 1979) has been interpreted as evidence of manufacture aimed in part at trade.

We do not have a good understanding of the organization of manufacturing either at the *oppida* or at the smaller settlements, largely because of the lack of good evidence of actual workshops. Perhaps the most important question is, were the artisans working for their own benefit, or did they work under the control of elite groups (Duval 1991)? For Gaul, where we have textual evidence as well as archaeological, Crumley (1974) and others have argued that the beginning of regular interaction with the Roman world during the second century BC led to the development of intensive competition among individuals and groups in temperate Europe for political influence with Rome, and for trade goods. Duval (1983) suggests that a new social group composed of artisans and merchants rose to prominence. The widespread evidence for the minting of coins (whatever their exact function in the economy may have been – see recent overview in Ziegaus 1993) from the second half of the second century BC, both at the *oppida* and at smaller settlements, could be interpreted in support of this model of growth in wealth and

status by artisans and merchants outside of the control of established elite groups.

The social units at the *oppida* were different from earlier ones, in that they were larger and considerably more complex. The larger community size and concentrated building, manufacturing, and trading activities required a more elaborate administrative structure than that needed by smaller communities. Haselgrove's (1988) ideas, developed from Rathje (1975), about investment in information processing and decision making, are relevant here. As societies become more complex, they need to devote disproportionately more energy to organization, including information gathering and processing, decision making, and administration. Such changes took place with the growth of the *oppida*.

Rathje (1975) predicts regular changes in material culture associated with these organizational changes, including growing standardization and a shift away from production of status goods that require high levels of labor investment, to simpler items that can be produced in large quantities with relatively little labor. The changes predicted by Rathje are apparent in the material culture of the late La Tène Period. The characteristic fibula forms of the later La Tène C and La Tène D phases are distinguished from earlier ones by the simplicity of design and structure, and especially by their general lack of individualizing ornament. The contrast with fibulae of La Tène phases A and B is striking (see for example fibulae of the different periods in Reinecke 1965). The same change is apparent in other items of personal ornament, notably glass bracelets (Gebhard 1989).

Changes in burial practice can be interpreted in a similar way. The flat-grave inhumation cemeteries of the fourth and third centuries BC are characterized by burials distinguished from one another by the grave goods (e.g. Waldhauser 1978, 1987). This individuality is particularly marked among women's burials with often uniquely ornamented neckrings, fibulae, and armrings, but it is also characteristic of men's graves. No two graves are just alike in their burial goods. During the second century BC the dominant burial practice in most of temperate Europe changed from inhumation with distinctive grave goods, to cremation with few or no goods (Krämer 1985). Thus in the burials, too, signs of individuality virtually disappear in the course of the second century BC in most of the regions where *oppida* occur. This change surely had a ritual aspect, but perhaps we need to view the ritual change as a part of the broader social change.

This trend toward increasing uniformity of material culture is seen in the *Viereckschanzen* - the rectangular enclosures that were sites of ritual activity. Before the second century BC, a variety of different kinds of enclos-ures, some circular, as for example the Goloring (Röder 1948), and some rectangular, as at Libenice (Rybová and Soudský 1962), as well as natural locations such as springs and rivers (Torbrügge 1971), were used as sites at which ritual practices were carried out, most clearly expressed in the deposition of offerings. The *Viereckschanzen*, which appeared on the landscape at about the same time as the *oppida*, represent a new standardization of ritual structure (Bittel 1981a). The new enclosures occur not only in association with *oppida*, but throughout the countryside as well, linked with smaller communities as well as with large ones.

Coins are perhaps the best example of Rathje's and Haselgrove's "directly economic form" of material cul-ture that played an integrating role at the *oppida*. They embodied value at the end of the Iron Age, yet they were mass-produced, and one coin was just like every other of its series. The most active period of the *oppida*, in the decades before and after 100 BC, corresponds to the time when silver and bronze coins proliferated, and most specialists now envision a real money economy at the major settlements (Steuer 1987; Kellner 1990). We lack good information about the social distribution of the lower-value coins; it is not clear whether they were available to most members of the *oppidum* communities, or restricted to elites (Polenz 1982). Future data on spatial patterning of coins on settlements should provide more information for understanding coinage in its social context.

Gold coins played a different role from silver and bronze. The hoards that contain gold coins, and often other gold objects as well (Furger-Gunti 1982), show that value was amassed and stored in this form. The amount of wealth represented by hoards such as Irsching (over 1000 gold coins) and Gaggers (some 1350) in Bavaria (Kellner 1990) was probably much greater than could have been accumulated by communities of earlier periods. Such treasures are likely to represent wealth accumulation by elites amassed through trade or toll collection (Crumley 1987c). Some hoards are geographically associated with the *oppida*, but others are not. As in the case of coin minting and locations of *Viereckschanzen*, the distribu-tion of the gold hoards supports a diffusion of wealth and status rather than its concentration in the *oppida*. Inter-pretation of the gold hoards is difficult. Both safe storage of bullion and offering of treasure to deities seem to have played a part in the deposition of the hoards (Furger-Gunti 1982; Kellner 1990:14).

Discussion

The major *oppida*, with larger populations than other sites and with substantial industrial production, required a social organization different from that of other Iron Age communities. Rathje's model provides a useful way of thinking about these questions as the archaeological evidence becomes more abundant. The information avail-able at present does not allow us to make any definitive statements about social statuses at the *oppida* compared to those at smaller sites, nor about social relations between the various communities.

The textual sources, in particular Caesar's account, suggest that late Iron Age Celtic society was highly stratified and that the strata were sharply defined from one another. The archaeological evidence from both settlements and graves, on the other hand, suggests a broad range of variation in status expression, a pattern that Roymans (1990) recognizes in his recent analysis of the material in northern Gaul. The situation is similar to that of the early Middle Ages, where written sources have been interpreted to indicate a rigid hierarchy of sharply defined statuses, but the archaeology suggests wide varia-tion instead (Christlein 1973). In working with Caesar's text, we need to bear in mind that he was most likely informed only by members of elite groups, he was a Roman viewing a foreign culture in terms of his own, and he was seeing a society under the stress of war (discussion in Chapman 1992; also see Dunham this volume).

The archaeological evidence suggests that all ranges of status in late Iron Age Celtic society were represented at the *oppida*, and that the smaller communities also included status variation. Recent results from excavations at Berching-Pollanten have been particularly revealing. There the material culture was similar to that at Man-ching, with the same sorts of iron tools, fine painted pottery, glass and sapropelite jewelry, keys, balances, and seventy-nine coins (Fischer, Rieckhoff-Pauli, and Spindler 1984; Kellner 1990:148). The data from other small sites, from France to Czechoslovakia, indicate that those communities also shared the material culture of the *oppida*. Even exotic imports such as Roman bronze vessels occur in the countryside as well as at the *oppida* (Werner 1978). The present archaeological evidence sug-gests that some of the *oppida* were flourishing economic centers, but not necessarily centers of social power or political importance. Caesar's assertions to the contrary probably reflect the special circumstances of the Gallic sites at the time of the Roman wars.

The development of the *oppida* cannot be ascribed to any single cause, but rather to a series of interrelated factors. An important one was the social and military instability of the second century BC, when many groups were moving in central Europe, seeking new homes or plundering indigenous communities. Part of this instability was the result of the return of Celtic groups from Mediterranean lands. Some migrated from Italy across the Alps after the defeats at the hands of the Romans late in the third and early in the second century BC. Mercenaries who had served in Mediterranean lands returned to their homelands. The *oppida* developed for community protection in this turbulent context.

The rapid expansion of manufacturing during the third and second centuries BC was an important factor in the growth of these large communities. The rapidly expanding craft industries benefited from more efficient supply, production, and transportation processes that resulted from the concentration of manufacturing in these large communities. The situation of the major *oppida* on routes of easy transportation underscores the role of commerce at these centers.

The social and political character of these communities developed after the *oppida* were established, as means for coping with the large populations and complex economic systems. The larger populations required the development of social organizations different from those at the small communities, but the extreme social and political structures described by Caesar for Gaul probably reflect the special conditions of a society under the stress of war with Rome, not typical configurations at *oppida* elsewhere.

The *oppida* are important for our understanding of the social evolution of the Celts because they were the first arguably urban communities that developed in Celtic lands (Collis 1984a). Our current evidence suggests that they were agglomerations of small settlement units, not unlike those at the unenclosed sites, with exceptional industrial activity in part of the enclosed areas, but with large tracts of sparsely settled land as well. Our present chronological understanding (Krämer 1985; Miron 1986, 1989; Gebhard 1991; Rieckhoff 1992) suggests that most of the *oppida* existed as large settlements for little over a century, and we need to regard them as special communities formed in response to particular social and military circumstances during the second and final centuries BC. Once those circumstances changed, in the course of the final century BC and the first century AD, these unusual communities lost their reasons for existence, and the settlements were abandoned.

PART IV

Evolution and ethnohistory: the protohistoric polities of Gaul and the British Isles

11
Modelling chiefdoms in the Scottish Highlands and Islands prior to the '45

ROBERT A. DODGSHON

Introduction

The Highlands and Islands of Scotland provide us with the most persistent forms of Celtic chiefdom. Only when the hopes of the 1745 Jacobite rebellion were dashed at Culloden in 1746 did central government assert its absolute authority over the region and only then can we speak of Highland chiefs finally giving way to the authority of the state. Their late survival means that the Highlands provide us with examples of Celtic chiefdoms that can actually be reconstituted, structurally and processually, through manuscript data. Sceptics might argue that Celtic chiefdoms were essentially an oral rather than literate culture, one whose inner logic was sustained across generations by *seanchaidhean*, or clan historians. The greater use of written records after *c.* 1500 could be ascribed to the fact that surviving chiefdoms were being transformed by alien ideas as the influence of the wider Scottish state spread into the region. But even conceding that such influences were at work, what remained was still a system whose organization and values were closer to those of a chiefdom than a feudal lordship, and whose documentation over the sixteenth to eighteenth centuries provides a valuable opportunity for exploring how such chiefdoms operated.

Though much has been written about the Highland clans, this opportunity for exploring how they operated as chiefdoms has hardly been seized. To a large degree, this neglect stems from the fact that most writers have been concerned with highlighting the individuality of clans rather than their shared characteristics. Furthermore, the handful of attempts which have tried to generalize about their character have concentrated on their socio-political

structure, saying little about other dimensions. Missing from the debate is any consideration of their ecology and of why chiefdoms should have been such a persistent feature of the region, of the role played by kinship in the life of the ordinary peasant as opposed to the major lineages and tacksmen, of whether they possessed a redistributive economy pivoted around the chief, and of whether we can identify distinct forms of chiefly behavior. Arguably, the failure to ask such questions arises from a failure to conceptualize chiefdoms and to ask whether they were driven by goals and strategies. In fact, very little use has been made of anthropological and archaeological models and how these might illuminate our understanding of Highland chiefdoms.

In response to these lacunae, I propose to consider five different aspects of the problem. First, I want to explore what we can call their ecology, the many ways in which the environmental context of chiefdoms helped to shape their development and persistence. Second, there is the question of kinship. That such ties bound the major lineages within chiefdoms is well documented but we need to ask how real were the ties of the ordinary kinsmen. Third, there is the question of whether we can speak of a chiefly economy based on redistributive exchange. As I will try to show, this links back to the problem of its ecological setting and how control over scarce resources was turned into social ranking or hierarchy. Fourth, inextricably bound up with their socio-political structure were specific forms of display centered around feasting and feuding. Fifth and finally, we need to bring these various dimensions of the problem together, to restore their unity as a system.

Highland chiefdoms: their ecological setting

The ecological setting of Highland chiefdoms has a bearing on three crucial questions: first, why did chiefdoms become such a prominent feature of local social organization, second, why did control over food play such a prominent role in their ideology, and, third, why did they persist for so long? Though tempting, it would be wrong to see the difficult, broken topography of the region as somehow generating chiefdoms as a social form. In a sense, the late survival of chiefdoms within the Highlands and Islands creates a false perspective over why they developed in the first place. As with other parts of Britain, forms of chiefdom must have been widespread throughout Scotland down to the early medieval period. Indeed, it is very easy to see a territorial unit like the thanage or shire as embodying some of the principles of a chiefdom (Dodgshon 1981:58–89). Once seen in this wider context, any deterministic link between the development of chiefdoms as a social form and the Highlands as a type of environment becomes untenable. However, this basic point made, there are ways in which the ecological setting of the Highlands may have influenced the local character of chiefdoms.

In principle, we can expect more fertile lowland areas to have provided more opportunity for the growth and interaction required by large or elaborate chiefdoms, whilst difficult mountainous regions would have favored more localized, flatter forms if only because the costs of maintaining physically – and demographically – larger forms would have been higher in such circumstances. In fact, such assumptions are not easily applied to the western Highlands and Islands. The problem is that whilst their ecological setting tended to insularize chiefdoms, to create fairly obvious lines of geographical segmentation, it did not necessarily inhibit the formation of complex alliance structures. This was especially true of the Hebrides and along the western seaboard. Though islands created a natural partitioning of territory, the fact remains that inter-island movement had lower costs than movement on the mainland. The very existence of the Lordship of the Isles makes this point emphatically. By any definition, this was a large, complex chiefdom. It flourished over the fourteenth and most of the fifteenth century. Though centered around Finlaggan on Islay, its constituent parts stretched from the western seaboard out across parts of both the Inner and Outer Hebrides (Macdonald and Macdonald 1896–1904).

Those components of the Lordship which survived after its collapse were almost as distended. The chiefdom formed around the Clanranald, for instance, stretched from South Uist and Benbecula eastwards across minor islands like Eigg, Rhum and Canna to districts along the western seaboard like Moidart and Arisaig (Fig. 11.1) (Scottish Record Office, hereafter SRO GD201/1257; SRO GD201/5/1235/124). The Macleod of Macleod controlled an equally sprawled estate (Fig. 11.1) (Macleod 1938–9: II, 69).

A second way in which the ecological setting of Highland chiefdoms affected their character was through the subsistence problems which beset the region. Patently, the control exercised over subsistence was a primary source of power and ranking in all agrarian societies. However, whilst acknowledging the universal value attached to subsistence, different habitats provide such societies with widely differing potentials when it comes to food production. Logically, we can expect fertile areas to have provided greater scope for the extraction of surplus by social hierarchies and, for this reason, greater scope for

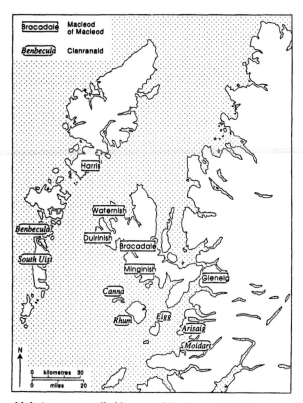

11.1 Areas controlled by two of the larger Hebridean chiefdoms: the Clanranald and the Macleod of Macleod.

the translation of food into other forms of consumption e.g. craft production, urban growth, standing armies. By comparison, marginal areas were caught in a subsistence trap. Low levels of output were usually combined with sharp fluctuations in output. The limitations which this marginality imposed on surplus extraction clearly gave less scope for the growth of social hierarchies. More significantly, it gave less scope for the translation of food into other forms of consumption. Arguably, the values and ideology developed around any system of social ranking would have found it difficult to escape from the fact that life and social order were about survival. Tighter margins and greater frequency of disaster would have worked to make the relations within and between chiefdoms more of a stark, competititve struggle over the basic resources of subsistence, over who controlled land and its product, food.

The ecological setting of Highland chiefdoms clearly places them in this latter category. When we analyze their relationships and ideology of behavior, the value and symbolism of food figures prominently. Their concern with basic questions of subsistence is understandable. Large areas can be classed as rocky, barren waste and low-yielding hill pasture. Arable consisted of scattered pockets of fertile cultivable soils, both along the valley bottoms of the interior and along the coastal margins of the west. Physically, the region is more suited to livestock farming than to cultivation. The combination of high rainfall, strong winds, wet springs, short summer growing season, and thin, acid soils made cropping a high-risk business. Even in the best of seasons, yields were generally low so that one can rarely speak of Highland communities having an abundance of food (Dodgshon and Olsson 1988:39–51; Dodgshon 1993:679–701). Equally relevant to the problem is the fact that the general abundance of land but limited supply of good arable meant the dividing line between sufficiency and crisis was fuzzy, one easily crossed when population grew or when climatic change (e.g. the Little Ice Age of the fifteenth to sixteenth centuries) remapped the limits of cropping.

Given the greater suitability of the region for livestock production, together with the more portable and storable nature of livestock, the question of why local communities built up such a strong reliance on cropping cannot be ignored. A significant factor may have been the greater energy yield of a crop-based economy relative to livestock production. Notwithstanding their differences in labor input, arable yielded more per unit of land than livestock. Under conditions of a growing population, developing a significant arable base to subsistence would have been a rational strategy, one that made more intensive use of both land and labor. In effect, such a strategy traded increased output in average years against the greater risks of failure during poor seasons. Of course, some of these risks could be combatted through the relations built up around simple rank systems, with chiefs offering a form of insurance, provided, that is, their control embraced a range of ecologies and, therefore, a range of different responses to crises.

The ecological setting of Highland chiefdoms is also relevant when we turn to the question of why they survived so long in the region. Put simply, we can see their survival as a matter of opportunity costs. Seen from Edinburgh, the difficult and isolated nature of the region made the costs of incorporating it into the wider state high. At the same time, the rewards of such incorporation would not have been attractive given the region's low potential for extracting surplus. Indeed, it is not without significance that when the Crown took temporary control of estates in Islay, Kintyre, and Ardnamurchan during the 1490s, it acquired a vast intake of food rents. Its response was to convert them into cash by selling the produce back to tenants (e.g. M'Neill 1897:646). Whether by virtue of its quality or the costs of moving it out of the region, such produce clearly was of no marketable value to the Crown. By this point though, the pressure to incorporate the region more fully into the Scottish state was driven by other factors so that its costs could be justified in other ways.

Highland chiefdoms: ties of kinship and alliance

Most of the chiefdoms that existed in the region over the fifteenth to seventeenth centuries can be documented using clan genealogies. These sources have been extensively used in studies of the kin ties that bound them together. However, the majority of such studies have stressed the individuality of particular clans or chiefdoms rather than their shared characteristics. There are, however, exceptions. A handful of studies are available showing how clans worked to establish themselves both affinally and territorially, how they built up their ties and alliances, and how they used their kinship ties to exploit their land economically and to control it politically (Cregeen 1968:153-92; Fox 1976:95–121; Wormald 1985). I want to restrict my discussion to two particular aspects of this problem: how chiefdoms established themselves as socio-spatial entities and the extent to which they were bonded agnatically.

Whereas later state systems organized society through an abstract territorialization of authority, one that transcended the social identity of its occupants, chiefdoms – to use Sahlins' words – organized territory through society (Sahlins 1968:5). Those in the Highlands and Islands were no exception. Socio-political order in the region was constituted through the prevailing order of chiefdoms, and not as a fixed territorial scheme imposed by a centralized administrative system. As chiefdoms expanded or contracted, this *de facto* pattern of socio-political order would have been continually reworked, simply because the one existed as a map of the other.

Given such a system, it follows that Highland chiefdoms needed to secure themselves in two ways, first, as social networks of kinship and alliance and, second, as controllers of land and its resources. Chiefs could employ a number of strategies. Naturally, those having control of fertile land were best placed. Not only did they have greater scope for packing their estates – cultivating men as well as land – they also had the material basis for contracting favorable alliances with other chiefs. It is surely no accident that Islay, the most fertile of the Hebridean Isles, was the centre of a large, complex chiefdom, the Lordship of the Isles (Storrie 1961:87-108).

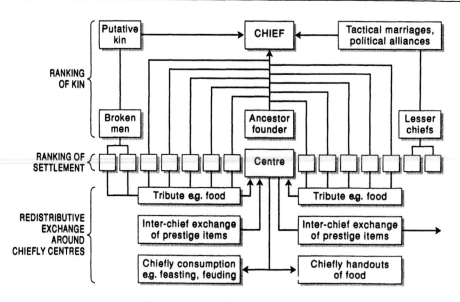

11.2 The socio-spatial structure of chiefdoms.

Tactical marriages were used by all successful chiefdoms to draw the kinsmen and resources of smaller, peripheral chiefdoms under their wing (Macpherson 1966:142). In fact, chiefly marriage patterns provided the opportunity for tactical thinking, with many chiefs having two or three wives during their lifetime and siring numerous children (Carter 1973:51–60; Sellar 1981:464–95; SRO GD50/28). Beyond marriage as a strategy of chiefly expansion, there also existed the possibility of chiefs forging a socio-political alliance. By the sixteenth century, we find such alliances being formally contracted via bonds of friendship: these bound two chiefs and their followers together; to behave toward each other as if they were kin and to do so, as one agreement put it, through "all hazards of disgrace and infamy" (SRO GD50/103). A recent study by Wormald has documented how the feudalized variant of these friendship bonds, or bonds of manrent, were used by emergent chiefdoms like the Campbells of Breadalbane to build up a powerful network of alliance (Wormald 1985).

Despite having a range of strategies to hand, chiefs must still have found difficulty in keeping their expansion as kin groups in balance with their command over the basic resources of land. A successful and expanding chiefdom might find itself with a sudden windfall of land but not the kinsmen to fill it. If faced with a sudden expansion of their territory, such as when the Campbells of Argyll took over parts of Knapdale and Mull in the seventeenth century, we cannot expect them to have filled

it with kin overnight; their biological response worked itself out more slowly than political opportunism. In fact, as Cregeen's work demonstrates, the solution was to put in Campbells as tacksmen over particular districts or townships, an emplacement which led ultimately to a subsequently more gradual process whereby Campbells were sublet townships or parts of a township by the tacksman as surplus men became available (Cregeen 1969:939).

We can assume this was a general solution to the problem. However, its implications have a direct bearing on the question of whether we can assume that Highland chiefdoms or clans were bound wholly by kinship. Contemporary documentary sources disclose that kinship structures operated at two levels. First, most Highland chiefdoms maintained details of the genealogical connections that bound them together at what we can call their level of socio-political control. Such genealogies provide us with a socio-political map, dividing the chiefdom into lineages or *sliochdeadh*, and each carefully ranked according to their genealogical distance from the ancestor/founder of the chiefdom and each assigned to a particular district (Fig. 11.2). This ideological fusion of kinship and space is underlined by the simple way in which the leading living member of each segment is invariably identified as Campbell of X or Mackenzie of Y, their position in the overall hierarchy of kin being inextricably linked to their emplacement in a particular district. Dr. Samuel Johnson made the same point in the diary of his visit to the

Highlands. The "chief of a clan is addressed by the name. The Laird of Dunvegan is called Macleod, but other gentlemen of the same name are denominated by the place where they reside, as Raasa, or Talisker" (Johnson 1971 edition: 153). In effect, clan genealogies record those connections which establish its control over a particular district. They provide a view of chiefly control from above.

The second form of kinship structure disclosed by contemporary sources provides us with a view from the bottom. When rentals and charters become available over the sixteenth century, they reveal many individual tenants as identified by a patronymic. As Samuel Johnson put it, the "distinction of the meaner people is made by their Christian names" (Johnson 1971 edition: 153). Most individuals were identified through their ties across two or three generations. Thus, a 1699 rental for Arisaig refers to a John McDoil VcCoil Vic Ewn as a tenant in the township of Booness (SRO GD201/1/362/3). Less frequently, we find individuals given a patronymic that spans four generations, such as the Donald MacCoil vic Ean vic Coil listed in a 1781 lease for Five Penny Borve (Lewis)(SRO GD46/1/212). Still more exceptionally, we find patronymics covering five generations, such as the Allane McAllane Vic Allane Vc Donil Vc Lauchlan cited in a charter of 1557 (SRO GD50/29) or the Roderick MacEan vic Coil vic Conachie vic Inish mentioned in a 1778 lease for North Bragar (Lewis)(SRO GD46/1/212).

Standard discussions of Highland chiefdoms too easily assume that the kin ties captured in patronymics are simply a close-focus version of the kin ties embodied in clan genealogies, the former slotting into the wider scheme mapped out by the latter. At first sight, this would seem borne out by the double identity which many individuals possess, recording themselves in rentals and leases by a patronymic plus a clan name as an alias or vice versa. Thus, a Breadalbane tack of 1577 refers to a Tarloch McEan VcTarloch alias Campbell (SRO GD50/29) whilst a rental of 1718 for Moydart mentions a John McEan vic Ewn alias McEachan (SRO GD201/5/1257/1). Putting the relationship in the reverse order, a 1701 rental of Badenoch lists a James McCallum alias Macpherson (SRO GD128/11/1), a 1718 rental for Arisaig lists a Donald McDonald alias McEan vic Alister (SRO GD201/5/1257/2), another of 1718 for South Uist lists a John McDonald alias McEan VcInish (SRO GD201/5/1257/5). Yet despite this juxtaposition, patronymics and clan names have no necessary connection. The problems to be overcome when the physical expansion of chiefdoms ran ahead of their biological capacity for filling such extra space inevitably meant that successful chiefdoms had to take a pragmatic approach to the question of how they were composed. However, in a society whose socio-political order derived from the order created by chiefdoms, this did not mean the abandonment of kinship as an ideological prop to the definition of chiefdoms. Rather was it a case of individuals having to assume the identity of a clan even if such ties were fictitious or presumed simply because such groupings were the only source of order in the Highlands. As a traditional Highland saying put it, a man without a clan was a broken man, broken because it gave him less favor when bidding for land and – in a world where chiefs provided protection for their kinsmen – it placed them outside of authority. The spirit of the former is captured in a note from a rental for the isle of Eigg: the Late Captain of Clanranald, it said "Referred to himself the power of keeping in his own Kinsmen and tenants on this Ile" (SRO GD201/5/1257/3). Likewise, when the would-be tenant, Andrew Macpherson, was described in a lease of 1618 for Dalcrombie (Inverness-shire) as "being of the maill [male] kynd of the clan Chattan," we can hardly doubt that it mattered to the granting of the lease (SRO GD80/3). The principle being applied extended to bonds of friendship. When Alex. MacIain MacAlister of Glengarry agreed a bond of friendship with Ewen Allanson of Lochiel in 1521, they agreed "to lease land to each other if they obtained it" (Macdonald and Macdonald 1896–1904: III, 377). The chief's role as protector is invoked in an offer of protection by a chief to the McGillekeyrs "as ane cheyf dois in the contreis of the helandis" (HMC *Fourth Report, Part 1, Report and Appendix, 1874*: 512; see also, Clan Donald Trust, Armadale, Lord Macdonald Papers RH4/90/19/8).

Once we grasp the ongoing need to squeeze individuals into a scheme that maintained an ideology of common kinship via the mantle of a common clan name, we can more easily understand some of the anomalies. We can, for example, understand why in the sixteenth century a Fraser of Lovat could offer a boll of meal to anyone who would take his name (Grant 1930:501), why – in 1552 – a William McOlcallum, his son Malcolm, and a Donald Roy McOlchallum Glass could renounce "McGregor their auld chief" and bind themselves to Colin Campbell "whome they have elected and chosen for their chief and master," a switch that simply swapped one alias for another (Menzies 1894:182). We can find other later instances of individuals switching between clan identities. Of course, the most notorious instance was when the MacGregors had their clan name proscribed in 1603 (Dodgshon 1989:184–5 and 195–6). Yet it would be wrong to see their proscription as a special case. In all

Table 11.1 *Aggregate rent for different parts of the Highlands and Islands showing the importance of rent payments in kind*

	Money Merks = mks Scots Pounds = lib	Meal Bolls = b Stones = st	Bere Bolls = b	Malt Bolls = b	Sheep	Cattle	Cheese Stones = st	Butter Stones = st	Hens	Geese
Islay (1542)	45. 0. 1 lib	2593 st	850 b		301	301	2161 st		301	301
Mull (1542)	340 mks	1360 b			1360	680	3400 st	640 st	4080	
North Kintyre (1542)	125. 0. 0. lib	380 st		74 b	41		307 st			
South Kintyre (1542)	162. 0. 4 lib	480 st		414 b	53	48	342 st			
Lewis (1580)		5760 b		—	640	1160				
Trotternish (1580)	160 mks	160 b		160 b		320			1280	
Ross of Mull (1587–88)	2. 14. 9 lib	432 st				48				
Badenoch [1603]	366. 0. 0. lib	175 b			89	89			382	
Islay (1614)	45. 0. 1 lib	2193 b			301	301	2161 st		301	301
Duirinish (1664)	2711. 6. 8 lib	244 b		55 b	57	/	81 st	87 st	4250	
Waternish (1664)	1636. 13. 4 lib	151 b		91 b	81	/	95 st	95 st	3280	
Bracadale (1664)	2122. 6. 8. lib	228 b		74 b	62	/		119 st	2960	
Minginish (1664)	1611. 6. 8. lib	220 b		88 b	92	/		104 st	3120	
Harris (1697)	2047 mks	180 b			96	55		149 st		

Source: Islay (1542), Mull (1542), North Kintyre (1542) based on M'Neill 1897:634ff. Lewis (1580) based on Skene 1877, Vol. III:429. Trotternish (1580) on *ibid.*:435. Ross of Mull (1587–8) on *Collectanea de Rebus Albanicus* 1847: 173–7 (Edinburgh: Iona Club). Badenoch (1603) on Macpherson 1893:503–13. Islay (1614) on Smith 1895:487–90. Duirinish (1664), Waternish (1664), Bracadale (1664), Minginish (1664), on Macleod 1938–9, Vol. I: 270–1. Harris (1697) on Macleod 1938–9, Vol II:85.

probability, the Crown was simply employing a device that already had some currency in the Highlands as individuals switched from declining or marginalized clans to more successful groups.

The redistributive economy of Highland chiefdoms

Highland chiefdoms can be associated with well-defined systems of redistributive exchange. We can identify two types, a well-defined one based on staples like food and cloth and another less well-defined flow based on prestige goods like weaponry and personal ornament (Fig. 11.2). Looking at the first of these, most Highland estates gathered rents made up in part of foodstuffs. Payments in the form of grain or meal were at the heart of these flows but alongside them we find townships being variously obligated to render sheep, poultry, calves, cattle, and whisky. Even when estates converted such payments into cash over the seventeenth and eighteenth centuries, their original composition in kind continued to be recorded (SRO GD112/9/45; SRO GD201/1/351/2; SRO GD46/1/ 267). The survival of rentals for various parts of the region enables us to reconstruct the gross quantities of food

involved in these payments (Table 11.1). Exactly what the various grain and meal payments constituted as a percentage of total crop is difficult to assess, but crude estimates would suggest that some tenants could have been paying as much as 20–30 percent of their crop as part of their rent (based on SRO E729/9/1). To this, of course, must be added the produce taken in as stock.

These manifest transfers of food were supplemented by further transfers between kinsman and chief via the custom of *cuid oidhche* or hospitality. The right of a chief and his "household men" to a night's hospitality from each tenant was a widespread burden on the latter (*Black Book of Taymouth* 1855:187–9). Its existence is attested in some of the earliest documentation for the region. When we start to get detailed references to it in the sixteenth century, we find it was an obligation capable of modification and abuse. On Lewis, it had been modified to the extent that "fighting men," men who elsewhere formed part of the chief's household men, were quartered directly on tenants, the latter being required to keep them in food and cloth (Skene 1877: III, 439). A more common abuse took the form of *sorning*. Groups of "idill men" would roam a district arbitrarily claiming hospitality from tenants. Some sorners may have invoked loose genealogical links to the local chief as the basis for sorning, but it is also clear that some were simply lawless and landless men abusing the principle of *cuid oidhche*, forcing hospitality out of tenants under duress. Attempts to eradicate sorning were made through enactments in local bailie courts from the early sixteenth century onward (Burnett 1889:703–4; SRO GD5O/136, August 12, 1700) and through leases issued by estates (*Black Book of Taymouth* 1855:237–9; Masson 1884:72–3, 92 and 534). A more general attempt at controlling the practice was made by an Act of Parliament in 1584 (*APS* October 24, 1584 and December 1, 1585) and, again, by the Statutes of Iona in 1607 (Masson 1889:26–30).

Although of a different order, smaller and less regular reverse flows of food can also be detected moving from chiefs to tenants during times of scarcity. In a risk-laden environment, especially when seen in terms of cropping, subsistence crises were a common but unpredictable part of the local economy. Clearly, in such circumstances, the social storage offered by chiefly systems of redistributive exchange provided an insurance against starvation. In many instances, though, the reverse flows of food that moved between chiefs and their kinsmen were token. The estate simply allowed tenants to keep the food that would otherwise have been remitted as rent. Captain Burt, an English officer who visited the Highlands in the mid-eighteenth century, suggested that "owing to the poverty of tenants," it was customary for "the Chief, or Laird, to free some of them, every Year, from all Arrears of Rent," with the average estate foregoing an entire year's rent *in cumulo* every five years! (Jamieson 1876 edition: I, 158). An 1829 report covering the Macdonald estate on Skye noted that "for some years past Lord Macdonald has been in the practice of allowing abatements on his estate indiscriminately to all the tenants without distinction" (Clan Donald Trust, Armadale, Lord Macdonald Papers GD221/5913; SRO E744/1/2). During serious crises, some estates went further and imported grain for distribution amongst tenants (Gray 1957:185–6). However, by the seventeenth century, these counterflows of food formed only part of an estate's potential response to crises. It could also accept cash payments – thereby enabling rent to be transferred from what was scarce (arable) to what was abundant (grass) through the sale of livestock (SRO E744/1). However, there is a difference between this solution and those mentioned earlier. The former exploit the considerable socio-political value of food, the latter are more concerned with its narrower economic value.

From the late seventeenth century onwards, Scottish chiefdoms were caught between these two sources of

value. The former was a source of support and status within the traditional value system of the chiefdom. Its profit and loss was to be measured in those terms. The latter introduced accountancy of a different sort, pressuring estates into the need for making cash profits. What we find by the eighteenth century is that this conflict over how the resources of the estate should be valued came to a head. The eventual collapse of the '45 rebellion undermined the socio-political significance of a large and loyal clan. However, Highland chiefs still felt obligated to help their tenants in times of need. Indeed, throughout the remainder of the eighteenth century and even early decades of the nineteenth, at a time when chiefs expanded their own cash needs, some continued to carry heavy rent arrears and to distribute food (Clan Donald Trust, Armadale, Lord Macdonald Papers GD221/5913; SRO GD46/17/59; Richards and Clough 1989).

Superimposed over the flows of basic commodities between tenants and their chief were more ill-defined flows of prestige items between chiefs or between chiefs and leading members of their major cadet branches. Three types can be distinguished. First, there were flows of cattle. As with other kin-based societies, cattle had a value that went beyond their immediate food value. The fact they were a storable food and could produce a yield (e.g. milk, cheese, calves) without the basic stock being consumed obviously enhanced their value. In the context of the western Highlands and Islands, a further factor may have been the vital role of livestock as a source of manure (Munro 1961:72–5). Indeed, some farms were assessed in terms of the number of cattle they carried (SRO E746/166). All else, it seemed, flowed from this fact. But whatever their use-values, and whatever their basic value as an item of exchange between tenants and their chief, cattle also had exchange value as a "prestige" item. In some instances, we find them used as *tochergude*, bridewealth, such as in the marriage between the son of Clanranald and the daughter of Rory Macleod of Dunvegan in 1613, the latter requiring Macleod to give the son of Clanranald "nine score of gud and sufficient quick ky" plus a further twenty if he "desyre thaime" (Macleod 1938–9: I, 52–4; SRO GD201/1/81). Their use in this form must have been fairly general, a means whereby the greater numbers of cattle gathered in as rent by those chiefs blessed with fertile land could be used, at a higher level of exchange, to contract more favorable alliances.

A second form of prestige item comprised items of personal ornament of a non-military kind, like rings, cloaks, and brooches. The *Book of Rights*, an Irish source thought to be of eleventh-century date, lists such items moving between high kings and territorial kings in Ireland

(Binchy 1962). Such detail is lacking for the west of Scotland, but successive Lords of the Isles (Macdonald and Macdonald 1896: I, 444) and others (Macdonald 1978:279) were famed for their liberality.

Military equipment probably formed a third type of prestige item. Indeed, given the role of feuding amongst Highland chiefdoms, there are good reasons for believing that such equipment may have been the most important type of gift moving between chiefs, or between chiefs and leading members of their clan. An interesting clue as to the symbolic value attached to such equipment is provided by the work of a vigorous school of stone masons who flourished in Argyll over the fifteenth and sixteenth centuries. Their work is represented for us by a range of grave slabs commemorating leading members of local kin-groups. For the present argument, what stands out about these slabs is the way in which they depict these individuals. Many are shown holding a two-handed claymore, and each is clad with shoulder mail, bascinet and aketon (Steer and Bannerman 1977:27). The symbolism is clear, their appearance as fighting men was bound up with their status. Such weaponry, though, could not have been freely available. It is precisely the sort of prestige item which we can expect chiefs to have controlled. Though references to ore smelting prior to the eighteenth century are scarce, some chiefs certainly maintained metalsmiths and armourers on their estate. In more than one instance, we find whole kin-groups associated with the craft of metalworking. The Gowans of Morvern and the McFederanes of Benderloch, for instance, were both renowned metalsmiths (Steer and Bannerman 1977:144–6). Where such smiths acted as hereditary smiths to an estate, we can expect their output of weaponry to have been carefully controlled by local chiefs. In what was possibly an exceptional case, we even find a galley, a fighting ship, given as part of a marriage settlement (Macleod 1938: I, 52-4).

Highland chiefdoms: forms of display behavior

Highland chiefdoms had two prime forms of display behavior: feasting and feuding. The former was clearly bound up with the ability of chiefs to gather in food as tribute or rent and can be regarded as an attempt to translate such payments directly into status. In character, these displays of feasting ranged from the modest to the monumental, the latter lasting for several days. Even chiefs with modest estates could entertain extravagantly, as when the chief of MacGregor entertained King James IV for eight days in 1506 (SRO GD50/93). We can only make sense of the latter if we see it as a means of building social credit. However, in a society where scarcities were

recurrent, feasting also served an ideological purpose. It symbolized the well-being of a chiefdom in a public and conspicuous way. The way in which food for a chief could be prioritized drew on the same point. When MacNeill of Barra finished his meal, a member of his household would ascend the topmost turret of Kisimuil Castle and proclaim that now that MacNeill had finished his meal, the rest of the world could start theirs. If a chief could not keep up appearances, then neither could his clan. There is a story about the Clanranald chief which makes a telling point. It tells how an heir who had been fostered with the Frasers on the mainland returned to South Uist to be inaugurated as Captain of Clanranald. Surprised at how many cattle were slaughtered for the feast which accompanied the occasion, he made the mistake of modestly suggesting that a few hens would do! His comment so struck at the self-belief of the clan, at their capacity to maintain the appearances of a clan, it reputedly abandoned him for a younger brother and precipitated a feud between Clanranald and the Frasers. In actuality, of course, feasting involved more than simply food: there were also pipers, harpists, clan historians and story tellers. As with petty craftsmen, we find such individuals being granted holdings rent free or as pure gift (e.g. SRO GD201/1257/5; Macphail 1914:279).

Like feasting, feuding was a form of display behavior closely tied to food and the control which chiefs sought to exercise over it. We can develop this connection in a number of ways. First, those involved in feuding were generally household men, so that their number was directly related to the overall amount of food gathered in by chiefs. Of course, as noted earlier, this capacity could be extended by making "fighting men" a direct burden on tenants. Where such arrangements prevailed, the distinction between "fighting men" and farmers was carefully drawn, the latter being compelled to remain on their farms. Second, feuding itself was food-focussed. Raids on rival clans routinely involved sorning on their farms, the destruction of standing corn, and the theft of cattle. In effect, feuding made food a central issue of inter-clan rivalry, reducing the capacity of one's rivals to feast and sustain fighting men whilst at the same time enhancing one's own capacity. When Sir Rory MacLeod and Donald Gorme Macdonald reached a "settlement of feud" in 1609, the settlement extended to all their "awin kin, freyndis, tennentis, dependaris and aleyris to haif" and settled all past "murthowris, heirshippes, spuilzeis of goodis, and raising of fyre commit by ather of thame agains utheris" (Macleod 1938: I, 47–8). Their feuding was part of a wider problem. Sixteenth-century entries in the *Register of the Privy Council*, a century when feuding was rife in the Highlands, document many instances of feuding in which stored corn was burnt and cattle stolen (Masson 1884:336, 362–3, 500–1 and 534). Third, the exploits of feuding provided a backcloth to feasting, the warp and weft out of which clan historians, *sean chaidh*, wove clan history. Naturally, feuding had its cost as well as its profit. Significantly, it was seen as a dimension of clan behavior that was played out according to accepted rules, one that was subject to its own in-built principles of accountancy. As Martin Martin said in 1600, by the custom of feuding they were "obliged to bring by open force the Cattel they found in the Lands they attack'd, or to die in the Attempt" but being "reciprocally us'd among them, was not reputed Robbery, for the Damage which one Tribe sustain'd by Essay of the Chieftain of another, was repair'd when their Chieftain came in his turn" (Martin 1716:10–12).

Modelling Highland chiefdoms: a synthesis

It will be apparent from what has been said so far that the different dimensions of Highland chiefdoms were not separate or discrete aspects of the problem. Running through each of them are common strands. In this final section I want to tease these strands out of the argument.

The key to Highland chiefdoms lies in the problems surrounding subsistence. Land and its product have socio-political value in any rural society. The degree to which this socio-political value is realized depends on certain opportunity costs. In the first place, a surplus has to be generated and abstracted by local chiefs. If still greater heirarchies are to develop based on regional elites or even more distant state rulers, then a still greater surplus has to be generated and abstracted. Of course, how far communities can be pressurized into supporting such elites depends on the kind of social relations that bound the different levels of the system, chief and kinsmen, lord and peasant and so on.

The organization of farming and prevailing technologies – their physical capacity to produce a surplus beyond subsistence – also affected the extent to which communities are coerced into supporting elite structures. For a region like the western Highlands and Islands, though, its low productivity acted as a limiting factor on the potential for elite structures. Would-be elites had to find better ways of generating a surplus and better ways of extracting it. Operating with equal force on the problem was the high cost of transport to and from the region. Needless to say, this was a particularly potent factor with regard to the exercise of power by the Scottish Crown. Looked at from outside, the high costs of controlling the region would not

have been offset by the surpluses that could be extracted, at least not given the types of farming system that prevailed down to the '45. It is in this context that we should see the long survival of Highland chiefdoms and their relatively late subjugation by the Scottish state.

There is, however, a further point to be made here. The low productivity of the region and the problems which would-be social hierarchies faced in generating surpluses meant that these problems dominated the ideology of Highland chiefdoms. Highland chiefdoms fought over land and its immediate product, food.

This was their distinguishing feature. Relatively little attempt was made to transform food into any other form of product. Food and the means to produce it was the drawthread that linked the different dimensions of Highland chiefdoms. In effect, we are faced with a system of chiefdoms based almost wholly around a primary circuit of production and consumption, with only minimal attempts to generate secondary circuits based on the transformed value of food, e.g. circuits based on petty commodity production. An attempt to summarize the relations and flows involved can be seen in Fig. 11.3. The key input is a chief's control over land. The old Highland sayings that a clan without land was a broken clan just as a man without a clan was a broken man make this very point. Of course, land is important in any rural society. For Highland chiefdoms, though, the kinship ties which bound them socially were shorn of much of their meaning unless intertwined with the tenurial ties which chiefs were able to articulate where they controlled land. The way in which major branches of a clan were tied to a particular place underlines this relationship between on the one hand valued kin ties and on the other a chief's ability to endow such branches with land. If a chief controlled resources beyond those needed by his own kin, it gave him scope to extend the socio-political framework of the chiefdom in other ways. Men without any kin ties to a chief could be given land (cf. Shipton 1984:613–34). In return for their food rent and loyalty, they were given the socio-political identity of the chief's clan and subsistence.

Having a well-settled estate provided a would-be chief with the basic resources needed to compete for greater status. There were different ways in which this could be done, but each depended ultimately on the ability of the chief to extract food from his estate. For this reason, we can posit a basic relationship between the chief's capacity to enhance his status and such variables as the size of his estate, its basic fertility, the number of people settled on it and the general productivity of the farming systems adopted. The different strategies by which chiefs filled their estates served to generate a food surplus as well as to expand the number of men owing allegiance to the chief. To a degree, the directness of the relationship between the number of men settled on the estate and the amount of surplus generated could be affected by the tacksman system, with some tacksmen being seen as intercepting the advantage due to those above them and beggaring those beneath them (Garnett 1799: I, 173). Otherwise, chiefs had a direct interest in packing their estates.

The food gathered in by chiefs and stored in their girnal or store house could be used to build socio-political status in four different ways (Fig. 11.3). First, when given out as "gift" during times of famine, it enabled a chief to foster the feeling that tenants, his kinsmen, were somehow dependent for survival on his liberality. Second, if chiefs had control over fertile land, their rent could involve cattle, a commodity that had a potential value as a form of bridewealth, enabling them to contract favorable marriage alliances. Third, and an equally powerful means of building socio-political status, was the extravagant consumption of food through feasting. The more legendary a chief's displays of hospitality, the more status he acquired. Fourth and finally, food had a central role to play in feuding. Not only was it vital for the support of fighting men, but also, it figured prominently in the ritual of feuding itself, with crops being destroyed and cattle being stolen. Indeed, more than other dimensions, feuding symbolized the degree to which Highland chiefdoms fought with food over food (Young 1971). The only dimension of Highland chiefdoms not mediated directly through exchanges of food was petty craft production.

In so far as Highland chiefdoms competed with each other for socio-political status, then we cannot expect them to have been stable affairs. By its very nature, the continual search for greater status created instability, with each chief trying to maximize the socio-political advantage to be gained from the productivity of both land and kin, from favorable marriage alliances, feasting, and feuding at the expense of other chiefs (Kirch 1980:39–48; Ekholm 1977:115–36). As with any competitive system, we can expect phases when some chiefs succeeded in gaining and multiplying these advantages, establishing themselves as the core of an elaborate hierarchy of ties and alliances. Complex chiefdoms, though, were fissiparous affairs, continually prone to collapse along the lines of weakness introduced by their segmentary structure, by the need to make family settlements between sons, and by the ambitions of others. For this reason, between these surges toward more asymmetrical and elaborate systems of socio-political order, we can expect phases when flatter, less complex systems prevailed, as petty chiefdoms jostled each other in expectation of being at the centre of the next

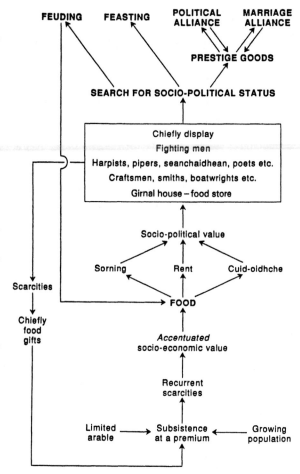

11.3 The structural and processual basis of Highland chiefdoms.

eruption of power. Unfortunately, because of its shallowness, the historical record for the Highlands only hints at such cyclical swings. Certainly, large complex chiefdoms did exist, like the Lordship of the Isles. Significantly, the collapse of the Lordship in the 1490s was followed by a phase of very active feuding, with minor or petty chiefdoms competing with one another for advantage. By this point though, other factors were starting to affect the situation. Increasingly, chiefs like Campbell of Argyll gained power and status through loyalty to the Scottish Crown.

Conclusion

There can be no question that the general character of Highland chiefdoms was affected by the projection of

Crown authority into the region long before their defeat at Culloden. From the late medieval period onwards, we find the more authoritative Scottish kings actively seeking to control even the remote and recalcitrant parts of the region, compelling chiefs to acknowledge the Scottish king as their superior and to accept a Crown charter for their estate. As one late fifteenth-century chief put it after returning from Edinburgh, whereas previously he had held his land on the point of sword, he now held it on the skin of a sheep (SRO GD201/1/361). In an ironic sense, his wry comment anticipated the great economic change that was to sweep over the Highlands from the 1740s onwards. Virtually at the same time as their political fate was decided, some chiefs began to introduce commercial sheep farming along the southern edge of the Highlands. In fact, economic changes of a kind had started to seep through the region back in the seventeenth century when some Highland chiefs began to behave as landlords by converting rents-in-kind from the more remote parts of their estates into cash rents, forcing tenants to engage the market. Tenants responded slowly, and most coped with the cash portion of their rents by selling livestock rather than by selling their scarce grain crop. Such changes worked to erode the traditional character of Highland chiefdoms. However, the extent of change prior to the '45 was not sufficient to turn them into a distinct form of chiefdom *sui generis*. We can still compare them structurally and processually with chiefdoms elsewhere.

12

Caesar's perception of Gallic social structures

SEAN B. DUNHAM

The perception of Celtic socio-political systems by scholars has long been affected by the writings of Classical authors. An author frequently cited is Julius Caesar, whose *Commentari de Bello Gallico* (*De Bello Gallico*) provides probably the best contemporary source on Gallic society from the first century before Christ. Caesar describes multiple socio-political systems among the people of Gaul. The Gauls, in the context of this essay, are those peoples called *Galli* by Caesar, and who called themselves *Celtae*, according to the same source (i.1). I propose a discussion of Caesar's perception of these socio-political systems, focussing particularly on the nature and context of Caesar's narrative as well as potential conclusions regarding Gallic social organization.

Social organization and social structure are difficult to recognize and interpret solely through the material evidence resulting from archaeological research. In the case of late Iron Age Gaul, interpretation of social organization has proved difficult owing to the number and scale of sites, and the proportionately small amount of data recovered from them. In view of the lack of archaeologically derived data concerning Gallic social structure, many scholars have relied on Classical sources to form a generalized view of Celtic culture throughout prehistoric Europe (Collis 1984b; Cunliffe 1988; Krämer 1960). Caesar's presence in Gaul and the written form of his narrative have caused Iron Age scholars to rely on the Classical evidence because of the perceived authority of the writer as observer. Up to now it has been expedient to rely on the authority of Classical authors when examining non-Classical peoples. A rethinking of this response to Classical texts is overdue.

Archaeological research has recently begun to challenge the traditional interpretation of Gallic social structures, which has resulted from the writings of Classical authors. A number of archaeological studies have produced evidence for a more socially complex European Iron Age than is suggested by the texts (Collis 1984b; Crumley 1974; Wells 1984). These studies have suggested that the archaeological culture and the societies described in the texts are quite different, reflecting very disparate social constructs (see especially Crumley 1974). Many of the textual studies have relied on an established literary tradition of Classical works, lumping together into a category of ancient ethnographies nearly a thousand years of scholarship pertaining to the Gauls – from Herodotus to Ammianus (Rankin 1987). This approach tends to treat the Gauls as a static culture. Classical texts should be reexamined as sources specific to the temporal and locational contexts to which they refer, as well as from the perspective of their relationship to a genre.

In anthropology and ethnohistory, it has been recognized that Western perceptions of others were filtered through Western cultural conciousness (Jaenen 1982; Marcus and Fisher 1986; Said 1978; Trigger 1982). Likewise, there is no reason to doubt that Classical authors (including Caesar) reported their observations of other peoples from the perspective of the Greco-Roman world. The peoples written about by the scholar are often quite different from those perceived by the observer, despite the fact that the first-hand observer is viewed as an authority. The same argument can be applied to Caesar's narrative. Caesar used Roman terms to define Iron Age Gaul. Modern scholars have continued to define Gallic peoples in these terms, without examining the meaning of such terms to a Roman, or the reason why such terms were employed by Caesar to describe non-Roman peoples. By attempting to understand Caesar's cultural context, some conclusions may be drawn concerning Gallic society from the perspective of Roman social organization.

Late Republican Rome is well understood by modern historians because of the wealth of textual information produced by Romans (and also Greeks) about themselves (e.g. Cicero, Livy, Polybius, and Tacitus). Caesar was a Roman writing about his military experience among the Gallic peoples. It is especially important to remember that he wrote about these people as he was conquering them. His purpose was not to elucidate the lifeways of the Gauls, but to explain his actions to his peers. The context of the narrative is Roman and the context of the archaeological record is Gallic. *De Bello Gallico* must be addressed from its Roman context if one is to use Caesar as a reference point in understanding Iron Age Gaul.

Caesar the Roman

Gaius Julius Caesar was born to a patrician family, the Julii, in 100 BC. According to Roman tradition, Caesar was a direct descendant of Romulus, Aeneas of Troy, and the goddess Venus on his father's side, and an heir to the ancient Roman monarchy on his mother's side. The Julii could boast of ten consuls, the highest Roman magistrate, in their family history. This is significant in that it was the goal of most Roman males of the patrician rank to have a successful political career, possibly (but rarely) culminating in a consulship. When Caesar was elected *praetor*, a judicial magistrate, in 62 BC, he was recognized by the senate as an able and ambitious man. In 59 BC he was elected consul, and the following year he began his Gallic campaign (Gelzer 1968).

In his time Caesar was considered one of the best orators in Rome, the consummate skill of a Roman senator. He wrote works on poetry, tragedy, and linguistic theory, in addition to his commentaries concerning his military pursuits, and he was considered a master of Roman rhetorical theory and its applications (Adcock 1956; Laistner 1947). Despite Caesar's accomplishments as an author and a general, it is important to stress that he was first and foremost a Roman senator who used these other skills to further his political career.

There is some scholarly disagreement concerning Caesar's purpose in writing *De Bello Gallico*. It is generally accepted that Caesar wished to convey his version of the campaign in Gaul (Adcock 1956; Smith 1952). The text is unusual for the context of late Republican Rome in that it was written in a form described as *commentarius* by the Romans. Latin literature was at this time dominated by oratory and history, and was most often written to further political ends. The *commentarius* form, by contrast, was usually used for private memoirs or official correspondence. Sometimes *commentarii* were used as sketches for scholars well versed in method and rhetoric to use in writing histories in the traditional manner. Caesar most likely wrote in this manner for a particular purpose. It has been suggested that this was a conscious break from the Greek rhetorical tradition that was prevalent in Rome at the time.

Caesar's contemporary, Cicero, wrote in 46 BC concerning *De Bello Gallico*:

> The commentaries are splendid; bare, straight and handsome, stripped of rhetorical ornament . . . He [Caesar] intended to provide material for others to use in the writing of history; but . . . he has frightened off all the men of sense from putting pen to paper. For there is nothing in history more attractive than clean lucid brevity. (*Brutus* 75)

This thought is paralleled by Caesar's general Hirtius in his preface to book viii of *De Bello Gallico*. Concerning the Gallic narrative, he notes that "contrary to the style, Caesar was not offering other historians a chance at writing the Gallic war, but denying them the opportunity."

Caesar's primary and most critical audience was his own senatorial class. The senate was an oligarchy of about 600 men who ruled the Roman Republic. His conquests in Gaul were not viewed favorably by all in Rome (viii.49–50; Syme 1939). It appears likely that Caesar wrote the commentaries to present his perspective on the campaign to the senate, in a manner which portrayed his actions in a fuller, more affable context than the official dispatches he sent to that body (Laistner 1947; Smith 1952). A secondary purpose was to maintain his popularity with the Roman masses via favorable propaganda concerning his exploits (Smith 1952). In this manner Caesar was able to state his case, and remain a political force, while absent from Rome.

Commentari de Bello Gallico

De Bello Gallico was Caesar's personal description of the conquest of Gaul (58–50 BC). Caesar's narrative offers modern scholars the best first-hand description of Gallic society in the first century BC. Unlike many of his contemporaries, Caesar was directly in contact with the Gauls. *De Bello Gallico* was probably written during the winters between 58 and 52 BC. Caesar wrote seven of the eight books; the eighth was written by Hirtius. All seven books written by Caesar relate to the Gallic conquest, as well as to Gaul and its people. The sixth book differs in that it contains a section (vi.11–29) that is not in the *commentarius* style and which scholars consider to be part of the Classical ethnographic tradition.

For the most part, Caesar's Gallic narrative has not attracted the critical attention of Classical scholars because of its *commentarius* form (Adcock 1956; Laistner 1947). The veracity of Caesar's account has been questioned because of internal contradictions in the text and the accounts of later Roman historians such as Suetonius (Rambaud 1953). Other scholars have contested this view, suggesting that the internal contradictions result from the nature of the text itself, and that the accounts of many of the later historians are, themselves, unreliable sources (Adcock 1956; Balsdon 1955; Rawson 1985). Caesar's audience had access to other information about the campaign and could have discovered fabrications perpetrated by Caesar (Balsdon 1955; Smith 1952). Furthermore, considering the political climate in Rome during the Gallic campaign, Caesar's political opponents would have used inaccuracies in his narrative to their advantage and possibly to remove Caesar from his office in Gaul (Beard and Crawford 1985; Dickinson 1963; Syme 1939). The evidence indicates that Caesar's narrative was a generally reliable account of the Gallic campaign from a Roman point of view.

Another controversy concerning Caesar's work which has received some scholarly attention is the authenticity of the sixth book. Book vi is important because it contains most of the ethnographic material concerning the Gauls and Germans. It has been argued that the ethnographic portions of book vi derive from the earlier work of Poseidonius (Tierney 1960). On the other hand, Caesar was undoubtedly familiar with Poseidonius' work, and he was quite capable of producing his own perception of Gallic culture (Nash 1976; Rawson 1985). Similarities between the ethnographic accounts of Caesar and surviving fragments of Poseidonius can be explained by the fact that both men were in Gaul within about a generation of one another. In other words, they both observed and were told about events and institutions which were part of the cultural milieu of late La Tène Gaul. Differences in their assessments can be attributed to the natures of their accounts. Poseidonius wrote a geography using the techniques and rhetoric of that tradition, even to the point of including allusions to Greek Heroic (Homeric) tradition in regard to Gallic social activities (Winter 1986; Tierney 1960). Caesar, on the other hand, as we have emphasized, related his military experiences in Gaul. His ethnographic digression in book vi may have been the result of a slow campaigning season. At issue, however, is the consideration of Caesar's perspective, that of his audience, and the context of the narrative itself. In view of the lack of critical review of this perspective, it is noteworthy that archaeologists invest so much uncritical stock in the contents of the text.

Caesar's perception of Gallic social structures

From Caesar the following general models for Gallic social organization can be reconstructed. A *civitas* was governed by a *senatus* and its elected magistrate (*vergobret* among the Aeduii), or in some cases a *rex*. In some instances a *civitas* seems to have been a confederation of two or more *pagi* which had their own magistrates and could function independently of the *civitas* (i.27; Nash 1978). Caesar also refers to councils (*concilia*) made up

of the leading men of Gaul (i.30; vi.3; vii.63), as well as the *principes* of individual *civites*. These councils were involved with issues concerning the Gallic *civites*. Caesar also describes a council of *druides* which met every year in the territories of the Carnutes (vi.13). This council was said by Caesar to deliberate on all issues and conflicts concerning Gaul.

Internal social structures were described by Caesar in terms that appear to reflect those used in the Roman Republic. This is not surprising, since Caesar understood that system best; it was, of course, his point of reference when he discussed the social organization of the Gauls in a work to be read by a Roman audience. Caesar uses the following Roman (Latin) terms to describe social organization in Gallic society: *reges, nobiles, principes, senatus, magistri, equites,* and *plebes*. All these terms would have had specific meanings to a Roman in the context of Roman society.

The Roman *rex* acted as a war leader, a priest, and a judge. During the Republican period the role of the *rex* was replaced by two annually elected magistrates called *consuls*. Caesar depicted Gallic *reges* as hereditary monarchs (v.25; v.54), elected magistrates (vii.32), and individuals with achieved status (ii.1; iv.21). He noted that when Gauls claimed the rank of *rex* without proper consent or support the claim could lead to conflict between factions or the death of the claimant (i.3; v.25; vii.4; 20).

Nobiles in Rome were those men whose ancestry included a *consul* (OLD *nobilis* sense 5). The term *nobiles* was associated with a particular family or lineage, who made up an hereditary elite. Caesar referred to the Gallic hostages who accompanied him to Britain as *principes* of every Gallic *civitas* (v.5). In the following passage (v.6) he called these same men *nobilitas*. The link to heredity or noble birth is illustrated in Caesar's description of Orgetorix, "the most noble among the Helvetii," (i.2) and Iccius, "of the highest nobility among the Remi." (ii.6) The passage contrasting Epodorix, "born of the highest rank," and Viridirarus, "his peer . . . but not in birth," may further reflect this usage (vii.39). Caesar also describes the destruction of the Aeduan *nobilitas, senatus,* and *equites* by the Germani (i.31; vi.12). This passage separates these three terms, suggesting different status. Caesar's use of the Roman term *nobiles* may reflect what he perceived as a similar ascribed rank in Gaul.

The *senatus* seems to have been part of the governing system of Gallic *civites* (ii.5; 28; iii.16; 17; v.54; vii. 32; 33; 55). This body may have been composed of what Caesar described as "older men who had some degree of wisdom or distinction" (iii.16). Within the senate there was a distinction between *principes* and other members of that body (ii.5; v.54). This distinction was probably one of social rank, and *principes* may have been related in some way to *nobiles* (v.5; 6). Caesar related that the *principes* of Gallic factions were thought by their followers to hold the highest prestige (vi.11). A Roman *princeps* was the leading man of the senate, usually the oldest and most prestigious senator, and he was always *nobilis*. In Republican politics the body of *consulares* (those who had held consular rank) were referred to collectively as the *principes* (OLD *princeps* sense 4b). Caesar seems to have used this term in a similar manner for Gaul (i.3; 13; 16; 30; ii.5; vi.4; vii.1; 32; 36; 38; 65). When the term was applied to the Gallic states it marked prestige (vi.12; vii.63).

The Roman senate was a council of elders, who originally acted as advisors for the king and later for the consuls. Caesar related that among the Aeduii no two members of the same family could hold magistracies or serve in the senate simultaneously (vii.33). This statement may hold the clue to the relationship between Gallic *principes* and *nobiles*. The *principes* may have been *nobiles* who held public office.

Gallic *magistri*, like their Roman counterparts, held public office. The best-illustrated Gallic magistrate was the Aeduan *vergobret* (i.16; 17; vii.32; 33; 37). The *vergobret* was described as an annually elected magistrate with regal authority and the power of life and death over his subjects. The *magistri* of the Helvetii are said to have organized troops and acted as judges (i.4). Caesar noted that the Gallic *civites* which were supposed to be the best run were those that required, by law, that anyone with knowledge of public concern report it to a magistrate and not spread it among the populace (vi.20). The magistrates shared information as they saw fit.

Equites present a problem in classification. It has generally been assumed that the Gallic *equites* were part of the noble class (*nobiles*). This was not made entirely clear in Caesar's account, nor does it correlate well with the Roman use of the term. Caesar stated that "in all of Gaul there are *two* classes of men who are in some degree of rank and honor *druides* and *equites*" (vi.13). According to Caesar, Gallic *equites* attained power (*gratia* and *potentia*) through their ability to make war (vi.15). This ability to make war was linked to their birth (family), wealth, and the number of clients (*ambactos* and *clientes*) they retained.

Roman *equites* were related to the senatorial rank in that the senators were equestrians who had secured a place in the senate. Originally the *equites* had formed a prestigious cavalry division. By Caesar's time they were those elites who fell within a particular census category

(after 67 BC, a property qualification of over 400,000 sesterces), but did not hold public office. Dumnorix (of the Aeduii) was said to have contracted the privilege of collecting the customs and taxes of his people (i.18). This gave him an opportunity to increase his own wealth and property. He was said, by Caesar, to have used his wealth for political bribery and the maintenance of private forces. These kinds of activities were not unknown among Roman *equites*. Dumnorix was also described as being the brother of the highest Aeduan magistrate. Since no two Aeduii from the same family could hold public office simultaneously, Dumnorix seems to have been an *eques* after the Roman fashion. It may be appropriate, in regard to the context of Caesar's narrative, to read his description of Gallic *equites* in terms of Roman *equites*.

Little specific data concerning the *plebes* can be directly gleaned from Caesar's account. This is not surprising, as Caesar was a patrician and most of his audience were of that order, or, if not, were members of the senate. Gallic *plebes* are described as venturing nothing by themselves and never taken into council. They were treated like *servi*. In fact, many enter into this state, and the *nobiles* have the same rights over them as masters over servants. Caesar argues that this status was brought about by debt, high taxes, and the wrongdoing of powerful men against the powerless (vi.13). In the early Roman Republic, the *plebes* were denied membership in the senate and were forbidden to marry into the patrician rank. By Caesar's time, the division between patrician and plebeian had changed and the *plebes* were moving towards greater legal status. However, the perceived boundary between these ranks was clearly recognized.

The following types of *plebes* were discussed in the narrative and fall into the following categories: *clientes*, *ambacti*, *obaerati*, and *vulgi*. In Rome *clientes* performed a service in return for some form of incentive. This label included artisans and agricultural workers. Although Gallic *clientes* may not have served in an identical way to their Roman counterparts their importance to Gallic society was presumably equal (Crumley 1987c). *Ambacti* is a Gallic term which might refer from its context to military service or to some type of retainer. Roman *obaerati* were those in debt or obligated in some other way to another. *Vulgus* simply means the people or the common people and is most likely literal in this context.

Druides are only referred to in book vi of *De Bello Gallico*. The word *druides* is Gallic, and is etymologically derived from terms denoting wisdom and truth (Partridge 1983). The concept of *druides* was not unknown to Caesar's peers, as noted by Cicero's comments, the work of Poseidonius, and the modern scholarship of

Chadwick (1966) and Tierney (1960), but the term is used only in the ethnographic section of book vi (vi.13–14). This is the book which is most often cited as a source for information on Gallic social structure, as well as the one which describes the function of *druides* in that society.

Caesar wrote that the *druides* were concerned with divine matters, sacrifices, and the interpretation of religion. They decided all disputes (public and private), and determined rewards and penalties. If their decision was not upheld or obeyed, they could ban groups or individuals from sacrifice. Those banned were avoided by others, unable to receive justice, and excluded from distinction. The *druides* met once a year, in the territory of the Carnutes, and heard disputes and passed judgments. They were exempt from military services, taxes, and all liabilities. One druid presided over all others. Upon his death the preeminent druid succeeded him. If there were multiple candidates, one was elected, or the decision was made through armed conflict (vi.13; vi.14).

Caesar's account attributes a certain amount of power to *druides* in pre-Roman Gaul. He accords them the tripartite duties of priests, philosophers, and judges (vi. 13–14). Although it might seem inevitable that Caesar would refer to this "order" in another part of *De Bello Gallico*, he does not. All the functions attributed to *druides* by the Classical authors were functions of Roman magistrates who were members of the senate (Beard and Crawford 1985). Caesar was himself a *praetor* (judicial magistrate), *pontifex* (priest), and man of letters while a Roman senator.

Diviciacus, a confidant of Caesar during the Gallic campaign, was said to be a druid by Cicero (*De Divinatione* i.41; 90). Caesar does not relate this. In fact, he refers to Diviciacus as one of the *principes* of the Aeduan *civitas* (i.3; 16). Caesar wrote that the *druides* presided over all disputes (vi.13). He also stated that *magistri* had this function (i.4; 16). *Druides* are described as being concerned with ritual and religion (vi.13). Caesar uses the term *sacerdotes* (priests) to describe members of the Aeduan *senatus* (vii.33). These examples seem to contradict Caesar's appraisal of the *druides*.

Caesar relates that one druid presided over all others (vi.13). Vercingetorix's father was said to have been the *princeps* of all Gaul (vii.4). When Vercingetorix's paternal uncle and the Avernian *principes* had him cast out from Gergovia for conspiring against the Romans (vii.4), Vercingetorix returned with an armed force, expelled his opponents, was declared *rex*, and was granted *imperium* over all the Gauls (vii.4). This incident parallels one of the processes described by Caesar for determining a new "high" druid (armed conflict). Since Caesar used the term

druides only in book vi, and these parallels and contradictions appear in other parts of his Gallic narrative, it is possible he chose to use Roman terms in the *commentarii* and a Gallic term (*druides*) in the ethnographic section. This seems to imply a link between the terms *druides* and *principes*.

It may be worthwhile to note that Cicero's discussion of Diviciacus as a druid centered around a discussion of the Roman Senate ruling the Republic through the control of and authority of religion (*De Divinatione* i.40–1; 89–90). "Among the ancients, those who ruled the state also had control of augury; For they considered that wisdom as well as divining were becoming to a king ... In our state the kings were augurs and later, private citizens endowed with the same priestly authority ruled the republic by the authority of religion." In reference to Republican Rome, it is a misconception of modern scholars to separate the functions of church and state (Beard and Crawford 1985). Likewise, no Classical author refers to druids exclusively as priests (Chadwick 1966). It has been suggested that Caesar used the term *druides* in book vi to acknowledge Poseidonius as a source and to update that narrative (Tierney 1960; Rawson 1985). Perhaps the term *druides* was introduced by Caesar in book vi as the Gallic equivalent to the Roman *senatus* or *principes*, to specify a difference between that status and those of *equites* and *plebes*.

Thoughts on Caesar's Gallic social structures

A model for Gallic social structure can be derived from *De Bello Gallico* when it is examined as a Roman product of the mid-first century BC, rather than from the perspective of the tradition of Classical ethnography. In early Republican Rome, the patricians, a group of elite families, controlled all political power and office-holding through the senate. The rest of the citizens, the plebeians, were by law deprived of such privileges. The Roman elite could be broken down into two groups: the senators and the equestrians. This parallels the historical model for Gallic social structure derived from the Classical ethnographers, which displayed an internally stratified aristocracy (*druides* and *equites*) and commoners (Crumley 1974). Perhaps Caesar simply "Romanized" the social organization of Iron Age Gaul.

The facts that Caesar used Roman terms to describe Gallic social structure, and that his purpose was *not* to write an ethnography, are relevant to any application of the Caesarian model of social structure to Iron Age Gaul. The resulting Gallic social structure is Roman in form. It does not assume that Gallic social structure was identical to Roman social structure, but acknowledges the context of Caesar's experience, and his Roman perception, in its construction. In fact, the Gallic *civitates* described by Caesar do not compare with the ideal government as represented by the Roman Republic (Cicero, *De Re Publica*; Polybius, *The Histories*).

Caesar describes a complex society of at least two discernible classes: *druides/equites* and *plebes*. This structure, as documented by Caesar, could represent the organizational system of a chiefdom or a state (since it mirrors Republican Rome), so it does not necessarily contradict the archaeological evidence. On the other hand, Caesar's observations of Gallic social structures do not directly support the archaeological data either. *De Bello Gallico* cannot be ignored as a source concerning Iron Age Gaul, nor should it be treated as a privileged source because of its written authority. It must be examined within its own cultural perspective and measured against its own cultural construction.

A contextual approach to Caesar's Gallic narrative, which acknowledges his Roman perceptions, creates a new perspective to be considered in our reconstruction of Gallic society. This perspective is not necessarily more correct than traditional models; it is simply different. As such, it can generate discourse which may provide greater insight into late La Tène society. For example, the ques-

tion "who or what were the druids?," a topic which has generated a great deal of both scholarly and popular interest (Piggott 1968; Chadwick 1966), becomes practically mundane. Instead of mysterious magician priests gathering mistletoe in an oak grove, an oligarchical elite with both judicial and religious duties is revealed.

Likewise, in order to address Gallic chiefdoms or Gallic states from the perspective of Caesar's narrative, it is necessary to rephrase the inquiry using his designations (such as *civitas*), along with their Roman definitions. The Roman terms and their Roman meanings might then be integrated with anthropologically derived models of social systems, and a possible baseline established for comparisons with archaeologically inferred reconstructions.

Archaeologists cannot continue to rely uncritically on Caesar to provide narrative for a past that is not well understood archaeologically. His narrative must be put back into the context of late Republican Rome, and his views accepted as those of a Roman describing non-Roman peoples. This is not, by any means, a final interpretation of Caesar's work. It merely suggests that Caesar's writings be examined within an appropriate context when considering Gallic culture in the first century BC.

13
Chiefdoms, confederacies, and statehood in early Ireland

D. BLAIR GIBSON

Introduction

In Ireland, political systems and social institutions similar in structure and complexity to those that preceded the advent of the earliest European states persisted long into the second millennium AD. From the time of the earliest written records down to the late twelfth century AD it is clear that chiefdoms were the predominant type of political system in Ireland. From the earliest times these chiefdoms ranged in complexity from simple polities to those that were structurally complex, often incorporating large tracts of territory and exhibiting much internal social stratification. It will be argued in this paper that by the twelfth century AD a complex regional chiefdom in southern Ireland had evolved to become a primitive state. The structure of the chiefdoms of the historic province of Thomond will be analyzed here with the objective of establishing the process by which an Irish chiefdom becomes transformed into a state. Statehood had special characteristics in Ireland, and these will be reviewed against the available data.

The methodology of chiefdom identification

According to Carneiro (1981:45), Earle (1978:3; 1987:289), and Johnson and Earle (1987:207), the chief characteristic of chiefdoms is that they are entities of regional scale which integrate local populations. These polities exhibit a permanent office of leadership and coordination in the person of the chieftain. Firth (1936), Sahlins (1958), and Kirchoff (1955) have described the social structure characteristic of chiefdoms, which has been termed *ramage* or conical clan structure. The entire chiefdom is composed of lineal descent groups that are encapsulated in more inclusive kin units which are themselves ranked within the chiefdom by proximity to a main line of descent. *Ramage* social structure, with its ranked multi-lineage segments, should be accepted as the social structure universal to all chiefdoms (Gibson 1990:28).

The social traits enumerated above are general attributes common to all chiefdoms. However, chiefdoms across the world would be expected to exhibit substantial variation in the specifics of organization, owing to differences in the level of complexity and scale between polities. Different subsistence strategies should also result in social institutions and structural nuances that would be specific to them. Documenting this variation in the social organization of chiefdoms is an important undertaking in light of the understanding that might be gained of the divergent courses of social evolution leading to state formation, as well as of the underlying structural and historical causes of variation in chiefdom and state structure.

The social structure of any society is reflected in part in the distribution of the populace over space, that is, by the spatial patterns of activity and residence. Since chiefdoms survived in Ireland into the late Middle Ages, chiefdom social structure is well suited to an examination utilizing both historical and archaeological sources of information. The following sections discuss the structure of the medieval chiefdoms of the historic province of Thomond in the west of Ireland from an analysis of the relationship between chiefdom capitals and historic territories.

Historic Irish settlement and capital organization

With the possible exception of the nucleated settlements associated with monasteries, up until the late Middle Ages Irish populations were distributed exclusively into scattered homesteads. Nucleated settlement was not introduced by the Norse settlers into Ireland until the ninth century AD, and the Irish themselves did not first begin to live in villages until the thirteenth and fourteenth centuries AD. Indeed, until the present century nucleated settlement remained the exception for the majority of the Irish population. The bulk of the population continued to live in spatially isolated households located upon their holdings.

Reflecting the general settlement pattern, the political centers of Irish chiefdoms did not consist of unitary, nucleated establishments, but instead were composed of elements that were spatially discrete, though often located in proximity to one another. The diagnostic elements that comprise the capitals of former Irish chiefdoms are three in number, and I have termed them the 'capital set'

13.1 Map of Ireland showing the province of Munster and the sub-province of Thomond (present-day County Clare).

(Gibson 1990:143). The first element of an Irish chiefdom capital is the principal homestead of the chiefly ramage. Throughout the Irish late Iron Age (*c*. 200–1173 AD), the principal homesteads of chieftains were large and surrounded by circular walls of earth or dry-laid stone. Those of paramount chieftains can be identified in documentary sources and located in space as far back in time as the tenth century AD (see for instance Hencken 1950; Eogan 1977).

The second element of the capital set was the ecclesiastical establishment patronized by the chiefly family. More often than not, this was a church or monastery located near to the homestead of its patrons. The third element of the capital set was the inauguration mound, the place where new chieftains assumed their office in a public ritual. This mound was usually a man-made feature such as an Early Bronze Age burial mound, said to be the resting place of some famous ancestor in the chiefly pedigree. Though the position of the chiefly homestead and the principal church could shift with the passing of time, the inauguration mound tended to stay fixed in

location, and so could be situated at some distance from the other two elements of the capital set at any point in time.

The simple chiefdom

My recent research has focussed on the reconstruction of chiefdoms in the historic province of Thomond (Ir. *Túaid-mumu*), a territory that is roughly coterminous with present-day County Clare, located in west-central Ireland (Fig. 13.1). Within Thomond my specific region of focus has been the northern section of Clare, a physiographic and cultural area called the Burren, which is encompassed by Burren Barony with additional sections in Inchiquin and Corcomroe Baronies to the south (Fig. 13.2). This region consists of rugged hilly terrain composed of extensively eroded and glaciated Carboniferous Limestone.

It is possible to reconstruct several small chiefdoms that formerly existed in this region between the eighth and twelfth centuries AD. Initially archaeological survey work and historical research focused upon the prehistoric settlement of Cahercommaun (Fig. 13.3). This large cashel-type site is located on the edge of a plateau overlooking a steep ravine. It is enclosed by three concentric walls of dry-stone construction, the innermost of which is nearly 10 m thick and 4 m high. The size of the site and the amount of stone contained in its walls makes it one of the largest sites of its age in County Clare. It was excavated in 1934 by Hugh O'Neill Hencken of the Third Harvard Expedition to Ireland, and was dated by him to the late eighth/early ninth centuries AD (Hencken 1938). This dating has subsequently been supported by radiocarbon determinations made on bone from the site's assemblage (Gibson 1990:247).

It has proved possible to reconstruct the chiefdom of which Cahercommaun was the likely principal chiefly residence. This was accomplished through the application of several premises that were derived from an examination of the historical geography of Irish chiefdoms in Thomond (Gibson 1990). Typically, chieftains' homesteads of the later Middle Ages in Thomond were located in the geographical center of their territories as was, for instance, the capital of the eponymous sixteenth century Gragans chiefdom of the O'Lochlainns in the Burren (Fig. 13.4). This chiefdom contained secular territories that were for the most part larger than the parishes, though their boundaries coincided.[1] In so far as an element in the name of one of these territories was the word *túath*, the Old Irish word for chiefdom, one may surmise that some of the secular territories predated the parishes that emerged in the twelfth century (Gibson

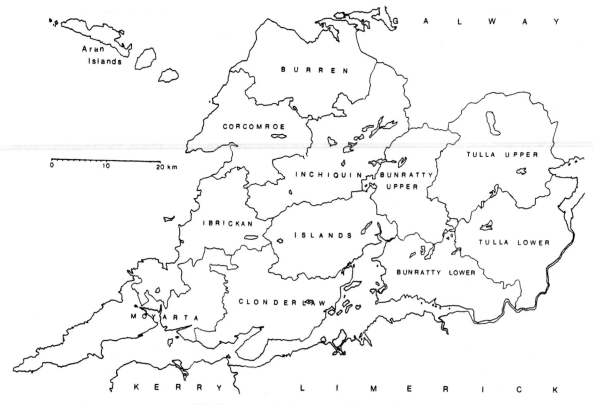

13.2 The present-day baronies of County Clare.

1990:97) (Fig. 13.4).[2] Most likely they were simple chief-doms in the early Middle Ages, and the parishes were carved out of them. This subdivision probably occurred on the basis of the distribution of aristocratic lineages within these territories.

The simple chiefdom pertaining to Cahercommaun, which I have termed *Tulach Commáin*, was reconstructed by combining the parishes of Carran, Kilcorney, and Killinaboy together (Fig. 13.5). Once this was accomplished, it became apparent that Cahercommaun was located in the geographical center of the territory. The two other elements of the capital set of this polity could also be identified with little difficulty: a nearby monastic community, *Tempal Chronáin*, was the principal ecclesiastical settlement, and a probable prehistoric burial mound, Tulach Commáin, was the most likely candidate for an inauguration mound. It was located within view of Cahercommaun, and bore the same personal name, Commán, that is incorporated into the place-name of the cashel (Cahercommaun = *Cathair Commáin* – "the dwelling place of Commán").

Other simple chiefdoms in the Burren were reconstructed through the technique of joining parish territories together. The matches were made by following lines of evidence such as place-name lore, and information on the attribution of parcels of land within the parishes provided by the surveys carried out by the English government in the late seventeenth century (Gibson 1990). The resulting territories reveal a patchwork of small, simple chiefdoms which contained on average 50 km² of land. Tulach Commáin was far larger than this, being 300 km² in extent, and so may have been the principal chiefdom of a larger entity, a *composite chiefdom*.

Composite chiefdoms and chiefdom confederacies

The Irish law texts recognized a political entity larger in scale than the simple chiefdom, called in Irish the *mór túath*, or "great chiefdom." These chiefdoms were made up of a number of simple chiefdoms arrayed around a central territory, the territory of the chiefdom of the leading ramage. These large chiefdoms were then compo-

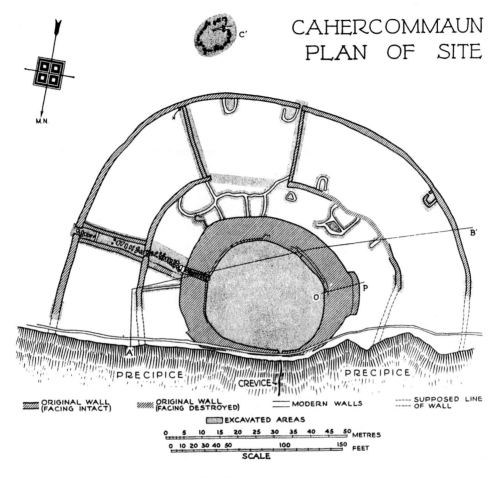

CAHERCOMMAUN
PLAN OF SITE

M.N.

PRECIPICE   PRECIPICE
CREVICE

▨▨▨ ORIGINAL WALL (FACING INTACT)   ▨▨▨ ORIGINAL WALL (FACING DESTROYED)   ═══ MODERN WALLS   ---- SUPPOSED LINE OF WALL

▨ EXCAVATED AREAS

0   5   10   15   20   25   30   35   40   45   50 METRES

0 10 20 30 40 50   100   150 FEET

SCALE

13.3 Cahercommaun.

sites of chiefdoms, and the pattern of the distribution of their constituent territories resembles a giant sunflower (Fig. 13.6). I have therefore termed chiefdoms of this type composite chiefdoms (1990:42). Several composite chiefdoms can be identified in Thomond with virtual certitude, and these predate the tenth century AD: they are those of the Corcu Mruad of northern Clare, the Corcu Baiscinn of southern Clare, and the Déis Tuaiscirt, later called the Dál Cais of eastern County Clare (Fig. 13.7).

Prior to the thirteenth century AD the chiefdom of the Corcu Mruad was co-extensive with the modern baronies of Burren and Corcomroe. These two baronies are within the Diocese of Kilfenora, which was established in the twelfth century upon the boundaries of the older chiefdom (Fig. 13.8). Three or four hundred years prior to the twelfth century (Iron Age IIb and earlier) the territory of the Barony of Inchiquin to the east probably constituted a

part of the Corcu Mruad chiefdom as well. This presumption rests upon the identification of Caherballykinvarga, a large and imposing cashel-type site, as the former capital of the Corcu Mruad. Including Inchiquin's territory within a Corcu Mruad composite chiefdom would position this site in the center of the resulting territory.

Many of the simple chiefdoms that have been reconstructed in the Burren would have been the constituent chiefdoms of the Corcu Mruad composite chiefdom. A proposed reconstruction of Corcu Mruad in its earliest state postulates that these simple chiefdoms were distributed radially around the capital territory of the composite chiefdom (Fig. 13.8). This central territory would have consisted of the present-day parishes of Kilfenora and Noughaval. The name Noughaval is an anglicization of *Nua Chabháil* (or *Chongbháil*), meaning "new habitation." The name refers to the twelfth century church and

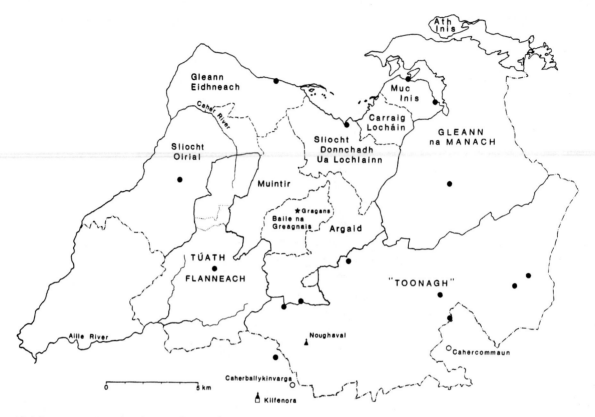

13.4 Reconstruction of early (pre-thirteenth-century) chiefdom territories in Burren Barony, Co. Clare. Empty circles: cashel sites. Full circles: tower-houses.

associated settlement there. This parish resulted from the subdivision of the territory at the heart of the Corcu Mruad chiefdom between the rival leading sections of the Corcu Mruad ramage, the O'Connors (Uí Conchobuir) and the O'Lochlainns. Noughaval retained a part of the function of the parent territory, becoming the ecclesiastical center of the O'Lochlainn chiefdom. Combining these two parishes results in a territory containing both the secular center Caherballykinvarga and Kilfenora (*Cill Fhinnabrach*), the cathedral of the diocese, and so the second element of the capital set of the Corcu Mruad. The third element of the capital set, the inauguration mound of the chieftains of Corcu Mruad, could either have been *Carn Mhic Táil* (Fig. 13.8), which was used as such by the Uí Conchobuir chieftains of Corcomroe in the Middle Ages, or *Cnoc an Carn*, a mound visible from Caherballykinvarga to the north (Fig. 13.5).

Another composite chiefdom, Déis Tuaiscirt, was the forerunner to the chiefdom confederacy of the Dál Cais. Prior to the ninth century AD, the leading ramages of this composite chiefdom were the Uí Cernaig and Uí Eichtígern. Their territories were in the south-center of the composite chiefdom near to the River Shannon (Fig. 13.9). Magh Adhair was the inauguration mound of the Dál Cais, and so presumably of the Déis Tuaiscirt as well.

Composite chiefdom to chiefdom confederacy

In 934 AD Rebachán mac Mothlai, abbot of Tuaim-Gréne (Tomgraney) and *ri* of the Dál Cais, died. This was the first time that Déis Tuaiscirt was referred to as Dál Cais in the annals (Ó Corráin 1972:114). Tuaim-Gréne is located far to the north-east within Déis Tuaiscirt (Fig. 13.9). Rebachán may or may not have been of the Uí Cernaig, but he was not of the main line of descent and Tuaim-Gréne was far from the former center of power (Ó Corráin 1973:55). In fact it lay near, if not within, the ninth century bounds of the chiefdom of the Uí Thairdelbaig (Fig. 13.9). Following Rebachán's death, paramount chieftainship over the Dál Cais fell to Cennétig mac

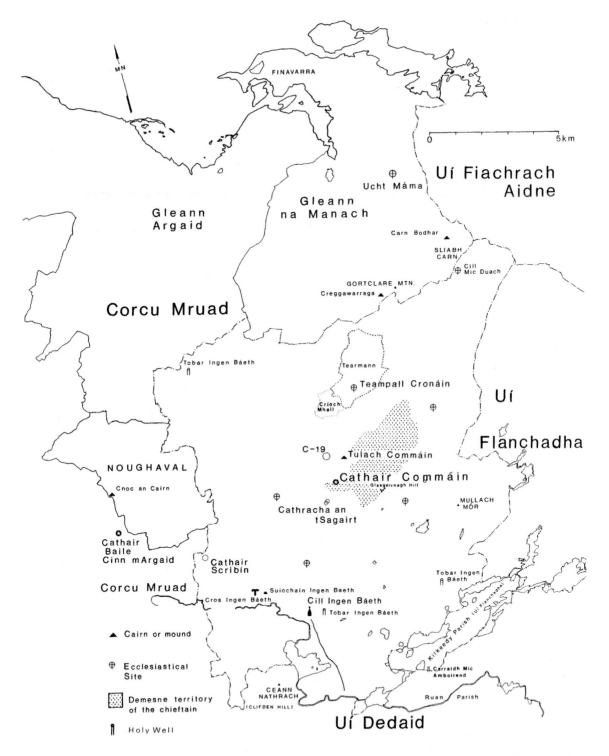

13.5 *The reconstructed eighth/ninth-century chiefdom of Tulach Commáin.* Cathair Baile Cinn mArgai *is a possible Irish rendering of Caherballykinvarga; and the names in large print (i.e.* Uí Flanchadha) *are those of neighboring chiefdoms.*

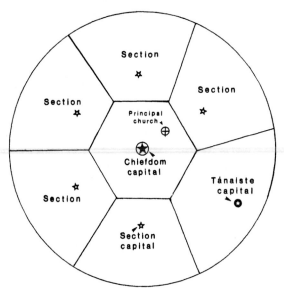

13.6 *Model of the structure of an Irish composite chiefdom based on sixteenth-century sources. Sections are multi-lineage aristocratic segments of the ruling ramage. Túaths were the antecedents of sections.*

Lorcán, chieftain of the Uí Thairdelbaig. Cennétig and his three sons, Lachtna, Mathgamain, and Brian, succeeded in driving Viking invaders out of Dál Cais and establishing their hegemony over the province of Munster.

Brian mac Cennétig, otherwise known as Brian Boruma (Boru), became one of the most powerful chieftains in Ireland. He succeeded in dominating the entire province of Munster. This does not mean, however, that he succeeded in establishing a state. The methodology of political domination by Brian of Thomond's chiefdoms can be clearly seen. Presumably after besting the chiefdoms of the Corcu Baiscinn and Corcu Mruad in battle, he replaced their chieftains with close relatives. He replaced the leaders of Corcu Baiscinn with a son, Mathgamain. The leaders of Corcu Mruad he replaced with the lineage of his father's brother Croscrach, headed by Máel Sechnaill mac Croscrach (Gibson 1990:382). This was not the first time that the ruling lineage of Corcu Mruad was replaced by one from Uí Thairdelbaig. In 925 AD the annals state that Anrudán mac Máel Gorm assumed the chieftainship of Corcu Mruad, and the genealogies place him in the Uí Thairdelbaig. The conquest of Corcu Mruad and hence the ascendancy of Uí Thairdelbaig over Déis Tuaiscirt/Dál Cais must go back at least this far. Other

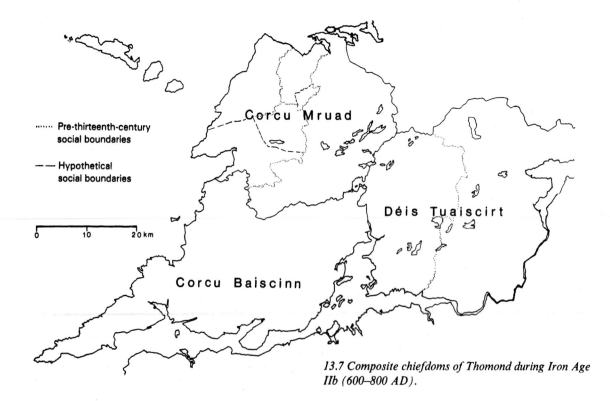

13.7 *Composite chiefdoms of Thomond during Iron Age IIb (600–800 AD).*

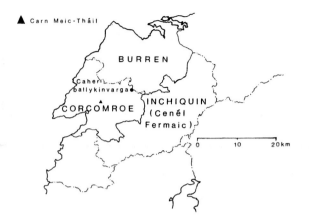

13.8 Chiefdom of the Corcu Mruad in Iron Age IIc–IId (800–1173 AD).

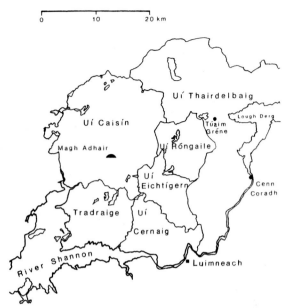

13.9 The composite chiefdom of the Déis Tuaiscirt/Dál Cais.

names in the Corcu Mruad genealogy in the ninth century such as Flaithbertach and Rechtabra are unusual for Corcu Mruad, and so probably also indicate previous external impositions (Gibson 1990:378–9).

Placing close kinsmen over conquered alien chiefdoms was a time-honored technique of pacifying enemies in Ireland. These impositions were not, however, accompanied by bureaucratic arrangements to weld these conquered territories into a state-like system. Indeed, the conquered chiefdoms still maintained their separate identities and territorial integrity. As time wore on, the imposed leaders were either overthrown in favor of the original leading ramage, as was apparently the fate of Anrudán mac Máel Gorm after the Norsemen forced the temporary decline in the power of the Uí Thairdelbaig. Alternatively, with the passage of time the descendants of the imposed leader would come to be identified with the local population, losing completely their connection to the ramage of their origins. The descendants of Mathgamain became the Mac Mathghamhna, the leading ramage of Corcu Baiscinn. The sons of Máel Sechnaill mac Croscrach and their descendants became leaders of the Corcu Mruad, and defended this chiefdom from attack from descendants of Brian Boruma, the Uí Briain, in 1054 AD (Gibson 1990:175).

Cénel Fermaic bordered upon Dál Cais directly and was presumably compelled to join this composite chiefdom before or during the tenth century (Fig. 13.8). This chiefdom contained the ramages of Uí Chuinn, Cénel Báeth, and Uí Dedaid under the leadership of the latter ramage. A genealogy was concocted which had the ramages of Cénel Fermaic sharing common descent with the Dál Cais (O'Brien 1976:152 A 41). Common descent

with Dál Cais was possible but unlikely for Cénel Fermaic. The personal names given to individuals in Irish aristocratic lineages were usually restricted to a small set, and used repeatedly over long periods of time. The names of the chieftains given in the genealogies of Cénel Fermaic show no affinity with those of the Dál Cais, but rather indicate a relationship with chiefdoms to the south, perhaps Ciarraige or Corcu Baiscinn (Gibson 1990:361). On this evidence the larger composite polity of the Dál Cais, consisting of the Dál Cais composite chiefdom together with Cénel Fermaic, can be properly termed a *chiefdom confederacy*. A chiefdom confederacy consists of a number of genealogically related and unrelated chiefdoms which were unified through coercion or common agreement. Chiefdom confederacies were legitimized through genealogies which promulgated a fiction of common identity through consanguineal links between founders. These genealogies simply described the political bonds between chiefdoms in the manner in which chiefdoms themselves were held to be structured internally.

Chiefdom confederacies were a common element of the political landscape of Ireland from the earliest times. The Connachta of Connaught and the Eóganachta of Munster were chiefdom confederacies that existed in the centuries prior to the tenth century (Sproule 1984). The Eóganachta of Munster had little internal cohesion. Eóganachta chiefdoms were just as likely to be geographi-

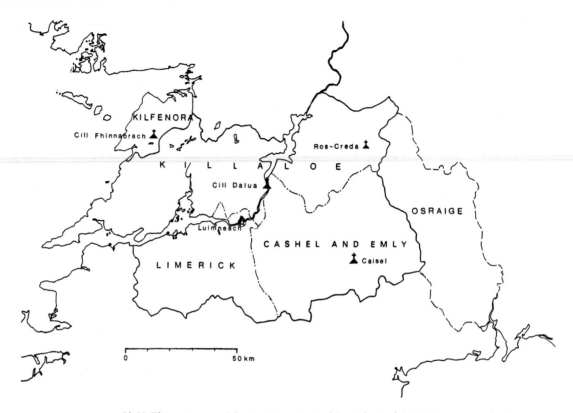

13.10 The core area of the primitive state of Muirchertach Uí Briain.

cally separated from each other as they were to border upon one another (Mac Niocaill 1972:34). Though the office of a paramount chieftain was held to exist at the head of the confederacy, it is likely to have been largely ritual and ceremonial until the eighth century. The "king" of Munster was no more than a *primes inter pares*.

The origins of statehood in Munster

Following the death of Brian mac Cennétig at the battle of Clontarf in 1014, chieftainship passed to his son Donnchad. The laxity of Brian's rule over Munster was demonstrated when the survivors of Clontarf were challenged by the previously subordinate Osraige of eastern Munster on their way home from the battle (Fig. 13.10). Following the death of Donnchad, the paramountcy of the Uí Thairdelbaig over Munster was reasserted in 1064 by Tordelbach Uí Briain, who was in turn succeeded by Muirchertach Uí Briain in 1086.

To Muirchertach Uí Briain goes the credit for the creation of the first state in Munster, perhaps the earliest state in Ireland. This assertion conjures up the problem of

how it is possible to recognize state organization in the historical record, distinguishable from the imprint of complex chiefdoms, as complex chiefdoms bear a strong structural resemblance to primitive states (see Gibson and Geselowitz 1988a; Service 1975).

As a first step toward resolving this issue we must remember that the paramount chieftain, or *rí riurech*, of an Irish composite chiefdom or chiefdom confederacy was first of all the leader or *rí* of his own chiefdom. The Uí Thairdelbaig chieftains of Dál Cais lived in homesteads within the boundaries of Uí Thairdelbaig. Brian's capital was at Cenn Coradh (Fig. 13.9), and this site remained the capital under Donnchad and Tordelbach, though they established additional strongholds in Munster. Muirchertach broke with tradition by moving his capital to the former Norse town of Luimneach (Limerick), outside the boundaries of his chiefdom (Fig. 13.10). Muirchertach's move represents a fundamental change in the nature of political leadership in Ireland, for it reflects the fact that the basis of Muirchertach's power was no longer his native *túath*, or chiefdom. The leadership of Munster then became extra-territorial, and was presumably divorced from the ties of fictive kinship that usually bound the aristocracy to a chiefdom's populace.

Long ago Sir Henry Maine made the observation that the transition to political society was accompanied by a change by which the individuals of a populace shift their sense of identity from the corporate group alone, to a territory with fixed boundaries (Maine 1861). These boundaries are a manifestation of the administrative power of the state bureaucracy, and the emergent power of the political center (see also Dodgshon 1987). However, the existence of fixed territorial boundaries alone cannot serve as a diagnostic feature of state organization, as chiefdoms and segmentary societies are also very often rigidly bounded (Service 1975).

During state formation the kinship principle that binds the members of a chiefdom together breaks down. This is just as dramatically, if not more incisively instanced by the growing autonomy of the ruling kin group both from the ruled and from the chiefdom's traditional aristocracy (Service 1975:294, 302). In the course of his brilliant career, Brian Boruma defeated a great many chieftains and came to dominate a vast area. However, the fact that throughout his reign Brian Boruma remained at Cenn Coradh within his traditional territory of Uí Thairdelbaig suggests that Brian remained a traditional Irish chieftain, drawing his primary support from his chiefdom and the Dál Cais confederacy. The wider polity that Brian ruled over was integrated solely by force, an interpretation supported by the fact that the military campaigns of Brian never ceased. True statehood came when Brian's successor Muirchertach moved his capital to a position central to his state but *outside* the bounds of Uí Thairdelbaig.

Another act of Muirchertach's that informs us that we are dealing with a state, and not a complex chiefdom, is the fact that in 1101 he bequeathed the site of Caisel to the Catholic church. Caisel was the prior capital of the Eóganachta confederacy, the center of "kingship" over Munster in the territory of the eponymous Eóganachta Caisel (see Fig. 13.10). Not only was their capital site passed over to the church, but lands were taken from the Eóganachta Caisel to support the foundation. As I stated above, Irish chieftains were wont to exert their influence by indirect means of control. No paramount chieftain would have dared to cede the capital site and land of another chiefdom away as Muirchertach did. The fact that Muirchertach was able to carry this deed off was a testimony to his greater powers. This ability to manipulate chiefdoms within Munster was also evidenced through Muirchertach's creation of the diocese of Killaloe in 1111 at the synod of Rathbraisel (Fig. 13.10). In addition to the Dál Cais homeland, Killaloe included

parts of some other chiefdoms such as the territory around the church of Ros-Creda, which was carved out of the chiefdom of Éli Uí Cherbail (Gleeson 1947:20; Gwynn and Gleeson 1962:120–7).

A reasonable approximation of the extent of the twelfth century state of Muirchertach Uí Briain may be gained by combining the dioceses of Killaloe, Limerick, and Cashel and Emly together (Fig. 13.10), as Killaloe and Limerick contain respectively the Dál Cais homeland and Muirchertach's capital, and the diocese of Cashel was created by Muirchertach. As has been stated above, Muirchertach had his chief residence at Luimneach, and, following time-honored precedent, this town also became the seat of the archbishopric of Munster.

The sphere of Muirchertach's influence stretched far beyond the territory shown in Fig. 13.10. Most if not all of the chiefdoms of Munster, and many chiefdoms in the provinces of Leinster and Connaught, had been defeated by him and had become client polities of his state. The dioceses of Limerick, Killaloe, and Cashel probably add up to the 'core area' of Muirchertach's state, the territory which was subject to direct bureaucratic regulation (Whittlesey 1944; Pounds and Ball 1964).

When the configuration of the state of Muirchertach is viewed against the location of the then secular and ecclesiastical capital at Luimneach, it is striking how the position of Luimneach expresses the principle of capital centrality, a principle extrapolated from an analysis of the geographical structure of Irish chiefdoms. Luimneach is positioned at a point where the borders of all three dioceses intersect; its location provides a pivot for these sub-territories. This may be a structural attribute common to many, if not all primitive states. In his study of the origins of the first state in Denmark, Klavs Randsborg found that the putative territories of this state converged upon the capital at Jelling (1980:77). The fact that the boundary of Limerick diocese takes in part of Clare suggests that the town/capital was provided with its own territory within the state.

Though little may be said about the social structure of Muirchertach's state, it may be profitably compared upon the basis of size and overt territorial structure with other early states. Colin Renfrew has claimed that all early civilizations were initially composed of territories of fairly uniform size with a central place as the political focus (Renfrew 1984:85). He terms this territorial unit an *early state module* (ESM). The state that has been described above fits the first criterion of an early state module in that it has a central place, but departs from the other key aspect singled out by Renfrew, that of size. Renfrew finds that the early state module averages about 1500 km^2 in extent (p. 97). Muirchertach's state was, however, about 9600 km² in size, or 6.4 times larger than the average ESM.

The difference in size between Renfrew's early state module, and Muirchertach's state may be related to a difference in the economic underpinnings of these polities. Renfrew's EMS sample consisted of the polities of the Maya lowlands, Mycenaean Greece, and Etruria. The latter two civilizations were supported by polyculture, whereas the Mayan polities pursued forms of intensive horticulture. The agricultural economies of these three areas were dependent upon vegetable foods that produced relatively high yields per hectare planted. The Irish subsistence economy was agropastoral in nature, livestock (chiefly cattle) providing a significant proportion of the diet in milk and meat. The dependency upon livestock would have been more pronounced in the west of Ireland, where the high rate of precipitation and low rate of evaporation restricts the amount of grain that can be grown. Pastoralism is land-extensive, providing fewer calories per hectare of land than agrarian production. This situation led to relatively low population densities in Ireland throughout the Middle Ages (Nicholls 1976). It is possible then that the territorial area of the ESM of an agrarian society will be substantially smaller than the ESM of an agropastoral state.[3]

It is interesting that the composite chiefdoms of Déis Tuaiscirt and Corcu Mruad do roughly approximate the size of the ESM. Déis Tuaiscirt was roughly 1200 km² and Corcu Mruad 1000 km² in area. To explain this finding one must simply apply conversely the logic of the preceding paragraph. The territorial equivalent of the EMS under a prevailing agropastoral economic regime will possess a simpler political system. A corollary of this explanation is the fact that among agropastoral societies, political control by aristocrats over the base population is exerted by indirect means through the creation of debt, which underpinned the institution of clientship (Buxton 1963; Gibson 1988, 1990; Patterson 1981; Webster 1990). There were probably a number of factors related to the agropastoral resource base that contributed to the fact of clientship being the dominant mode of staple finance in Ireland. Cattle as a resource cannot be as readily increased, renewed, or harvested as agricultural products. Nor do herders need any facilities such as terraces or irrigation canals that are susceptible to management. Furthermore the relatively sparse and dispersed populations instanced by cattle raising, and the broken topography, increased the costs of goods transport and communication. These conditions of pastoral production mitigate against direct managerial controls

over production. Instead aristocrats expropriated livestock, food, and labor from the base population through patron/client relationships.

In Ireland the system of clientship was extended into the sphere of political relations between aristocrats, so that instead of displacing a defeated rival, a chieftain bound him into a clientship contract with the obligation of payments of tribute. This system of indirect rule gave the larger-scale Irish political units a federate character. The territories of Irish chiefdoms tended to endure for centuries within larger polities, with boundaries remaining relatively unchanged, despite political changes in leadership at the top due to this system of administration.

This state of Muirchertach may be termed a *primitive state*. Unlike complex agrarian states, it probably lacked a large complex bureaucracy with a multitude of specialized officials overseeing the economic and juridical aspects of state administration. At this state of research, it is even unclear whether the territories were administered by chieftains appointed by Muirchertach, or whether Muirchertach retained the aboriginal chieftains as clients in the traditional Irish fashion. It may not be too far fetched to speculate that Muirchertach entrusted territorial administration to church officials, seeing as the dioceses that were set up by Muirchertach were carved out of, and to a certain extent displaced, former chiefdoms. It is fair to assume that some manner of simple bureaucracy existed with economic and juridical aspects, as stewards and judges constituted an important part of the retinues of Irish chieftains before and after Muirchertach's time.

Conclusions

Acknowledgment of the historic autochthonous attainment of state-level complexity has been denied to the Irish because of the perceived weakness and instability of their institutions of leadership (see Dodgshon 1987; Nicholls 1976). The Irish centers of government lacked large bureaucracies and were not associated with nucleated settlement. Political power was also somewhat transitory in nature, ebbing and flowing rapidly with the arrival and departure of individual leaders. Up to the destruction of the Irish aristocracy in the late seventeenth century, no one leader had managed to integrate the entire island into a single state-level polity.

The historic "statelessness" of the Irish, however, really reflects the failure of scholars to interpret the Irish situation in terms of the prevailing subsistence context. The Irish economy was agropastoral with an emphasis on cattle raising. The Irish population lived, then, in the scattered homesteads typical of pastoralists rather than in nucleated settlements (Gibson 1988). The mobility of the economic base demanded that the financing of the aristocratic sector must be achieved through the control of people through contracts between commoner and aristocrat, rather than through the control of land (Patterson 1981; Gerriets 1983). Goods for the political economy of the aristocrats were then mobilized through patron–client relationships. This form of goods mobilization entailed a smaller bureaucratic sector associated with kingship than one would encounter in an agrarian setting.

Nevertheless, states did appear in Ireland in the early Middle Ages. In Munster, state-level complexity was achieved, following a long period of development, with the reign of Muirchertach Ui Briain. One hallmark of this historic Irish primitive state was the emergent autonomy of the king and his bureaucracy, with the consequent abandonment of the procedure whereby territorial expansion was accompanied by an expansion of the fictional kinship lattice to include the leading families of conquered chiefdoms. The departure of the king from his traditional territory entailed a dissolution of the ideological basis of the chiefdom: the fiction of common descent. Subsequent to Muirchertaich's reign, O'Brien lineages carved out estates from subject chiefdoms without seeking to identify themselves with the populace.

Muirchertach initiated another important change in imposing the diocesan system of territorial administration upon his state. These ecclesiastical territories were the first territorial units of any kind in Ireland not to be coterminous with the boundaries of preexisting chiefdoms. More than any other act, the creation of these territorial units indicated the supplanting of the tradition of retaining conquered chiefdoms as subordinate administrative units, by a new regime whereby the state held a monopoly on power. The area which had been reorganized on this basis could be said to be the 'core area' of Muirchertach's state. This core area centered upon Muirchertach's new capital at Luimneach, which also became the seat of the archbishopric of Munster. In their discussion of the core areas of early European states, Pounds and Ball (1964) note that one trait which typifies the capitals of core areas is the presence of the seats of archbishops.

As the Middle Ages progressed, the Irish primitive state experienced gradual but significant change in its organization and institutions. The primitive bureaucracy expanded as stewards became entrusted with the supervision of subject territories. This change went hand in hand with the transformation of the political economy from one of goods mobilization from subject chieftains through tribute, to the establishment of rent. This explica-

tion of the origin of the state in Ireland underlines the fact that the trajectory of social evolution in any instance assumes a character specific to the mode of subsistence. It is not only possible for pastoralists to achieve state-level complexity without external stimulus; it is also evident from this study that the states of agro-pastoralists assume a structure that is distinct from the structure of agrarian states. The shift to the direct administration of territories by stewards is a further indication of the demise of indirect rule through chiefdoms.

As it arose in the twelfth century, centuries after other European states had flourished and declined, some social scientists may dismiss the polity of Muirchertach Ui Briain as a "secondary state," that is, a state which has come into being as a result of direct contact with other adjacent or nearby states. Rating states as "pristine," or better yet "primary," or as "secondary" may have some relevance when evaluating the importance of factors such as the existence of a slave trade in contributing to the origins or character of a state. However one must countenance the fact that state organization cannot be invoked at will; societies must be sufficiently populous and complex, with solid economic underpinnings to make the transition to statehood. It is a fallacy to suppose that mere exposure to state organization is sufficient to enable the creation of a state by a population.

The Irish had been exposed to the idea of the state for quite some time before the advent of Muirchertach. Christianity had been introduced to Ireland from the fourth and fifth centuries. The structure of the ecclesiastical hierarchy on the continent emulated a state, and states are portrayed in the Gospels. There is also reason to suppose that some Irish had become exposed to the Roman Empire in Britain and on the continent prior to its collapse. These influences were obviously not sufficient to prod the Irish toward political systems that were more hierarchical and centralized. On the contrary, the Catholic church in Ireland came to emulate the structure of Irish chiefdoms during the first millennium AD.

The invading Norsemen of the eighth and ninth centuries were also not influential in providing a model for Irish statehood, as their polities were not rigidly centralized and their settlements were confined to coastal entrepôts. Brian Boruma may have fancied himself as the Gaels' savior from the Norsemen, but they had been in Ireland for over a century before he commenced his career in the late tenth century, and they exerted no overarching political influence. They were, however, influential in introducing novel weapons and fighting tactics to Ireland, such as the use of ships in military campaigns. Their entrepôts and exchange networks probably entailed increases in the volume of trade and communication with the rest of Europe over the exchanges that had been facilitated by Ireland's ecclesiastical contacts. The role of exchange in promoting state formation in Ireland has yet to be explored.

As a state, then, the polity of Muirchertach must be considered to be a "precocious state" in the terminology of Service (1975:20). It was not the *earliest* state in the British Isles, but was the first state of its kind among the polities of Ireland. In his examination of the origins of the Zulu primitive state, Service described a process whereby an unstable militarist polity created by the leaders Dingiswayo and Shaka gave way to a state characterized by administrative changes introduced by Shaka's successor and brother Mpande that leant the political system stability (1975: Ch.5). Superficially the history of the O'Brien state would seem to offer a striking parallel to this case, with Brian Mac Cennétig's military conquests being succeeded by a true state with a stable administration under his descendants Turlough and Muirchertach Uí Briain. However the process of state formation in Ireland was probably more gradual, protracted and less dramatic than the Zulu example. The expansion of the Déis Tuaiscirt/Dál Cais composite chiefdom had commenced several centuries prior to Brian Mac Cénnetig's arrival, and the consolidation of the O'Brien state trans-

pired during the century following his death in 1014. Given the fact that the O'Brien state came into being in gradual, incremental stages, one is tempted to conclude that this was an organization generated largely by autochthonous processes.

Notes

1 Like *Baile na Greagnais* around the seat of the chieftain at Gragans, the small territories of *Carraig Locháin* and *Muc Inis* represent demense land owned by the chiefly lineage. The towerhouse at Muc Inis was inhabited by the chieftain's son (Source: *Books of Survey and Distribution*).

2 The Old Irish period of the language was from the seventh to ninth centuries.

3 County Clare as a whole contains 3447 km² (Finch 1971:1). In 1659 the county had a population of 16,914 (Frost 1978:384), and a population density of 4.9 persons per km². This census was taken eight years after the struggle of the Irish Confederation against Cromwell, which probably resulted in a reduction in the population. Even with substantially higher population numbers the landscape cannot be said to have been densely peopled at this time.

14

Clans are not primordial: pre-Viking Irish society and the modelling of pre-Roman societies in northern Europe

NERYS THOMAS PATTERSON

Contemporary documentation is available for the modelling of European Iron Age societies but its interpretation is problematic. Roman authors saw things in Roman terms and gave overwhelming attention to the customs of the elite. The other sources close to the social conditions of the Iron Age, the writings of the medieval Celtic scribes, have with only a few exceptions (Gibson, this volume; Clarke 1972; Mytum 1992) been treated gingerly by archaeologists (e.g. Edwards 1990:8; Bintliff 1984b:172). Celticists themselves have encouraged avoidance of these sources by maintaining that the most informative sources, the law-tracts, were merely the "ruins" of a prehistoric system and were almost unintelligible.[1] This view has recently been challenged from several angles (McCone 1990; Ó Corráin et al. 1984; Patterson 1989, 1990, 1991). There are difficulties in understanding Celtic legal writing, but they consist of linguistic and cultural unfamiliarity and do not mean that the texts cannot be interpreted productively as to their social significance.

The picture of Irish society that is obtainable from the Irish vernacular law-tracts is especially relevant to two archaeological disputes regarding the European Iron Age. One is whether elite formation was based primarily on control of domestically generated increases in agrarian wealth (Bintliff 1984b), or on control of the circulation of manufactured prestige items (Wells 1984; Rowlands 1980, 1984). The Irish case shows how control of agrarian production was a sufficient condition for the emergence of stratification under pre-modern European agrarian conditions, but also suggests that other factors had to have been present for disparities in agricultural power to produce class divisions.

The second theoretical issue on which Irish evidence can be brought to bear is the importance of kinship in the organization of pre-Roman European societies. Some scholars envisage only extended families as the kinship-based groups in ranked Iron Age communities (Humphreys 1978; Rowlands 1980:19ff.; Audouze and Büchsenschütz 1992:175–6), but others have postulated "segmentary" lineages and/or clans (Charles-Edwards 1972[2]). Sometimes this assumption is embedded in terminology, as in the case of early Iron Age high-status burials in Slovenia which have been labelled *Sippenhügel*, clan-mounds (Bintliff 1984b:161, citing the primary literature).

Assumptions that kinship groups must have been extensive and multifunctional in pre-state Europe stem from an anthropological model of social evolution, exemplified by Fried's *Evolution of Political Society*. In this Fried discussed ranking (i.e. the establishment of many status distinctions between individuals without strong class solidarity between members of the same rank), as a pristine form of social stratification that developed within *pre-existing* extensive kin-groups. For Fried the crucial evolutionary change was that between mobile band-societies where property relations were minimum, to fixed-residence, property-owning groups which were either lineages or clans (Fried 1967:124–75). But in the Irish case clans did not form the matrix of stratification. Instead, clan oligarchies came into being as a result of advancing social stratification which was not, initially, based on control of productive property so much as on control of the use of effective force. In a nutshell: warlords fathered clan-lords.

Fried would object, of course, that the Irish case was *not* one of pristine social differentiation, for as is shown below, outside influences were crucial to early Irish development. But for archaeologists modelling pre-state European societies that is exactly the point: where Rome had influence there were no "pristine" social systems. Hence models such as Fried's do not apply to much of Iron Age Europe, and the assumption must be abandoned that lineages and clans were necessarily present as an intermediary "stage" of development from egalitarian to state systems. Irish clans and lineages emerged under particular conditions that may not have been common elsewhere in late Iron Age Europe. Once consolidated they impeded other possibilities for social change, tending to an entrenched "conservatism" – a clannish world-view. The Irish clan system lasted with modifications until the sixteenth century and radical social reorganization only occurred after conquest (Nicholls 1972).

A model of early Irish society

The following remarks are based on my survey of the published editions of the primary written sources and the relevant secondary literature in archaeology, history, and text criticism (Patterson 1991 and 1994). My views do not differ much from those of such modern authorities on Irish social history as Byrne, Ó Corráin, and Nicholls, but being based on an application of sociological/anthropological perspectives they place greater emphasis on systemic interrelationships. I also maintain, to the contrary of Binchy's theory, that patrilineal kinship became more not less important as a principle of social organization in Ireland during the early Middle Ages (Binchy 1936, 1943; Patterson 1990, 1991).

Clans do not jump off the pages of the old Irish record: they steal up on the researcher. In sagas one meets regionally based aristocracies such as the "men of Leinster." However, the military aristocracy overflowed these regional boundaries time and again, so that dynastic clans were actually trans-regional organizations. In contrast to the sagas, the annals usually mention only personal groups at the local level, such as a leader and his *muintir* (household). The lawyers offer yet another perspective on society. With only a few important exceptions, the law-tracts evade discussion of social groups, concentrating on relationships between individuals in dyads. Yet by piecing together information from all these sources a picture of the organization of a clan, *cenél*, and a lineage, *fine*, is obtained.

Before we can describe clans, however, we must first envisage them "on the ground." Clans were distributed within and across petty "kingdoms,"[3] *tuatha*, units that might have their own "kings" and chief judges (Kelly 1989: 17, 52–3). Based on findings by historical geographers, I have suggested that a *túath* usually had a minimum complement of agrarian resources: extensive waste for summer transhumant grazing; woodland for swine and dry cattle; low moorland for winter grazing of sheep; meadow for wintering cattle and horses; arable land for crops and gardens (Patterson 1991:88–93). Settlements were scattered at mid-elevations across this diversified terrain and consisted of small clusters of nuclear families (about four or five), each in its own dwelling, probably constituting extended families or shallow lineages. The law-tracts stress an ideal of self-sufficiency in resources and equipment for each farming unit – that is, each got access to all the types of land in the area and each should have the gear and hands to work the unit fully. Typical *túath* size was about 16 km in diameter and many scholars have shown that the *túath* corresponded closely with the later medieval barony (for references see Patterson 1991:92–3). The origins of *túath* political unity probably lie in repeated interaction between members of scattered communities on the upland wastes during summer. Recourse to the waste in spring was motivated by (i) the natural upland migration of sheep at winter's end (ii) the dangerous proximity of starving cattle to domestic crops in the absence of investment in infrastructure (stockade fencing). Down to modern times dispersed communities that shared summer pastures appointed someone to sort out the disputes that arose between them from trying to balance everyone's rights (which often involved complicated substitutions): this local official was still called a "king" or "judge" in the nineteenth century (Patterson 1991:90–21).

The social composition of the *túath* was variable: one clan might coincide with one *túath* (Binchy 1978: *CIH* 429.20), but more commonly there were present branches of far-flung ruling dynasties, along with remnants of previous ruling clans. The *túath* thus provided the elite with a sort of net that held in place a labor force consisting of those persons who could not escape when a new clan overtook the area, for want of adequate mobile resources (livestock) and external social connections. These would have been the lower echelons of clan society. As members of defeated groups they were allowed to remain *in situ* on terms of lowered status and diminished security as landholders. Those who escaped survived as clans in marginal lands, whence a bid for a return to the old lands might be mounted in future (Smyth 1982).

The basic social entity then was the clan not the *túath*. In essence it was a low-energy war-machine – what it did, as a group, was produce enough labor and food surplus to support its own warrior elite that rode on horseback to stand-up fights and cattle-raids. There was little prehistoric investment in military infrastructure: only about sixty hillforts have been noted (Raftery 1972, 1976), and horsemanship lagged behind developments in central Europe (Raftery 1991:51). The food surplus was directly consumed by the elite at seasonal feasts, especially during the winter period of *cóe*, 'guesting and feasting' (Binchy 1940; Simms 1978). Feasts were basic to the establishment of supra-local alliances, and in literature are the scene of boasting, brawling, and competition, as well as covert surveillance of the strength of the host group and the availability of marriage partners.

The food surplus was provided by tributary clients, known in Irish scholarship as base-clients (*dóer-céile*), each of whom was contracted to an individual lord (*flaith*). Ideally the lord was the client's superior kinsman, and if an adequate patron could be found within his own clan the small-farmer was supposed to contract with him in preference to a more distant kinsman or a non-kinsman. But competition within the elite was beyond the scope of legal regulation and a small-farmer could lawfully contract with as many as three lords within or outside his clan (Kelly 1989:29–32). The basic form of the food-supplying contract was that a lord gave a small-farmer a number of cattle and received a legally fixed amount of food-renders in return. The lord's 'gift' (*rath*) was made over in two parts. The first consisted of a number of cows equal in value to the amount that the recipient would have received as his honor-price were someone liable to compensate him for some serious injury. The lord was then entitled to a share of honor-price payments to his client and the latter was limited as to his autonomy in legal actions – he could hardly side with his lord's rival's clients in a dispute, for example. The client also owed his lord general help – joining his posse, erecting ramparts around his residence, and helping bring in his crop. (There must have been limitations on these demands, but no clear evidence exists.) The second payment was the bulk of the "gift," and it was on this that the client owed return payments. A *bóaire*, a substantial but plebeian farmer, would take twelve cows in fief, while lesser ranks of farmers took less. The food render owed for this loan consisted mainly of prepared and processed food such as meat, malt, cheese, bread, honey, leeks, and candles. Evidently, domestic labor and management (preparation, storage, transportation, and liability for spoilage of food) were the main economic targets of domination, not herdsmanship.

In fact, it was because lords controlled stock-raising themselves – by maintaining large herds in wilderness areas (Lucas 1989:68–124; Patterson 1991:93–7), and by raiding enemies – that they were in a position to supply peasants with extra stock. The latter in turn were liable to shortfalls in their required numbers of milch-cows because small-scale herds are demographically unstable (Dahl and Hjort 1976). This in itself would not have been a problem in a highly buffered agrarian regime (such as Neolithic leaf-fodder pastoralism with light plowing and digging), but Iron Age integrated mixed farming was not flexible at the lower ends of the scale of production.

The key problem for the small farmer was that he needed to maintain adequate production in a number of competing areas of farming: he needed oxen to plow, bulls to breed, reserve cattle (barren cows) in case his dairy-herd sickened, milch cows and their young (to keep the dams in milk). All these were after the same finite amount of grass – finite within the radius of the distance traversable from a fixed food storage and processing center

during the winter season. In the cultivation sector he needed livestock for manure and traction; the stock in turn needed fodder for the winter. Where reliance on cattle as a direct source of food was high, the problem of herd balance was important to resolve. One response to these problems was hamlet communitarianism – peasants pooled their oxen in joint-plowing contracts and the shared plow team worked all their arable. But social pressures (customary obligations, debts, and cattle theft) brought further problems in the pastoral sector, encouraging the peasant to have a dependable relationship with someone who kept cattle on a grander scale than he and his neighbors: someone who could meet all their stock needs with ease and rapidity. The Irish cattle-clientship contract shows that the small-farmers found it acceptable to trade a lower living standard – paying food-renders – for greater security in their total farming operation. Once committed, the peasant tended to be tied into a dependent way of life because the contract could not be terminated in less than seven years (on pain of a fine equivalent of the lord's honor-price), even if the loan were no longer needed. Other factors, examined below, also constrained him to dependence.

In addition to these contracts with base-clients, men of the clan elite had a wide variety of other contracts that can only be itemized here: 'free' clients seem to have kept reserves of cattle for their lords (Patterson 1991: 125–30); superior lords contracted political alliances with lesser lords by conferring prestigious gifts, including weaponry, riding horses, hunting dogs, and slaves (Dillon 1962); alliances at all levels were cemented by marriage and the "lending" of children in fosterage. Within a fully developed clan the elite would have made many such contracts with lower members of the clan and with peers and superiors in other clans. The lower ranks, however, were expected to bring their business to their senior kin.

Stratification within the clan was fine tuned. There were many ranks of lordship, distinguished from each other by only small differences in numbers of clients (each lord had one block of five clients more than the rank below him, according to the law-tract on status, *Crith Gablach*: Binchy 1941; Mac Néill 1923). The farmers were also divided into several ranks according to their degree of agrarian self-sufficiency: he who had to borrow most was least. Social mobility was very possible: a farmer who produced surplus stock could extend credit to his neighbors and begin to receive some of the renders payable to lords. The laws imposed a barrier, however: men who were not descended from lords could not in their own lifetime obtain true lordly renders (beer and beef: the makings of a feast). It took three generations to cross the farmer/lord divide: the ranks of society were thus divided into proto-classes by control of the distribution of cattle to farmers (Patterson 1991:168–76).

But though riven by internal competition, the clan was solidary in the face of other comparable social groups. In addition to infra-clan clientship, there existed defense-mechanisms that protected, one by one, all the cells from which the complex group was built. The smallest clan sub-unit, the *gelfhine*, was a three-generation patrilineal group.[4] Men in this group inherited the entire estate of their nearest kinsman who died heirless. But if the group as a whole died out its lands were distributed to agnatic kin as far as fourth cousins, a lineage known as the *fine*. Its members' rights to collateral inheritance were exactly balanced by their obligation to pay the same amount as they might get in inheritance as a contribution to wergeld (*cró*) when one of the group required indemnity. The inheritance rights thus shored up the solidarity of the group as to payment of reparations, protecting individuals from the danger of debt-slavery in lieu of wergeld, and protecting the group as a whole from the vendetta.

Less threatening than vendetta, but still dangerous, was debt. As in archaic Greece (Finley 1982:62–76), agrarian debt was a slippery slope that could end in landlessness or slavery. The Irish clans, however, developed a web of legal constraints on individual autonomy which forestalled the danger of loss of land to settle debt. The most basic rule was that no one could put at risk, whether by taking someone's part in a legal suit or by making a dangerous economic transaction, more than a proportion of his or her inherited property. This proportion (possibly one third of a person's inherited dairy herd [Patterson 1991:251–4]), was the amount known as the honor-price; it could be used by an adult without consulting anyone else to go about everyday business. If a person acquired more by personal effort (as in a cattle raid), the difference was his or hers to use at will, but if a loss ensued, permission (and a loan, presumably) had to be received from the head of kin, before taking further action. The *fine* also possessed a veto power in the contract most likely to incur debt, that of clientship with a lord. Here the basic rule was that no one could take in fief more animals than he had the right to depasture on the commons, a right also linked to a man's honor-price – his heritage of stock and the land required to support it. This device was a response to the possibility that an individual's holdings of livestock could fall below the numbers for which he had inherited pasture rights; land rights flowed down through the clan by descent, but stock holdings were influenced by luck, husbandry, and political patronage. To prevent the conflicts that would arise if a man borrowed more cattle in clientship than his hereditary pasture rights could support, legal custom allowed close kin to return the cows and cancel the contract.

Another legal aspect of group defensiveness was suretyship (Kelly 1989: 167–72; Patterson 1991:Ch. 11.). The surety was a legal guarantor who intervened between the principals in a transaction to ensure compliance by the party for whom he stood surety. In Irish law it seems that any non-trivial transaction was secured by several sureties on each side, so that when a contract was in danger of violation a cross-cutting network of obligations was invoked which involved the honor and reputation of a number of local people of good social standing. The main function of the various types of surety was to compel payment either by the liable principal, or his next of kin, or one of the other sureties. The ultimate surety, who could use force to effect compliance, was ideally a senior kinsman and a member of the noble grades (Patterson 1991:316–50). By spreading liability for the debt within the group, sureties warded off the danger of distraint, which was the only sanction on compliance to law in this society. Distraint (forcible seizure of property) resulted in fines and interest payments on the impounded cattle, and was far more expensive than immediate settlement. Distraint might also escalate into violence. The surety, like a modern bail bondsman, could put up the required payments *at once* – then deal with the debtor afterwards. The latter did not have an easy time simply because it was his kinsman who served as his surety: landlessness and debt-slavery within the clan might result.

Security in this society obviously depended on keeping a firm grip on one's own assets and a sharp eye on one's kinsmen's. The minutely graded ranking system was an outgrowth of these anxieties rather than a cause of it, though once it was legally formalized and socially symbolized through sumptuary codes, rank-consciousness acquired its own momentum. One of the strongest forces keeping it alive over centuries was the practice of isogamous marriage, in which people of the same rank married each other, often within close degrees of consanguinity. Under early Irish marriage customs each spouse contributed a proportion of the conjugal fund: the woman's share was either equal to the husband's, or half as much. Consciousness of individual property was so strong that divorce settlements were based on a complicated formula that gave each partner the major part of the profits of his or her own original input into the fund. Divorce was anticipated, and the cultural ideal was that as long as neither spouse damaged the other's interests, "they should part as they came" – with their property and rank unscathed (Patterson 1991: 288–96).

Application of the Irish model to European Iron Age societies

Irish cattle-clientship shows one way in which elite control of the pastoral sector of agriculture could have stimulated initial phases of social stratification in environmentally similar parts of prehistoric Europe. However, the Irish clan system was much more than a hamlet-based or even a *túath*-based hierarchy and if we try to explain the whole social system in terms of controls in the agrarian sector we run into difficulties. Principally, it must be explained how lords, being possessed of coercive power, were not more oppressive to the peasants than they were. Secondly, it must also be shown why peasants, having some power to resist social domination, yielded to the extent that they did when one of the results of cattle-clientship was more mouths for them to feed, in their own families *and* their lords'.

The Irish aristocracy was very aware that it was they who stood to benefit from clanship and they consciously promoted farmers' adherence to clans by acknowledging the latter's clan-kinship and their "ownership" rights in clan-lands. The farmer in turn gained a sense of social security that offset his actual servility. Keating, the seventeenth-century Gaelic historian, commented that Irish lords did not dispossess the tenantry and establish big estates as did English lords because it was necessary in Ireland to give every man ownership rights in his land so as to induce him to fight for it – and thus for his neighbor and lord – and not take flight when the enemy appeared (Comyn 1902:69). The bond between lord and man was still based in part on cattle-loans in the sixteenth century, and farmers could still undercut a noble's power by withdrawing their loyalty and adhering to other lords (Nicholls 1978). This was only possible because the Irish population remained at low levels until the early modern period. Smyth (1982:5) gives estimates ranging from 12,000 persons for the Uí Dunlainge, a powerful early medieval clan in the relatively fertile south-east, to a mere 500–700 for weak groups in the same area, such as the Fotharta. In the same range is Byrne's estimate of an average of 3000 persons of all ages per *túath* (1971:7). Population pressure was so slight that huge areas of forest remained intact until after the Norman Conquest, providing havens for men fleeing social pressures (McCone 1990:203–23). The Irish farmer drew bargaining power from the demographic underdevelopment of Ireland and used it to gain social security within the clan system.

Returning to the lord's coercive power – in what did it reside? A consensual/functional explanation (the perceived benefits of cattle-lordship, leading farmers grate-

fully to support a local elite) is inadequate to explain the clan as something more than a sporadic formation. I would suggest that the Irish clans (and the comparable clans of medieval Wales, Scotland, and the Western Isles), were social formations that were generated during a period of greatly intensified militarism – that they were not the outcome of long-term autochthonous prehistoric social evolution, but arose during interaction between the peoples of these remote parts of Europe with the wealth of the Roman Empire, especially when this became vulnerable during the withdrawal of Roman forces from Britain. The main type of evidence for this view is archaeological (Laing 1985). This points to major political disturbances and the final collapse of old patterns of regional political organization in Ireland (Mac Néill 1911). These may have been declining over a long period, owing to the isolation of Ireland during the period of Roman occupation of adjacent *Britannia*, a process beginning perhaps as early as the Roman colonization of Gaul. When records become available, i.e. from late- and post-Roman Britain, it appears that numbers of old tribal groups had vanished, and that organized Irish raiding parties, comparable to later Vikings, were pillaging and settling western Britain on a grand scale. St. Patrick refers in the *Confessio* to being carried off to captivity in Ireland along with many thousands of others (Bieler 1953 *Confessio* #1). Both archaeological findings and signs of great language change at this time suggest that Ireland was temporarily inundated by wealth and labor from Roman Britain (Laing 1985). New dynasties emerge toward the end of this period of raiding – chiefly, the Uí Néill and the Eóganachta, whose origin-legends refer to this period, to overseas adventures, and to wealth in slaves (Mac Néill: 1919; Dillon and Chadwick 1972; Morris 1975).

The foundation of the clan system during this period is probable because lords now acquired a new power-basis – small-scale demesne farming performed by bond labor, organized rather like the Welsh lord's *maenor* (Gerriets 1987). The labor force for such relatively intense farming was generated by the slave-raids referred to above and was certainly unavailable on this scale previously. Mytum (1992) has suggested that Irishmen also settled in the Irish colonies in Roman North Britain and Wales, learned local farming techniques, and transmitted these back to Ireland through normal kinship channels (marriage, alliance, fosterage, etc.). Demesne mixed farming, using a middle- to heavy-weight plow, permitted the development of the big household, *muintir*, whose members are associated, like the *familia* of the Roman *villa*, or the *teulu* of the Welsh *llys*, with military activities. This development explains the existence, attested in early annals entries, of small, horse-borne strike-forces that enabled the lords, as a class, to intimidate the farmers, as well as to fight each other.

But given the difficulties inherent in policing a dispersed population in a wild landscape, another mechanism had to be in place. This too, I believe, arose under specific historical circumstances. It is apparent from both legal texts and early annals and genealogies that the rise of the two main dynastic federations in the fifth century (the Eóganachta originating in the south-west and Uí Néill in the center-east), was facilitated by their command of vassal groups, aithech-túatha. Some of these were obligated only to supply matériel or productive services, but others performed military duties for the ruling dynasty of the territory, in return for which they received conditional "rights to land." In this respect they were in the opposite ideological position of farmer "landowning" clan-members, whose rights to land inhered in their descent claims and were contingent only on being good clansmen, not on martial prowess. (Indeed a "good" free man is even described in the tract Miadshlechta as one who only fought on "the day of battle" – once a year! [Patterson 1991:333–4].)

It was this implicit rivalry between low-status clan-members and the vassal peoples that kept the lords in power. The aithech-túatha served to constrain the farmers to remain within their clans as its base producers, to a large extent by being interspersed between clan lands and thus preventing groups of farmers from expanding into whatever good land existed on their own perimeters and shaking off the debts of cattle-loans which kept them tied to their lords. Relations with the aithech-túatha, and with the forest-based flana, neither of which were kinsmen to clan "landowners", also offered the lords a sort of rudimentary "police" that could scout out those attempting to set up independent communities beyond the control of a lordship. The distribution of aithech-túatha is visible at the macro-level on maps, based on eighth- and ninth-century data, that show the interspersal of free clan-lands with those of aithech-túatha (Ó Corráin 1972: [maps] 4,18). This practice is demonstrated as a tactic of warfare in the Táin, where the strong battalion of the Gailioin was divided up into small groups and interspersed among the other "tribal" contingents so as to prevent them pursuing their own interests (O'Rahilly 1967:345–7 = p.147). The principle could also be applied at the micro-level by lords who had power of temporary allocation over clan-lands that had fallen vacant on failure of heirs. Such a practice would account for the considerable attention given in the law tracts to various categories of landless men temporarily settled on clan lands under the direct control of a chief.

A conundrum now presents itself: if the lords' power derived in part from these vassals, but in order to induce the vassals to serve, the lords already had to have power, then how did this political complex emerge? The answer is probably to be found in the developments referred to above, namely the enrichment of Irish war-lords during the period when Irishmen raided and settled the western coasts of Britannia. The military vassals, the aithech-túatha, I suggest, developed in a conquest-state type of social situation in the late fourth and fifth centuries, which, however, dissipated long before state formation was achieved, leaving only dispersed nodes of entrenched power. Access to booty in Britain permitted not only the development of agriculture but the payment of mercenary armies (indeed Mytum argues that some Irishmen were mercenaries for Rome [Mytum 1992:25–8]), and the rise of new dynastic clan confederacies, the Uí Néill and the Eógnachta, at this time. Toward the end of the initial phase of aggression, measuring perhaps about a hundred years from the barbarica conspiratio of 367 to the second Saxon attack on Ireland in 471, enough wealth and military power was concentrated in the hands of the elite that Irish leaders were able to turn to internal social domination – and perhaps had to, given Anglo-Saxon dominance in southern Britain. In this context they settled aithech-túatha on land in payment for warrior services, generated support for permanent household war-bands (including mercenary body-guards) through demesne farming, and organized their own kin into stratified clans that served the nobility's need for stable socio-economic support without a heavy input of supervision and coercion from above. But beyond this level of political centralization they were unable to go because of the low productivity of the native economic system and the cessation of further external opportunities for large-scale raiding.

What preceded the stratified clans discussed in this paper is hard even to guess; some scholars have emphasized that group nomenclature seems to imply lower levels of social differentiation – tribes and lineages without stratification, as opposed to conical clans. The evidence, however, consists only of an archaic stratum of tribal names derived from divinities, contrasted with later group nomenclature based on patronyms (Mac Néill 1911). Such evidence is consistent with the existence of a theocracy of some sort, exercising power over societies in which kinship groups might not have extended much beyond shallow lineages of three or four generations in depth. Given the great political and legal influence of the druid priesthood in both pre-Roman Gaul and pre-Christian Ireland, inter-group social integration on the basis of cult-alliance rather than extended kinship is a possibility during early stages of social development in western Europe. An example of organization along such lines comes (from outside the Celtic-language zone) from early medieval Angeln (upper Schleswig-Holstein and Jutland). Here settlements were surrounded by unpopulated waste where numerous slain individuals received bog-burials. Davies and Vierck envisage a cult-alliance focussing on the bogland with social groups circulating within the bog-bounded territories. In such a case, kinship groups and geographical areas would not meaningfully coincide ((1974:224–7, 228), nor would large corporate descent groups be likely to emerge. But whatever the plausibility of this conjecture, it is plain that neither terminology nor archaeology proves the existence of marked social stratification or large clan structures in pre-literate Ireland. In fact Mac Néill (1921:114–76) pointed out that in the oldest strata of the Irish texts kinship terms suggest only the existence of small social groups based on kinship.

With this model of Irish society in mind let us consider the significance of the following similarities and contrasts between Gaul, as described by Caesar, and Ireland.

1. *A functionally bifurcate elite.* In both cases the elite was divided into the intellectually influential and the militarily powerful (Caesar, *De Bello Gallico* [*BG*] vi.13). Obviously the Irish druids did not long survive the Christian conversion,[5] but the prestige and professionalism of the lay judiciary in medieval Ireland is unmatched in other parts of Europe, and can only be explained as a devolved survival of the bifurcate structure found also in Gaul.

2. *Legal sanctions.* In both societies, the main penalty for offense was reparation payments to the victim, or next of kin, adjudicated by druids in Gaul (*BG* vi.13), or judges in Ireland. As in Athens (MacDowell 1972:116), the homicide, until he made amends, was ostracized from ritual gatherings, deprived of his own legal entitlements, and shunned (Kelly 1989:221–2; Patterson 1991:316–17).

3. *Lordship.* Political leadership was vested in an oligarchy of wealthy warriors; ritual kingship died out in pre-conquest Gaul, and Irish kingship, though ritualized in many ways, was still a preeminently secular function. In both societies, a noble's status depended on the numbers of his retainers, which depended on his individual wealth and acumen (*BG* vi.15).

4. *Factionalism.* Caesar said that factions divided all groups, from the independent polity (*civitatus*) to the household (*domus*) (*BG* vi.11). The same was true of Ireland, where competition tended to whittle down to two balanced groups in opposition to each other, with third parties getting eliminated (Ó Corráin 1971:7–39).

5. *Inter-group hostage taking and treaties.* This is well attested for both societies, where chiefs' sons were the normal pawns (*BG* vi.12; Kelly 1989:278–9).

6. *Informal suppression of conflict.* In a fissiparous political structure unimportant people could cause a lot of political damage. In the more successful Gaulish 'tribes' political gossip was formally restricted to the ears of magistrates (*BG* vi.20). In Ireland the estates of lawyers and monasteries, which often served as travellers' hostels, were typically located between political zones on the routes frequented by travellers. Ordinary people did not occupy these border areas (Ó Ríain 1972; Edwards 1990:104–5).

7. *Filiation.* Caesar states that Gauls differed from other people chiefly in that "they do not allow their own sons to approach them openly until they have grown to an age when they can bear the burden of military service" (*BG* vi.18). This alludes to fosterage, which in Ireland was also a source of great prestige to both father and son (Kelly 1989: 86–90). In Gaul a custom of paternal avoidance may have arisen because the son's presence might look as if the father could find no one to foster him: avoidance would eliminate irksome ambiguity. If so, the Gaulish custom indicates even more anxiety about status there than in Ireland.

8. *Marriage.* Irish isogamy and property-matching is closely paralleled in Caesar's description of the (upper-class?) Gaulish marital economy: "The men, after making due reckoning, take from their own goods a sum of money equal to the dowry they have received from their wives and place with the dowry. Of each such sum account is kept between them and the profits saved" (*BG* vi.19).

These similarities between Gaul and Ireland make the differences all the more interesting.

1. *Clientship.* This relationship in Gaul seems more degraded than in Ireland: Caesar's references to the "slavishness" of the clients' position (*BG* vi.13), is more reminiscent of the Irish *fuidir*, who had lost his land through debt and entered a totally dependent relationship with a lord.

2. *Military service.* Gaulish leaders employed *ambacti* as well as *clientes* in warfare (*BG* vi.15; iii.2). Edwards (ibid.) suggests that *ambacti* had higher status than clients and were similar to the *soldurii* of the Aquitani. The latter seem to have been a sworn brotherhood of fighters; they are reminiscent of socially uprooted Irish professional fighters, *ambue* ("cowless men"), fian (*Männerbund*), and *dibergach* ("marauders"). These, along with the military vassals settled on land for services, were amongst the forces enabling the Irish lord to dominate (Mac Néill 1941–3). In Ireland, however, they faded away (McCone

1990:223), presumably because the booty-economy that sustained such groups died out during the sixth century. There are references to such men taking fiefs of cattle from lords into the wilds with them (McCone 1990: 211). This poor reward-base for mercenaries persisted, for when they next appeared in Ireland on a large scale (thirteenth-century *gallowglass* from the Scottish islands), they were supported mainly through grants of rights to extract food from the farmers, and gifts of horses.

Gaul and Ireland thus had much in common but differed in that Gaul experienced prolonged proximity to the slave-based and coin-using economies of the Mediterranean, which presented an early and prolonged stimulus to mercenary military group formation. In Ireland, on the other hand, mercenaries were only an ephemeral large-scale phenomenon. Consequent on these differences in military orientation these two "Celtic" societies diverged in other ways. Irish society became stratified within the cocoon of the clan, producing rank and class divisions while denying them through kinship. Gaulish society, in contrast, had moved toward the alienation of social classes, based on the elite's ability to realize the cash-value of the farmers' land and labor in a commoditized system where money could buy military services in a direct and flexible way.

Contrasts in population densities are co-factors in the development of these differences, for Gaul on the eve of the Roman conquest was far more populous than pre-modern Ireland. Diodorus Siculus estimated 50,000–200,000 persons for tribes in Gaul; Caesar's tribal estimates ranged from the Helvetii at 263,000 to the Latovici at 14,000 (Wells 1984:171). Even allowing for exaggeration by Caesar, the contrast with estimated Irish population dimensions, cited above, is great. The Irish farmer, though hemmed in by *aithech-túatha*, could, if he effected an escape from his creditors, hold out in the woods for a time or attach himself to another lord: the Gaulish farmer, in a more crowded (and less wooded?) landscape, might have found this harder – escaping, he might more readily have encountered spies and slave-traders than new friends.

Behind rising populations, in turn, lies the Iron Age intensification of agriculture in Gaul. In contrast, Irish participation in the conversion to iron tools was slow (Raftery 1975), and presumably little improvement in cultivation occurred during the second half of the first millennium BC (Herity 1991). Unless decisive evidence to the contrary is available, it seems obvious, as Cunliffe argues (1988:80–105, 169–70), that the main reason for this difference between Gaul and Ireland was the difference in their respective proximity to the commodity markets of the Mediterranean and their ability to absorb and transform a growing surplus into money and power.

Notes

1 The law-tracts were written in Old Irish mainly between the sixth and eighth centuries, and were transcribed with modifications, glosses, and commentaries until the sixteenth century (see Kelly 1989).

2 In his most recent publication, however, Charles-Edwards concludes that there is no evidence for the existence of "deep lineages" from the "Common Celtic period" (1993:472). He still adheres to the view that there were four-generation agnatic lineages in late prehistoric Ireland and Wales, though the evidence for this is also murky (see Note 4 below).

3 Although the term *rí* (= Lat. *rex*) was used of a chief of a *túath* and of larger political federations, a king was just an overlord (a *flaith*) of his high-status kinsmen and allied clan chiefs, *primus inter pares*.

4 It has long been maintained that the group of first cousins, the *gelfhine*, acquired new legal importance following changes in Irish society that reduced the scale of solidary kin-groups by a degree of relationship (from the second-cousin group, *derbfhine*). See Charles-Edwards (1993) and Mytum (1992). But in a 1990 paper I showed that the textual evidence for such a theory is at best inconclusive, while other supportive evidence, e.g. for population growth, is lacking (Patterson 1991: Appendix).

5 Irish druids are attested in the earliest (sixth-century?) stratum of law-tracts emanating from south-west Ireland (Binchy 1978: *CIH* 1612.8 = Mac Néill 1923:277 #37).

Bibliography

Adams, R.McC. 1966. *The Evolution of Urban Society*. Chicago: Aldine.

Adcock, F.E. 1956. *Caesar as Man of Letters*. London: Archon Books.

Allen, T. F. H. and T.B. Starr 1982. *Hierarchy: Perspectives for Ecological Complexity*. Chicago: University of Chicago Press.

Anderson, B. 1991. *Imagined Communities: Reflections on the Origin and Spread of Nationalism*. (Revised edition). London: Verso.

Appadurai, A. 1986. Introduction: commodities and the politics of value. In A. Appadurai (ed.) *The Social Life of Things: Commodities in Cultural Perspective*, pp. 3–63. Cambridge: Cambridge University Press.

APS[Acts of the Parliaments of Scotland], 1814–75, Vols. I–XI. London: T. Thomson and Vol. XII Edinburgh: A. Anderson.

Arcelin, P. 1992. Société indigène et propositions culturelles massaliotes en basse Provence occidentale. In M. Bats, G. Bertucchi, G. Congès and H. Tréziny (eds.) *Marseille Grecque et la Gaule. Etudes massaliètes 3*, pp. 305–36. Lattes: ADAM Editions.

Arcelin, P. and B. Dedet 1985. Les enceintes protohistoriques du Midi méditerranéen des origines à la fin du IIe s. av. J.-C. In B. Dedet and M. Py (eds.) *Les Enceintes protohistoriques de Gaule méridionale*, pp. 11–37. Caveirac: Association pour la Recherche Archéologique en Languedoc Oriental.

Arcelin-Pradelle, C. 1984. *La Céramique grise monochrome en Provence*. Supplement 10 of the *Révue Archéologique de Narbonnaise*. Paris: Boccard.

Arnold, B. 1991a. *The Material Culture of Social Structure: Rank and Status in Early Iron Age Europe*. Ph.D. dissertation. Ann Arbor: University of Michigan Microfilms.

1991b. The deposed Princess of Vix: The need for an engendered European prehistory. In D. Walde and N. Willows (eds.) *The Archaeology of Gender*, pp. 366–74. Proceedings of the 22nd Annual Chacmool Conference. Alberta: University of Calgary.

1995. Cups of bronze and gold: drinking equipment and status in early Iron Age Europe. In D. Meyer and P. Dawson (eds.) *Debating Complexity*. Proceedings of the 26th Annual Chacmool Conference. Alberta: University of Calgary.

n.d. "Drinking the Feast": alcohol and the legitimation of power in Iron Age Europe. In M. Dietler (ed.) *Drinking in the Past: Archaeological Perspectives on Alcohol and its Social Roles*. Cambridge: Cambridge University Press.

Audouze F. and O. Büchsenschütz 1989. *Villes, villages et campagnes de l'Europe celtique*. Paris: Hachette.

1992. *Towns, Villages and Countryside of Celtic Europe*. H. Cleere (trans.) London: Batsford.

Balsdon, J.P.V.D. 1955. Review of Michel Rambaud *L'Art de la déformation historique dans les Commentaires de César*. In *Journal of Roman Studies* 45:161–4.

Bateson, G. 1972. *Steps Toward an Ecology of Mind*. New York: Ballantine.

Bats, M. 1992. Marseille, les colonies massaliètes et les relais indigènes dans le trafic le long du littoral méditerranéen gaulois (VIe–Ier s. av. J.-C.). In M. Bats, G. Bertucchi, G. Congès and H. Tréziny (eds.) *Marseille grecque et la Gaule*. Etudes Massaliètes 3, 263–78. Lattes: ADAM Editions.

Beard, M. and M. Crawford 1985. *Rome in the Late Republic*. New York: Cornell University Press.

Benoit, F. 1965. *Recherches sur l'Hellénisation du Midi de la Gaule*. Aix-en-Provence: Publications des Annales de la Faculté des Lettres 43.

Benveniste, E. 1969. *Le Vocabulaire des Institutions Indoeuropéennes*. Paris: Editions de Minuit.

Berry, B.J.L. 1961. City size distributions and economic development. *Economic Development and Cultural Change* 9:573–88.

Berry, W.E. 1987. Southern Burgundy in Late Antiquity and the Middle Ages. In C.L. Crumley and W.H. Marquardt (eds.) *Regional Dynamics: Burgundian Landscapes in Historical Perspective*, pp. 447–607. San Diego: Academic Press.

Bersu, G. 1946. The Wittnauer Horn, a hill-fort in Switzerland. *Antiquity* 20:4–8.

Biel, J. 1985. Die Ausstattung des Toten. In D. Planck, J. Biel, G. Süsskind and A. Wais (eds.) *Der Keltenfürst von Hochdorf: Methoden und Ergebnisse der Landesarchäologie*, pp. 78–105. Stuttgart: Konrad Theiss Verlag.

1990. Vorgeschichtliche Siedlungsreste in Eberdingen-Hochdorf, Kreis Ludwigsburg. *Archäologische Ausgrabungen in Baden-Württemberg 1989*:97–99.

1991. Fortsetzung der Siedlungsgrabung in Eberdingen-Hochdorf, Kreis Ludwigsburg. *Archäologische Ausgrabungen in Baden-Württemberg 1990*: 89–93.

Bieler, L. (ed.) 1953. *The Works of St. Patrick*. Westminster Md: Newman Press.

Binchy, D.A. 1936. The family membership of women and the legal capacity of women in regard to contracts. In D.A. Binchy (ed.) *Studies in Early Irish Law*, pp. 180–6; 207–38. Dublin:Hodges, Figgis and Co.

1940. *Aimser Chue*. In J. Ryan (ed.) *Feil-sgribhinn Eoin Mhic Néill*, pp. 18–22. Dublin: The Sign of the Three Candles.

1943. The linguistic and historical value of the Irish law tracts. (*Sir John Rhys Lecture of the British Academy*). Reprinted in D. Jenkins (ed.) *Celtic Law Papers*. Brussels 1971, pp. 73–107.

1958. The Fair of Tailtiu and the Feast of Tara. *Ériu* 18:113–38.

Binchy, D.A. (ed.) 1941. *Crith Gablach*. Dublin: The Stationary Office.

1962. *Lebor na Cert*. Book of rights, Dublin: Irish Texts Society.

1978. *Corpus Iuris Hibernici* 1–6. Dublin: Dublin Institute for Advanced Study.

Binford, L. 1967. Smudge pits and hide smoking: the use of analogy in archaeological reasoning. *American Antiquity* 32(1):1–12.

1971. Mortuary practices: their study and their potential. In J.A. Brown (ed.) *Approaches to the Social Dimensions of Mortuary Practices*, pp. 6–29. Washington DC: Memoirs of the Society for American Archaeology 25.

Bintliff, J.L. 1984a Iron Age Europe, in the context of social evolution from the Bronze Age through to historic times. In J. Bintliff (ed.) *European Social Evolution: Archaeological Perspectives*, pp. 157–226.

Bintliff, J.L. (ed.) 1984b. *European Social Evolution: Archaeological Perspectives*. Bradford: University of Bradford Press.

Bittel, K. 1934. *Die Kelten in Württemberg*. Römisch Germanische Forschungen 8. Berlin.

1981a. Religion und Kult. In K. Bittel, W. Kimmig, and S. Schiek (eds.) *Die Kelten in Baden-Württemberg*, pp. 85–117. Stuttgart: Konrad Theiss Verlag.

1981b. Die Kelten und Wir. In K. Bittel, W. Kimmig and S. Schiek (eds.) *Die Kelten in Baden-Württemberg*, pp. 15–20. Stuttgart: Konrad Theiss Verlag.

1981c. Keltischer Ahnenkult? In K. Bittel, W. Kimmig and S. Schiek (eds.) *Die Kelten in Baden-Württemberg*, pp. 87–97. Stuttgart: Konrad Theiss Verlag.

Bittel, K., W. Kimmig and S. Schiek (eds.) 1981. *Die Kelten in Baden-Württemberg*. Stuttgart: Konrad Theiss Verlag.

Bittel, K. and A. Reith 1951. *Die Heuneburg an der oberen Donau*. Stuttgart: W. Kohlhammer.

Black Book of Taymouth, 1855. Edinburgh: Bannatyne Club.

Bocquet, A. 1991. L'archéologie de l'Age du Fer dans les Alpes occidentales françaises. In A. Duval (ed.) *Les Alpes à l'Age du Fer*, pp. 91–155. Paris: CNRS.

Boserup, E. 1965. *The Conditions of Agricultural Growth*. London.

Boudet, R. 1987. *L'Age du Fer récent dans la parie méridionale de l'Estuaire Girondin (du Ve au Ier Siècle avant notre ère)*. Périgueux: Editions Vesuna.

Bouloumié, B. 1978. Les tumulus de Pertuis (Vaucluse) et les œnochoés "rhodiennes" hors d'Etrurie. *Gallia* 36:219–41.

1985. Les vases de bronze étrusques et leur diffusion hors d'Italie. In M. Cristofani, P. Moscati, G. Nardi and M. Pandolfini (eds.) *Il Commercio Etrusco Arcaico (Atti dell'Incontro di Studio, 5–7 Dicembre 1983)*. Quaderni del Centro di Studio per l'Archeologia Etrusco-Italica 9, pp. 167–78. Rome: Consiglio Nazionale delle Ricerche.

1987. Le rôle des Etrusques dans la diffusion des produits étrusques et grecs en milieu préceltique et celtique. In *Hallstatt-Studien, Tübinger Kolloquium zur westeuropäischen Hallstatt-Zeit*, pp. 20–43. Weinheim: VCH Verlag, Acta Humaniora.

1992. *Saint-Blaise (fouilles H. Rolland). L'Habitat protohistorique, les céramiques grecques*. Aix-en-Provence: Publications de l'Université de Provence.

Bouloumié, B. and C. Lagrand 1977. Les bassins à rebord perlé et autres bassins de Provence. *Revue Archéologique de Narbonnaise* 10:1–31.

Bourdieu, P. 1977. *Outline of a Theory of Practice*. Cambridge: Cambridge University Press.

Bradley, R. 1984. *The Social Foundations of Prehistoric Britain*. London: Longman.

1985. *Consumption, Change and the Archaeological Record: The Archaeology of Monuments and the Archaeology of Deliberate Deposits*. Occasional Paper 13. Edinburgh: University of Edinburgh Department of Archaeology.

1990. *The Passage of Arms*. Cambridge: Cambridge University Press.

Braudel, F. 1979. *Civilisation matérielle: economie et capitalisme, XV–XVIIIe siècle*. Paris: Armand Colin.

Brun, P. 1987. *Princes et princesses de la Celtique: le premier Age du Fer en Europe, 850–450 av. J.-C.* Paris: Editions Errance.

1988a. Les "résidences princières" comme centres territoriaux: élements de vérification. In J.P. Mohen, A. Duval and C. Eluère (eds.) *Les Princes Celtes et la Méditerranée*, pp. 129–43. Rencontre de l'Ecole du Louvre. Paris: Réunion des Musées Nationaux.

1988b. L'entité Rhin-Suisse-France orientale: nature et évolution. In P. Brun and C. Mordant (eds.) *Le Groupe Rhin-Suisse-France oriental et le notion de civilisation des champs d'Urnes*, pp. 599–618. Nemours: APRAIF.

Brun, P. and P. Pion 1992. L'organisation de l'espace dans la vallée de l'Aisne pendant l'Age du Bronze. In C. Mordant and A. Richards (eds.) *L'Habitat et l'occupation du Sol à l'Age du Bronze*, pp. 117–28. Paris: CTHS.

Brunaux, J.-L., P. Meniel and F. Poplin 1985. *Gournay I: les fouilles sur le sanctuaire et l'oppidum*. Revue Archéologique de Picardie. Paris: Editions Errance.

Brunaux, J.-L. and A. Rapin 1988. *Gournay II: boucliers et lances: dépôts et trophées*. Revue Archéologique de Picardie. Paris: Editions Errance.

Büchsenschütz, O. 1984. *Structures d'habitats et fortifications de l'Age du Fer en France septentrionale*. (Mémoires de la Société Préhistorique Française). Paris: Société Préhistorique Française.

1988. Les habitats hallstattiens et la Méditerranée. In J.P. Mohen, A. Duval and C. Eluère (eds.) *Les Princes celtes et la Méditerranée*, pp. 165–78. Paris: Rencontres de l'Ecole du Louvre. Paris: Réunion des Musées Nationaux.

1989. Neue Ausgrabungen im *oppidum* Bibracte. *Germania* 67(2):541–50.

Büchsenschütz, O., S. Krausz and C. Soyer 1992. Le village celtique des Arènes à Levroux (Indre): état des recherches. In D. Vuaillat (ed.) *Le Berry et le Limousin à l'Age du Fer: artisanat du bois et des matières organiques*, pp. 245–52. Guéret: Actes du XIIIe Colloque de l'AFEAF, May 1989.

Büchsenschütz, O. and I.B.M. Ralston 1987. Réflexions sur l'économie de la Gaule d'après César et les données archéologiques. *Mélanges Colbert de Beaulieu*, pp. 163–73. Paris.

Büchsenschütz, O. and I.B.M. Ralston (n.d.). Approaching diversity in the late Iron Age of western temperate Europe (Iron Age symposium, Cambridge 1988).

Bujna, J. 1982. Spiegelung der Sozialstruktur auf latènezeitlichen Gräberfeldern im Karpathenbecken. *Pamatky archeologicke* 73:312–431.

Bulliot, J.-G. and H. de Fontenay 1875. *L'Art de l'emaillerie chez les Eduens avant l'ère chrétienne*. Paris: Champion.

Burgess, C.B. 1980. *The Age of Stonehenge*. London: Dent.

Burnett, G. (ed.) 1889. *The Exchequer Rolls of Scotland Vol. 12, 1502-1507*. Edinburgh: H.M. Register House.

Buxton, J. 1963. *Chiefs and Strangers: A Study of Political Assimilation among the Mandari*. Oxford: Clarendon.

Byrne, F.J. 1971. Tribes and tribalism in early Ireland. *Ériu* 22:28–66.

Cadoux, J.-L. 1986. Les armes du sanctuaire gaulois de Ribemont-sur-Ancre (Somme) et leur contexte. In A. Duval and J. Gomez de Soto (eds.) *Actes du VIIIe Colloque sur les Ages du Fer en France non-méditerranéenne, Angoul 1984*. Aquitania Supplement 1, pp. 203–10.

1991. Organisation spatiale et chronologie du sanctuaire de Ribemont-sur-Ancre. In J.-L. Brunaux (ed.) *Les Sanctuaires celtiques et le monde méditerranéen*. Paris: Editions Errance, Dossiers de Protohistoire 3.

Caesar. *The Gallic War*. 1963. H. J. Edwards (ed. and trans.). Loeb Classical Library. Cambridge: Harvard University Press.

Cannon, A. 1989. The historical dimension in mortuary

expressions of status and sentiment. *Current Anthropology* 30:437–58.

Carneiro, R.L. 1970. A theory of the origin of the state. *Science* 169:733–8.

1981. The chiefdom: precursor of the state. In G.D. Jones and R.R. Kautz (eds.) *The Transition to Statehood in the New World*, pp. 37–79. Cambridge: Cambridge University Press.

Carter, I. 1973. Marriage patterns and social sectors in Scotland before the eighteenth century. *Scottish Studies* 18:51–60.

Chadwick, N. 1966. *The Druids*. Cardiff: University of Wales Press.

Champion, T.C. 1985. Written sources and the study of the European Iron Age. In T.C. Champion and J.V.S. Megaw (eds.) *Settlement and Society: Aspects of West European Prehistory in the First Millennium BC*, pp. 9–22. New York: St Martin's Press.

Chapman, M. 1992. *The Celts: The Construction of a Myth*. New York: St. Martin's Press.

Chapman, R., I. Kinnes and K. Randsborg (eds.) 1981. *The Archaeology of Death*. Cambridge: Cambridge University Press.

Charles-Edwards, T.M. 1972. Kinship, status and the origins of the hide. *Past and Present* 56:3–33.

1993. *Early Irish and Welsh Kinship*. Oxford: Clarendon Press.

Chaume, B., L. Olivier and W. Reinhard 1994. Keltische "Fürstensitze" westlich des Rheins. *Archäologie in Deutschland* 4:53–4.

Chausserie-Laprée, M. 1985. *Le Quartier de l'Ile à Martigues*. Martigues: Musée d'Art et d'Archéologie.

Childe, V. G. 1925. *The Dawn of European Civilization*. London: Kegan Paul.

1926. *The Aryans: A Study of Indo-European Origins*. London: Kegan Paul.

1934. *New Light on the Most Ancient East: The Oriental Prelude to European Prehistory*. London: Kegan Paul.

1945. Directional changes in funerary practices during 50,000 years. *Man* 4:13–19.

1951. *Social Evolution*. New York: Schuman.

Christaller, W. 1966. *Central Places in Southern Germany*. First published in Jena 1935. C. W. Baskin trans. Englewood Cliffs: Prentice-Hall.

1972. How I discovered the theory of central places. In P.W. English and R.C. Mayfield (eds.) *Man, Space, and Environment*, pp. 601–10. Oxford: Oxford University Press.

Christlein, R. 1973. Besitzabstufungen zur Merowingerzeit im Spiegel reicher Grabfunde aus West- und Südwestdeutschland. *Jahrbuch des Römisch-Germanischen Zentralmuseums* 20:147–80.

Čižmář, M. 1989. Erforschung des keltischen Oppidums Staré Hradisko in den Jahren 1983–1988 (Mähren, CSSR). *Archäologisches Korrespondenzblatt* 19:205–68.

Claessen, H. and P. Skalník 1978a. The early state: theories and hypotheses. In H. Claessen and P. Skalnik (eds.) *The Early State*, pp. 3–29. The Hague: Mouton.

1978b. The early state: models and reality. In H. Claessen and P. Skalnik (eds.) *The Early State*, pp. 637–50. The Hague: Mouton.

Clarke, D.L. 1972. A provisional model of an Iron Age society and its settlement system. In D. L. Clarke (ed.) *Models in Archaeology*, pp. 801–69. London: Methuen.

Clavel-Levêque, M. 1989. *Puzzle gaulois: les Gaules Mémoires, Images, Textes, Histoire*. Centre de Recherches d'Histoire Ancienne 88. Annales Littéraires de l'Université de Besançon 396. Paris: Les Belles-Lettres.

Cohen, A. 1974. *Two Dimensional Man: An Essay on the Anthropology of Power and Symbolism in Complex Societies*. Berkeley: University of California Press.

Collis, J.R. 1977. Iron Age henges? *Archaeologica Atlantica* 2:55–63.

1981. A theoretical study of hillforts. In G. Guilbert (ed.) *Hill-Fort Studies*. Papers presented to Dr. A.H.A. Hogg, pp. 66–76. Leicester.

1982. Gradual growth and sudden change: urbanisation in temperate Europe. In C. Renfrew and S. Shennan (eds.) *Ranking, Resource and Exchange: Aspects of the Archaeology of Early European Society*, pp. 73–8. Cambridge: Cambridge University Press.

1984a. *Oppida: Earliest Towns North of the Alps*. Sheffield: Department of Archaeology and Prehistory, University of Sheffield.

1984b. *The European Iron Age*. London: Oxford University Press.

1986a. Central place theory is dead: long live the central place. In E. Grant (ed.) *Central Places, Archaeology and History*, pp. 37–9. Sheffield: Department of Archaeology and Prehistory, University of Sheffield.

1986b. Adieu Hallstatt! Adieu La Tène! In A. Duval and J. Gomez de Soto (eds.) *Actes du VIIIe Colloque sur les Ages du Fer en France non-Méditerranéenne, Angoulême 1984*, pp. 327–30. Aquitania: Supplément 1.

Forthcoming. Les Celtes, culture, contacts, conflits et

confusion. *Actes de XVIe Colloque de l'AFEAF, Agen.* May 1992.

Colson, E. 1969. African society at the time of the scramble. In L.H. Gann and P. Duignan (eds.) *Colonialism in Africa, 1870–1960,* Vol. I, pp. 27–65. Cambridge: Cambridge University Press.

Comyn, D. 1902. *The History of Ireland by Geoffrey Keating. Foras Feasa ar Eirinn,* Vol. I. London: Irish Texts Society.

Corney, M. 1989. Multiple ditch systems and late Iron Age settlement in central Wessex. In M. Bowden *et al.* (eds.) *From Cornwall to Caithness,* pp. 111–28. British Archaeological Reports 209. Oxford: British Archaeological Reports.

Cregeen, E. 1968. The changing role of the house of Argyll in the Scottish highlands. In I.M. Lewis (ed.) *History and Social Anthropology,* A.S.A. Monograph Number 7, pp. 153–92. London: Tavistock Publications.

1969. The tacksmen and their successors: a study of tenurial reorganisation in Mull, Morvern and Tiree in the early eighteenth century. *Scottish Studies* 13: 931–44.

Crumley, C.L. 1974. *Celtic Social Structure: The Generation of Archaeologically Testable Hypotheses from Literary Evidence.* Anthropological Papers 54, Ann Arbor: University of Michigan Museum of Anthropology.

1976. Toward a locational definition of state systems of settlement. *American Anthropologist* 78:59–73.

1979. Three locational models: an epistemological assessment of anthropology and archaeology. In M.B. Schiffer (ed.) *Advances in Archaeological Method and Theory* Vol. II, pp. 141–73. New York: Academic Press.

1987a. A dialectical critique of hierarchy. In T.C. Patterson and C.W. Gailey (eds.) *Power Relations and State Formation,* pp. 155–69. Washington, D.C.: American Anthropological Association.

1987b. Historical Ecology. In C.L. Crumley and W.H. Marquardt (eds.) *Regional Dynamics: Burgundian Landscapes in Historical Perspective,* pp. 237–64. New York: Academic Press.

1987c. Celtic settlement before the conquest: the dialectics of landscape and power. In C.L. Crumley and W.H. Marquardt (eds.) *Regional Dynamics: Burgundian Landscapes in Historical Perspective,* pp. 403–30. New York: Academic Press.

1988. Region, nation, history: dynamic definitions of otherness. Unpublished paper presented at American Anthropological Association Eighty-Seventh Annual Meeting, Phoenix, Arizona, November 16–20, 1988.

Crumley, C.L. and P.R. Green 1987. Environmental setting. In C.L. Crumley and W.H. Marquardt (eds.) *Regional Dynamics: Burgundian Landscapes in Historical Perspective,* pp. 19–39. San Diego: Academic Press.

Crumley, C.L. and W.H. Marquardt (eds.) 1987. *Regional Dynamics: Burgundian Landscapes in Historical Perspective.* San Diego: Academic Press.

Crumley, C.L., W.H. Marquardt and T.L. Leatherman 1987. Certain factors influencing settlement during the later Iron Age and Gallo-Roman periods: the analysis of intensive survey data. In C.L. Crumley and W.H. Marquardt (eds.) *Regional Dynamics: Burgundian Landscapes in Historical Perspective,* pp. 121–72. San Diego: Academic Press.

Cunliffe, B.W. 1984. *Danebury: An Iron Age Hillfort in Hampshire,* Vol. II. London: Council for British Archaeology Research Reports 52.

1987. *Hengistbury Head, Dorset, Vol. I: The Prehistoric Settlement 3500 BC – AD 500.* Monograph 13. Oxford: Oxford Committee for Archaeology.

1988. *Greeks, Romans and Barbarians: Spheres of Interaction.* New York: Methuen.

Dahl, G. and A. Hjort 1976. *Having Herds: Pastoral Herd Growth and Household Economy.* Stockholm Studies in Social Anthropology 2. Stockholm.

Dalton, G. 1978. The impact of colonization on aboriginal economies in stateless societies. *Research in Economic Anthropology* 1:131–84.

Davies, W. and H. Vierck 1974. The contexts of tribal hideage: social aggression and settlement patterns. *Frühmittelalterliche Studien* 8:223–93.

Debord, J. *et al.* 1989. Les fossés couverts du site gaulois tardif de Villeneuve-Saint-Germain (Aisne). In F. Audouze and O. Büchsenschütz (eds.) *Architectures des Ages des Métaux, fouilles récentes,* pp. 121–35. Paris: Dossiers de Protohistoire 2.

Déchelette, J. 1927. *Manuel d'archéologie préhistorique, celtique, et gallo-romaine,* Vol. IV. Paris: Picard.

Dedet, B. 1992. *Rites funéraires protohistoriques dans les Garigues languedociennes: approche ethno-archéologique.* Paris: CNRS.

Dehn, W. 1951. Die gallischen "oppida" bei Cäsar. *Saalburger Jahrbuch* 10:36–49.

de Marinis, R. 1988. Nouvelles données sur le commerce entre le monde méditerranéen et l'Italie septentrionale du VIIe au Ve siècle avant J.-C. In J.-P. Mohen, A. Duval and C. Eleuère (eds.) *Les Princes celtes et la Méditerranée,* pp. 45–56. Rencontres de l'Ecole du Louvre. Paris: Réunion des Musées Nationaux.

Demoule, J.-P. 1989. D'un âge à l'autre: temps, style et société dans la transition Hallstatt/La Tène. In M. Ulrix-Closset and M. Otte (eds.) *Hallstatt: la civilisation Hallstatt*, pp. 141–71. Liège: Etudes et Recherches Archéologique de la Université de Liège 36.

Demoule, J.-P. and M. Ilett 1985. First-millennium settlement and society in northern France. In T.C. Champion and J.V.S. Megaw (eds.) *Settlement and Society: Aspects of West European Prehistory in the First Millennium B.C.*, pp. 193–221. Leicester: Leicester University Press.

de Navarro, J.M. 1972. *The Finds from the Site of La Tène I: Scabbards and the Swords Found in Them*. London: The British Academy.

Denton, G. and W. Karlen 1973. Holocene climatic variations – their pattern and possible cause. *Quaternary Research* 3(2):155–205.

Dickinson, J. 1963. *Death of a Republic: Politics and Political Thought at Rome 59–44 BC*. New York: Macmillan.

Dietler, M. 1989. Greeks, Etruscans and thirsty barbarians: Early Iron Age interaction in the Rhône basin of France. In T. Champion (ed.) *Center and Periphery: Comparative Studies in Archaeology*, pp. 127–41. London: Unwin Hyman.

1990a. *Exchange, Consumption, and Colonial Interaction in the Rhône Basin of France: A Study of Early Iron Age Political Economy*. Ph.D. Dissertation. Ann Arbor: University of Michigan Microfilms.

1990b. Driven by drink: the role of drinking in the political economy and the case of Early Iron Age France. *Journal of Anthropological Archaeology* 9:352–406.

1992. Commerce du vin et contacts culturels en Gaule au Premier Age du Fer. In M. Bats, G. Bertucchi, G. Congès and H. Tréziny (eds.) *Marseille grecque et la Gaule*. Etudes Massaliètes 3, pp. 401–10. Lattes: ADAM Editions.

1994a. Feasts and commensal politics in the political economy: food, power, and status in prehistoric Europe. In P. Wiessner and W. Schiefenhövel (eds.) *Food and the Status Quest*. Oxford: Berg Publishers. In press.

1994b. "Our Ancestors the Gauls": archaeology, ethnic nationalism, and the manipulation of Celtic identity in modern Europe. *American Anthropologist* 96(3):584–605.

Dillon, M. (ed. and trans.) 1962. *Lebor na Cert. The Book of Rights*. London.

Dillon, M. and N. Chadwick 1972. *The Celtic Realms.*

Second edition. London: Weidenfeld and Nicolson.

Dodgshon, R.A. 1981. *Land and Society in Early Scotland*. Oxford: Clarendon Press.

1987. *The European Past*. London: Macmillan Educational.

1989. 'Pretense of blude' and 'place of thair duelling': the nature of Scottish clans, 1500-1745. In R.A.B. Houston and I.D. Whyte (eds.) *Scottish Society: 1500–1800*, pp. 169–98. Cambridge: Cambridge University Press.

1993. Strategies of farming in the western highlands and islands prior to crofting and the clearances. *Economic History Review* 46:679–701.

Dodgshon R.A. and E.G. Olsson 1988. Productivity and nutrient use in eighteenth century Scottish highland townships. *Geografiska Annaler* 70B:39–51.

Drda, P., K. Motyková and A. Rybová 1991. L'acropolis de Závist. In J.-L. Brunaux (ed.) *Les Sanctuaires celtiques et le monde méditerranéen*. Paris: Editions Errance, Dossiers de Protohistoire 3.

Driehaus, J. 1974. Review of H. Zürn *Hallstattforschungen in Nordwürttemberg*. *Prähistorische Zeitschrift* 49:152–62.

Duval, A. 1983. Autour de Vercingetorix: de l'archéologie à l'histoire économique et sociale. In J. Collis, A. Duval and R. Perichon (eds.) *Le Deuxième Age du Fer en Auvergne et en Forez*, pp. 298–335. Sheffield: University of Sheffield.

1991. Celtic society in the first century B.C. In S. Moscati *et al.* (eds.) *The Celts*, pp. 485–90. New York: Rizzoli.

Duval, A. and J. Gomez de Soto (eds.) 1986. *Actes du VIIIe Colloque sur les Ages du Fer en France non-méditerranéenne, Angoulême 1984*. Aquitania: Supplément 1.

Duval, P.-M. 1986. Sources and distribution of chieftaincy wealth in ancient Gaul. In D.E. Evans, J.G. Griffith and E.M. Jope (eds.) *Proceedings of the Seventh International Congress of Celtic Studies*, pp. 19–24. Oxford: Cranham Press.

Duval, P.-M. and V. Kruta (eds.) 1979. *Les mouvements céltiques du Ve au Ier siècle avant notre ère*. Paris: CNRS.

Earle, T.K. 1976. A nearest-neighbor analysis of two Formative settlement systems. In K. V. Flannery (ed.) *The Early Mesoamerican Village*, pp. 196–223. New York: Academic Press.

1978. *Economic and Social Organization of a Complex Chiefdom: The Halela District, Kaua'i, Hawaii*. University of Michigan, Museum of Anthropology, Anthropological Papers 63.

1987. Chiefdoms in archaeological and ethnohistorical perspective. *Annual Reviews in Anthropology* 16: 270–308.

1989. The evolution of chiefdoms. *Current Anthropology* 30(1):84–8.

Edwards, N. 1990. *The Archaeology of Early Medieval Ireland*. Philadelphia: University of Pennsylvania Press.

Egger, R. 1961. *Die Stadt auf dem Magdalensberg*. Vienna: Böhlau.

Eggers, H.J. 1951. *Der Römische Import im Freien Germanien*. Hamburg: Atlas der Urgeschichte.

1986. *Einführung in die Vorgeschichte*. Third edition. Munich: Serie Piper.

Eggert, M. 1988. Riesentumuli und Sozialorganisation: Vergleichende Betrachtungen zu den sogennanten "Fürstengrabhügeln" der späten Hallstattzeit. *Archäologisches Korrespondenzblatt* 18:263–74.

1989. Die "Fürstensitze" der Späthallstattzeit: Bemerkungen zu einem archäologischen Konstrukt. *Hammaburg* NF 9:53–66.

Ekholm, K. 1977. External exchange and the transformation of central African societies. In J. Friedman and M.J. Rowlands (eds.) *The Evolution of Social Systems*, pp. 115–36. London: Duckworth.

Eogan, G. 1977. The Iron Age – Early Christian settlement at Knowth, Co. Meath, Ireland. In V. Markotic (ed.) *Ancient Europe and the Mediterranean*, pp. 68–76. Warminister: Aris and Phillips.

Evans, D.E. 1977. The contribution of (non-Celtiberian) Continental Celtic to the reconstruction of the Celtic "Grundsprache". In K.H. Schmidt (ed.) *Indogermanisch und Keltisch*, pp. 66–88. Wiesbaden: Ludwig Reichert Verlag.

Feinman, G. and J. Neitzel 1984. Too many types: an overview of sedentary pre-state societies in the Americas. In M. Schiffer (ed.) *Advances in Archaeological Method and Theory*, Vol. 7, pp. 39–102. New York: Academic Press.

Feugère, M. and C. Rolley 1991. *La Vaiselle Tonds-Républicaine Bronze*. Dijon: Université de Bourgogne.

Finch, T.F. 1971. *The Soils of County Clare*. National Soil Survey of Ireland, Soil Survey Bulletin 23. Dublin: An Foras Talúntais.

Finley, M.I. 1982. *Economy and Society in Ancient Greece*. New York: Viking Press.

Firth, R. 1936. *We, the Tikopia*. Boston: Beacon Press.

Fischer, F. 1981a. Die Kelten und ihre Geschichte. In K. Bittel *et al*. (eds.) *Die Kelten in Baden-Württemberg*, pp. 45–76. Stuttgart: Konrad Theiss.

1981b. Stadt, Gesellschaft und Siedlung. In K. Bittel *et al*. (eds.) *Die Kelten in Baden-Württemberg*, pp. 77–84. Stuttgart: Konrad Theiss.

1981c. Sinsheim-Dühren. In K. Bittel, W. Kimmig and S. Schiek (eds.) *Die Kelten in Baden-Württemberg*, pp. 471–2. Stuttgart: Konrad Theiss.

1982. Frühkeltische Fürstengräber in Mitteleuropa. *Antike Welt: Zeitschrift für Archäologie und Kulturgeschichte* 13:1–72. Feldmeilen: Raggi Verlag.

1987. Der Westkreis der Hallstatt-Kultur im Überblick. In *Hallstatt-Studien: Tübinger Kolloquium zur westeuropäischen Hallstatt-Zeit 1980*, pp. 1–19. Weinheim: VCH Acta humaniora.

1988. Südwestdeutschland im letzten Jahrhundert vor Christi Geburt. In D. Planck (ed.) *Archäologie in Württemberg*, pp. 235–50. Stuttgart: Konrad Theiss.

Fischer, T., S. Rieckhoff-Pauli and K. Spindler 1984. Grabungen in der spätkeltischen Siedlung im Sulztal bei Berching-Pollanten. *Germania* 62:311–63.

Fitzpatrick, A. 1985. The distribution of Dressel 1 amphorae in northwestern Europe. *Oxford Journal of Archaeology* 4:305–40.

Fletcher, R. (n.d.). What is Manching? A material behavior enquiry. Iron Age Symposium, Cambridge 1988.

Fleury, B. 1986. Late Iron Age chronology in the light of new material from the Aisne Valley (Northern France). *Institute of Archaeology Bulletin* 23:29–46.

Flouest, J.-L. 1990. Inventaire des amphores massalières des régions Berry, Bourgogne et Franche-Comté. In M. Bats (ed.) *Les Amphores de Marseille grecque*, pp. 253–8. Etudes Massaliètes 2. Aix-en-Provence: Publications de l'Université de Provence.

Flouest, J.-L. and I.M. Stead 1977. Une tombe de La Tène III à Hannogne (Ardennes). *Mémoires de la Société d'Agriculture, Commerce, Sciences et Arts de Département de la Marne* 92:55–72.

Fox, R.G. 1976. Lineage cells and regional definition in complex societies. In C.A. Smith (ed.) *Regional Analysis*, Vol. 11, *Social Systems*, pp. 95–121. New York: Academic Press.

Frankenstein, S. and M.J. Rowlands 1978. The internal structure and regional context of early Iron Age society in southwest Germany. *Institute of Archaeology Bulletin* 15:73–112.

Freidin, N. 1982. *The Early Iron Age in the Paris Basin, Hallstatt C and D*. Oxford: British Archaeological Reports International Series 1, pp. 1–82. Marseille: Société Anonyme du Sémaphore de Marseille.

Fried, M. 1960. On the evolution of social stratification and the state. In S. Diamond (ed.) *Culture in History*. New York: Columbia University Press.

1967. *The Evolution of Political Society*. New York: Random House.

Friedman, J. and M.J. Rowlands 1977. Notes towards an epigenetic model of the evolution of "civilization." In J. Friedman and M.J. Rowlands (eds.) *The Evolution of Social Systems*. London: Duckworth.

Fröhlich, S. 1990. Zum Grabhügelfeld von Emsbüren. *Archäologie in Deutschland 1990* 4:45–6.

Frost, J. 1978 [1893]. *The History and Topography of the County of Clare . . .* Dublin: The Mercier Press.

Fulford, M. 1987. Calleva Atrebatum: an interim report on the excavation of the *oppidum*, 1980–6 *Proceedings of the Prehistoric Society* 53:271–8.

Furger-Gunti, A. 1982. Der "Goldfund von Saint-Louis" bei Basel und ähnliche keltische Schatzfunde. *Zeitschrift für Schweizerische Archäologie und Kunstgeschichte* 39:1–47.

Fustel de Coulanges, N.D. 1908. *Histoire des institutions politiques de l'ancienne France: la Gaule romaine*. Paris: Hachette.

Gamble, C. 1981. Social control and the economy. In A. Sheridan and G. Bailey (eds.) *Economic Archaeology: Towards an Integration of Ecological and Social Approaches*, pp. 215–29. British Archaeological Reports International Series 96. Oxford: British Archaeological Reports.

1986. Hunter-gatherers and the origin of states. In J.A. Hall (ed.) *States in History*, pp. 22–47. Oxford: Basil Blackwell.

Gamst, F.C. 1970. Peasants and elites without urbanism: the civilization of Ethiopia. *Comparative Studies in Society and History* 12(4):373–92.

Garnett, T. 1799. *Observations on a Tour through the Highlands and Part of the Western Isles of Scotland*. Vols. I and II. London: J. Stockdale.

Gasco, Y. 1984. Les tumulus du Premier Age du Fer en Languedoc Oriental. *Archéologie en Languedoc* 9:1–246.

Gebhard, R. 1989. *Der Glasschmuck aus dem Oppidum von Manching*. Wiesbaden: Franz Steiner.

1991. *Die Fibeln aus dem Oppidum von Manching*. Wiesbaden: Franz Steiner.

Gelzer, M. 1968. *Caesar: Politician and Statesman*. Oxford: Oxford University Press.

Geoffrey of Monmouth 1929. *Historia Regum Britannie of Geoffrey of Monmouth*. R. Ellis Jones (trans.). London: Longmans, Green and Co.

Gerriets, M. 1983. Economy and society: clientship according to Irish laws. *Cambridge Medieval Celtic Studies* 6:43–86.

1987. Kingship and exchange in Pre-Viking Ireland. *Cambridge Medieval Celtic Studies* 13: 39–72.

Geselowitz, M.N. 1994. Labor specialization in late Iron Age temperate Europe: the evidence from the Kelheim iron. In P.S. Wells (ed.) *Settlement, Economy, and Cultural Change at the End of the European Iron Age: Excavations at Kelheim in Bavaria, 1987–1991*, pp. 77–82. Michigan: International Monographs in Prehistory.

Gibson, D.B. 1988. Agro-pastoralism and regional social organization in early Ireland. In D.B. Gibson and M.N. Geselowitz (eds.) *Tribe and Polity in Prehistoric Europe*, pp. 41–68. New York: Plenum.

1990. *Tulach Commáin: A View of an Irish Chiefdom*. Ph.D. dissertation. Ann Arbor: University Microfilms International.

Gibson, D.B. and M.N. Geselowitz. 1988a. The evolution of complex society in late prehistoric Europe: toward a paradigm. In D.B. Gibson and M.N. Geselowitz (eds.) *Tribe and Polity in Late Prehistoric Europe*, pp. 3–37. New York: Plenum.

Gibson, D.B. and M.N. Geselowitz (eds.) 1988b. *Tribe and Polity in Late Prehistoric Europe*. New York: Plenum.

Giddens, A. 1979. *Central Problems in Social Theory*. Berkeley: University of California Press.

Ginsburg, N. 1961. *Atlas of Economic Development*. Chicago: University of Chicago Press.

Giraldus Cambrensis 1978a. *Expugnatio Hibernica: The Conquest of Ireland*. A.B. Scott and F.X. Martin (trans. and eds.). Dublin: Royal Irish Academy.

1978b. *The Journey through Wales/The Description of Wales*. L. Thorpe (trans.). London: Penguin Books.

1982. *The History and Topography of Wales*. J.J. O'Meara (trans.). London: Penguin Books.

Gleeson, D. F. 1947. *Roscrea: A History of the Parish from Earliest Times to the Present Day . . .* Dublin: Sign of the Three Candles.

Goessler, P. 1950. Geschichte in der Vorgeschichte. *Praehistorische Zeitschrift* 34:5–17.

Gosden, C. 1985. Gifts and kin in early Iron Age Europe. *Man* (NS) 20:475–93.

Goudineau, C. 1989. L'apparition de l'écriture en Gaule. In J.-P. Mohen (ed.) *Le Temps de la Préhistoire*, Vol. I, pp. 236–8. Paris: Société Préhistorique Française.

Goudineau, C. and C. Peyre 1993. *Bibracte et les Eduens: à la découverte d'un peuple gaulois*. Collection Hauts Lieux d'Histoire. Paris: Editions Errance/Centre archéologique européen du Mont-Beuvray.

Grant, E. (ed.) 1986. *Central Places, Archaeology, and History*. Sheffield: Department of Archaeology and Prehistory.

Grant, I.F. 1930. *Social and Economic Development of Scotland before 1603*. Edinburgh: Oliver and Boyd.

Gray, M. 1957. *The Highland Economy 1750-1850*. Edinburgh: Oliver and Boyd.

Green, M. 1986. *The Gods of the Celts*. Totowa, NJ: Barnes and Noble.

Grenier, A. 1924. *Les Gaulois*. Paris.

Guichard, V., P. Pion, F. Malacher and J. Collis 1993. A propos de la circulation monétaire en Gaule chevelue aux IIe et Ie siècles avant J.-C. *Revue Archéologique du Centre* 32:25–55.

Guillaumet, J.-P. and P. Barral 1991. Le sanctuaire celtique de Mirebeau-sur-Bèze, Côte d'Or. In J.-L. Brunaux (ed.) *Les Sanctuaires celtiques et le monde méditerranéen*, pp. 193–5. Paris: Editions Errance, Dossiers de Protohistoire 3.

Guinot, N. 1987. Position of the dialects of the Morvan and Charolais in linguistic history. In C.L. Crumley and W.H. Marquardt (eds.) *Regional Dynamics: Burgundian Landscapes in Historical Perspective*, pp. 387–98. San Diego: Academic Press.

Gunn, J. 1994. Global climate and regional biocultural diversity. In C.L. Crumley (ed.) *Historical Ecology*, pp. 67–97. Santa Fe: School of American Research Press.

Gunn, J. and R.E.W. Adams 1981. Climatic change, culture, and civilization in North America. *World Archaeology* 13(1):85–100.

Gwynn, A. and D. Gleeson 1962. *A History of the Diocese of Killaloe*. Dublin: M.H. Gill.

Hachmann, R. 1970. *Die Goten und Skandinavier*. Berlin: Walter de Gruyter.

Haffner, A. 1965. Späthallstattzeitliche Funde aus dem Saarland. *Bericht der Staatlichen Denkmalpflege im Saarland* 12:7–34.

1989. *Gräber – Spiegel des Lebens: Zum Totenbrauchtum der Kelten und Römer am Beispiel des Treverer-Gräberfeldes Wederath-Belginum*. Mainz: Philipp von Zabern.

Harding, A. 1984. Aspects of social evolution in the Bronze Age. In J. Bintliff (ed.) *European Social Evolution: Archaeological Perspectives*, pp. 135–45. Bradford: University of Bradford Press.

Harding, D.W. 1990. Changing perspectives in the Atlantic Iron Age. In I. Armit (ed.) *Beyond the Brochs: Changing Perspectives on the Later Iron Age in Atlantic Scotland*, pp. 5–16. Edinburgh: University of Edinburgh Press.

Härke, H. 1979. *Settlement Types and Patterns in the West Hallstatt Province*. British Archaeological Reports International Series 57. Oxford: British Archaeological Reports.

1982. Early Iron Age hill settlement in west central Europe: patterns and developments. *Oxford Journal of Archaeology* 1(1):187.

1989. Die Anglo-Amerikanische Diskussion zur Gräberanalyse. *Archäologisches Korrespondenzblatt* 19: 185–94.

Haselgrove, C.C. 1986. Central places in British Iron Age studies: a review and some problems. In E. Grant (ed.) *Central Places, Archaeology, and History*, pp. 3–12. Sheffield: Department of Archaeology and Prehistory.

1987. Culture process on the periphery. In M.J. Rowlands *et al.* (eds.) *Center and Periphery in Ancient World Systems*, pp. 104–24. Cambridge: Cambridge University Press.

1988. Coinage and complexity: archaeological analysis of socio-political change in Britain and non-Mediterranean Gaul during the later Iron Age. In D.B. Gibson and M.N. Geselowitz (eds.) *Tribe and Polity in Late Prehistoric Europe*, pp. 69–96. New York: Plenum.

1989. The later Iron Age in southern Britain and beyond. *Britannia Monograph* 11:1–18.

1990. Later Iron Age settlement in the Aisne Valley. *Actes du XIIe Colloque de l'Association française pour l'étude de l'Age du Fer, Quimper.*

Hassan, F.A. 1994. Population ecology and civilization in ancient Egypt. In C.L. Crumley (ed.) *Historical Ecology*, pp. 155–81. Santa Fe: School of American Research Press.

Hencken, H. O'N. 1938. Cahercommaun: a stone fort in County Clare. Extra volume of the *Journal of the Royal Society of Antiquaries of Ireland*. Dublin: Hodges and Figgis.

1950. Lagore Crannog: an Irish royal residence of the 7th to 10th centuries A.D. *Proceedings of the Royal Irish Academy* 53C:1–247.

Herity, M. 1991. The phases of the Irish Neolithic. *Journal of Indo-European Studies* 19(1/2).

Hill, J.D. 1989. Rethinking the Iron Age. *Scottish Archaeological Review* 6:16–23.

Hingley, R. 1984. Towards social analysis in archaeology: Celtic society in the Upper Thames Valley. In B. Cunliffe and D. Miles (eds.) *Aspects of the Iron Age in Central Southern Britain*, pp. 72–88. Oxford: Oxford Committee for Archaeology.

1989. Iron Age settlement and society in Central and Southern Warwickshire. In A. Gibson (ed.) *Midlands Prehistory*, pp. 122–57. British Archaeological Reports 204. Oxford: British Archaeological Reports.

HMC [Historical Manuscript Commission] 1874. *Fourth*

Report of the Royal Commission on Historical Manuscripts. London: HMC.

Hobsbawm, E.J. 1983. Introduction: inventing traditions. In E. Hobsbawm and T. Tanger (eds.) *The Invention of Tradition*, pp. 1–14. Cambridge: Cambridge University Press.

Hodder, I. 1979. Economic and social stress and material culture. *American Antiquity* 44:446–54.

1988. Material culture texts and social change: A theoretical discussion and some archaeological examples. *Proceedings of the Prehistoric Society* 54:67–75.

Hodson, F.R. 1968. *The La Tène Cemetery of Münsingen-Rain.* Acta Bernensia 5. Berne: Stämpfli.

1977. Quantifying Hallstatt: some initial results. *American Antiquity* 42:394–412.

1979. Inferring status from burials in Iron Age Europe: some recent attempts. In B.C. Burnham and J. Kingsbury (eds.) *France Before the Romans*, pp. 157–91. London: Thames and Hudson.

Hoffman, M.A., H. A. Hamroush and R. O. Allen 1986. A model of urban development for the Hierakonpolis region from Predynastic through Old Kingdom times. *Journal of American Research in Central Egypt* 23:175–87.

Hubert, H. 1934. *The Greatness and Decline of the Celts.* New York: Arno Press Reprint.

Humphreys, S. 1978. *Anthropology and the Greeks.* London: Routledge and Kegan Paul.

Isaac, B.L. 1975. Resource scarcity, competition, and cooperation in cultural evolution. In I.A. Brady and B.L. Isaac (eds.) *A Reader in Culture Change*, Vol. I, *Theories*, pp. 125–43. Cambridge, Mass.: Schekman.

Jacobi, G. 1974. *Werkzeug und Gerät aus dem Oppidum von Manching.* Wiesbaden: Franz Steiner.

Jaenen, C.J. 1982. "Les Sauvages Ameriquains": persistence into the 18th century of traditional French concepts and constructs for comprehending Amerindians. *Ethnohistory* 29:43–56.

James, E. 1988. *The Franks.* Oxford: Blackwell.

Jamieson, R. (ed.) 1876. *Burt's Letters from the North of Scotland.* 5th edition (first published 1754). Edinburgh: R. Fenner.

Jansová, L. 1986. *Hrazany: das keltische Oppidum in Böhmen.* Prague: Ceskoslovenské Akademie Ved.

Joachim, H.-E. 1968. *Die Hunsrück-Eifel Kultur am Mittel-Rhein.* Cologne: Böhlau.

1973. Ein reich ausgestattetes Wagengrab der Spätlatènezeit aus Neuwied, Stadtteil Heimbach-Weis. *Bonner Jahrbücher* 173:1–44.

Joffroy, R. 1979. *Vix et ses trésors.* Paris: Tallandier.

Johnson, A. and T.K. Earle 1987. *The Evolution of Human Societies.* Stanford: Stanford University Press.

Johnson, G.A. 1982. Organizational structure and scalar stress. In C. Renfrew, M.J. Rowlands and B.A. Segraves (eds.) *Theory and Explanation in Archaeology*, pp. 389–422. New York: Academic Press.

Johnson, S. 1971. *A Journey to the Western Islands of Scotland.* M. Lascelles (ed.) New Haven: Yale University Press.

Jones, G.D. and R.R. Kautz (eds.) 1981. *The Transition to Statehood in the New World.* Cambridge: Cambridge University Press.

Jucker, H. 1973. Altes und Neues zur Grächwiler Hydria. In *Zur griechischen Kunst: Festschrift Hans-Jörg Bloesch*, pp. 42–62. Berne: Francke Verlag.

Kellner, H.-J. 1990. *Die Münzfunde von Manching und die Keltischen Fundmünzen aus Südbayern.* Stuttgart: Franz Steiner.

Kelly, F. 1989. *A Guide to Early Irish Law.* Dublin: Dublin Institute for Advanced Studies.

Kilian-Dirlmeier, I. 1970. Zur jüngeren Hallstattzeit im Elsass. *Jahrbuch des Römisch-Germanischen Zentralmuseums* 1970:84–93. Mainz: Phillip von Zabern.

Kimmig, W. 1969. Zum Problem späthallstättischer Adelssitze. In K.H. Otto and J. Hermann (eds.) *Siedlung, Burg und Stadt: Studien zu ihren Anfängen.* Festschrift Paul Grimm. Schriften der Sektion für Vor- und Frühgeschichte 25, pp. 95–113. Berlin: Deutsche Akademie der Wissenschaften.

1983a. *Die Heuneburg an der oberen Donau.* Führer zu archäologischen Denkmälern in Baden-Württemberg 1. Stuttgart: Konrad Theiss Verlag.

1983b. Die griechische Kolonisation im westlichen Mittelmeergebiet und ihre Wirkung auf die Landschaften des westlichen Mitteleuropa. *Jahrbuch des Römisch-Germanischen Zentralmuseums Mainz* 30:5–78.

Kimmig, W. and W. Rest 1959. Ein Fürstengrab der späten Hallstattzeit von Kappel-am-Rhein. *Jahrbuch des Römisch-Germanischen Zentralmuseums Mainz* 1: 179–216.

Kipp, R.S. and Schortman, E.M. 1989. The political impact of trade in chiefdoms. *American Anthropologist* 91(2):370–85.

Kirch, P.V. 1980. Polynesian prehistory: cultural adaptation in island ecosystems. *American Scientist* 68:339–48.

Kirchoff, P. 1955. The principles of clanship in human society. *Davidson Journal of Anthropology* 1:1–11.

Kluge, J. 1987. Die latènezeitliche Besiedlung des Kelheimer Beckens, Niederbayern. University of Münster: Doctoral dissertation.

Kossack, G. 1954. Pferdegeschirr aus Gräbern der älteren Hallstattzeit Bayerns. *Jahrbuch des Römisch-Germanischen Zentralmuseums Mainz* 1:11–178.

1959. *Südbayern während der Hallstattzeit* Vols. I and II. Berlin: Walter de Gruyter and Co.

Kostrzewski, J. 1950. *Compte-rendu des fouilles de Biskupin.* Poznan.

Krämer, W. 1960. The *oppidum* at Manching. *Antiquity* 34:191–200.

1975. Modell von Gehöften im keltischen Oppidum Manching. *Ausgrabungen in Deutschland 1950–1975* 3: 327. Mainz: Römisch-Germanisches Zentralmuseum.

1985. *Die Grabfunde von Manching und die Latènezeitlichen Flachgräber in Südbayern.* Wiesbaden: Franz Steiner.

Krämer, W. and F. Maier 1970–89. *Die Ausgrabungen in Manching,* 11 vols. Stuttgart.

Kristiansen, K. 1982. The formation of tribal systems in later European prehistory: northern Europe. In C. Renfrew *et al.* (eds.) *Theory and Explanation in Archaeology: The Southhampton Conference,* pp. 241–80. New York: Academic Press.

Kruta, V., M. Szabó and E. Lessing 1978. *Les Celtes.* Paris: Hatier.

Kurz, S. 1987. Nachhallstattzeitliche Funde aus dem Grabhügelfeld vom Burrenhof. *OPUSCULA: Tübinger Beiträge zur Vor- und Frühgeschichte* 2. Festschrift Franz Fischer. Universität Tübingen: Institut für Vor- und Frühgeschichte.

Labov, W. 1972. *Language in the Inner City: Studies in the Black English Vernacular.* Philadelphia: University of Pennsylvania Press.

Lagrand, C. 1963. La céramique "pseudo-ionienne" dans la vallée du Rhône. *Cahiers Rhodaniens* 10:37–82.

Laing, L. 1985. The Romanisation of Ireland. *Peritia* 4:261–78.

Laistner, M.L.W. 1947. *The Greater Roman Historians.* Berkeley: University of California Press.

Lamb, H. H. 1977. *Climate: Past, Present, and Future,* 2 vols. London: Methuen.

Lappe, S. 1979. Keltische Glasarmringe und Ringperlen aus Thüringen. *Alt-Thüringen* 16:84–111.

Legendre, J.-P. 1989. Organisation spatiale et "pouvoir princier" dans la région de Hagenau (Bas-Rhin) à la fin de l'époque hallstattienne. *Revue Archéologique de l'Est et du Centre-Est* 40:199–203.

Lemonnier, P. 1990. *Guerres et festins: paix, échanges et compétition dans les Highlands de Nouvelle-Guinée.* Paris: Maison des Sciences de l'Homme.

Lengyel, L. 1969. *Le Secret des Celtes.* Paris: Choisy-le-Roi.

Lerat, L. 1958. L'amphore de bronze de Conliège (Jura). *Actes du Colloque sur les Influences Helléniques en Gaule,* pp. 89–98. Dijon: l'Université de Dijon.

Le Roy Ladurie, E. 1971. *Times of Feast, Times of Famine: A History of Climate since the Year 1000.* New York: Doubleday.

Lewis, H. 1978. Warfare and the origin of the state: another formulation. Paper presented at the Post-Plenary Session: The Study of the State. Tenth International Congress of Anthropological and Ethnological Sciences, New Delhi, India, December 21, 1978.

Lewuillon, S. 1990. Affinités, parentés et territoires en Gaule indépendante: fragments d'anthropologie. *Dialogues d'Histoire Ancienne* 16:2–59.

Liebschwager, C. 1972. Zur Frühlatènekultur in Baden-Württemberg. *Archäologisches Korrespondenzblatt* 2:143–8.

Lorenz, H. 1986. *Rundgang durch eine keltische "Stadt".* Pfaffenhofen: W. Ludwig.

Losch, A. 1954. *The Economics of Location.* W. H. Woglom and W. F. Stolper (trans.). New Haven: Yale University Press. (Originally published in 1943).

Lucas, A.T. 1989. *Cattle in Ancient Ireland.* Kilkenny: Boethius.

McCone, K. 1990. *Pagan Past and Christian Present.* Maynooth: An Sagart.

McCulloch, W.S. 1945. A heterarchy of values determined by the topology of nervous nets. *Bulletin of Mathematical Biophysics* 7:89–93.

Macdonald, A. and A. Macdonald 1896–1904. *The Clan Donald,* 3 vols. Inverness: Northern Counties Publishing Company.

Macdonald, J. 1978. *Clan Donald.* Loanhead: Macdonald Publishers.

MacDowell, D.M. 1972. *The Law in Classical Athens.* Ithaca: Cornell University Press.

McGuire, R. 1983. Breaking down cultural complexity: inequality and heterogeneity. In M.B. Schiffer (ed.) *Advances in Archaeological Method and Theory,* Vol. VI, pp. 91–142. New York: Academic Press.

MacKendrick, P. 1987. The Romans in Burgundy. In C.L. Crumley and W.H. Marquardt (eds.) *Regional Dynamics,* pp. 431–45. San Diego: Academic Press.

Macleod, R.C. (ed.) 1938–9. *The Book of Dunvegan,* 2 vols. Aberdeen: Third Spalding Club.

M'Neill, G.P. (ed.) 1897. *The Exchequer Rolls of Scotland,* Vol. XVII, *A.D. 1537–1542.* Edinburgh: HM Register House.

Mac Néill, E. 1911. Early Irish population-groups: their

nomenclature, classification, and chronology. *Proceedings of the Royal Irish Academy* 29C: 59–114.

1919. *Phases in Irish History*. Dublin: Gill and Son.

1921. *Celtic Ireland*. Dublin: M. Lester Ltd.

1923. Ancient Irish law: the law of status or franchise. *Proceedings of the Royal Irish Academy* 36 C:265–316.

1941–3. Military service in medieval Ireland. *Journal of the Cork Historical and Archaeological Society*, Series 2:46–8; 6–16.

Mac Niocaill, G. 1972. *Ireland Before the Vikings*. Dublin: Gill and Macmillan.

Macphail, J.R.N. (ed.) 1914. *Highland Papers*, Vol I. Second series, Vol. V. Edinburgh: Scottish History Society.

Macpherson, A.G. 1966. An old highland genealogy and the evolution of Scottish clans. *Scottish Studies* 10:142.

Maier, F. 1985. Vorbericht über die Ausgrabung 1984 in dem spätkeltischen Oppidum von Manching. *Germania* 63:17–55.

1986. Vorbericht über die Ausgrabung 1985 in dem spätkeltischen Oppidum von Manching. *Germania* 64:1–43.

Maine, Sir H. 1861. *Ancient Law*. London: J. Murray.

Malacher, F. and J.R. Collis 1992. Chronology, production and distribution of coins in the Auvergne. In M. Mays (ed.) *Celtic Coinage: Britain and Beyond*, pp. 189–206. The Eleventh Oxford Symposium on Coinage and Monetary History. British Archaeological Reports 222. Oxford: British Archaeological Reports.

Mann, M. 1986. *The Sources of Social Power*, Vol. I. Cambridge: Cambridge University Press.

Maquet, J. 1961. *The Premise of Inequality in Ruanda: A Study of Political Relations in a Central African Kingdom*. Oxford: Oxford University Press.

Marcus, G. and M. Fisher 1986. *Anthropology as Cultural Critique*. Chicago: University of Chicago Press.

Marquardt, W. and C. Crumley 1987. Theoretical issues in the analysis of spatial patterning. In C. Crumley and W. Marquardt (eds.) *Regional Dynamics*, pp. 1–18. New York: Academic Press.

Martin, M. 1716. *A Description of the Western Islands of Scotland*. Second edition. London: A. Bell.

Masson, D. (ed.) 1884. *Register of the Privy Council*, Vol. VI, *1599-1604*. Edinburgh: HM Register House.

Masson, D. (ed.) 1889. *Register of the Privy Council*, Vol. IX, *1610-1613*. Edinburgh: HM Register House.

Meduna, J. 1970. Das keltische Oppidum Staré Hradisko in Mähren. *Germania* 48: 34–59.

Megaw, J.V.S. 1970. *Art of the European Iron Age*. New York: Harper and Row.

Meniel, P. 1984. *Contribution à l'histoire de l'élevage en Picardie*. Revue Archéologique de Picardie. Numéro spécial. Amiens.

Menzies, D.P. 1894. *The Red and White Book of Menzies: The History of the Clan Menzies and its Chiefs*. Glasgow: privately printed.

Metzler, J. 1992. Les sanctuaires gaulois en territoire trévire. In J.-L. Brunaux (ed.) *Les Sanctuaires celtiques et le monde méditerranéen*, pp. 28–41. Dossier de Protohistoire 3. Paris: Edition Errance.

Metzler, J., R. Waringo, R. Bis and N. Metzler-Zens 1991. *Clemency et les tombes de l'aristocracie en Gaul belgique*. Luxembourg: Dossiers d'Archéologie du Musée National d'Histoire et d'Art.

Milisauskas, S. 1978. *European Prehistory*. Studies in Archaeology. New York: Academic Press.

Milisauskas, S. and J. Kruk 1984. Settlement organization and the appearance of low-level hierarchical societies during the Neolithic in the Bronocice microregion, southeastern Poland. *Germania* 62: 1–30.

Miller, D. 1982. Structures and strategies: an aspect of the relationship between social hierarchy and cultural change. In I. Hodder (ed.) *Symbolic and Structural Archaeology*, pp. 89–98. Cambridge: Cambridge University Press.

Millett, M.J. 1990. *The Romanization of Britain*. Cambridge: Cambridge University Press.

Minsky, M. and S. Papert 1972. *Artificial Intelligence Progress Report* (AI Memo No. 252). Cambridge, MA: Massachusetts Institute of Technology, Artificial Intelligence Laboratory.

Miron, A. 1986. Das Gräberfeld von Horath. *Trierer Zeitschrift* 49:7–198.

1989. Das Frauengrab 1242: zur chronologischen Gliederung der Stufe Latène D2. In A. Haffner (ed.) *Gräber: Spiegel des Lebens*, pp. 215–28. Mainz: Philipp von Zabern.

Moberg, C.-A. 1977. La Tène and types of society in Scandinavia. In V. Markotic (ed.) *Ancient Europe and the Mediterranean*, pp. 115–20. Warminster: Aris and Phillips.

Morel, J.-P. 1981. Le commerce étrusque en France, en Espagne et en Afrique. In *L'Etruria mineraria: Atti del XII Covegno di Studi Etruschi e Italici, Firenze 1979*, pp. 463–508. Florence: Leo Olschki.

Morris, I. 1987. *Burial and Ancient Society: The Rise of the Greek City-State*. Cambridge: Cambridge University Press.

Morris, J. 1975. *The Age of Arthur: A History of the British Isles from 350–650*. London: Weidenfeld and Nicolson.

Motyková, K., P. Drda and A. Rybová 1982. The Celtic stronghold of Závist. *Pamàtcky Archeologické* 73:432–54.

1988. Die bauliche Gestalt der Akropolis auf dem Burgwall Závist in der Späthallstatt- und Frühlatènezeit. *Germania* 66:391–436.

1990. Die Siedlungsstruktur des Oppidums Závist zum heutigen Forschungsstand. *Archäologisches Korrespondenzblatt* 20:415–26.

Munro, R.W. 1961 *Munro's Western Isles of Scotland and Genealogies of the Clans 1549*. Edinburgh: Oliver and Boyd.

Murray, M.L. 1994. Kelheim: the landscape survey. In P.S. Wells (ed.) *Settlement, Economy, and Cultural Change at the End of the European Iron Age*, pp. 96–134. Michigan: International Monographs in Prehistory.

n.d. a. Fields of discourse: the evolution of social space during the Bronze/Iron Age transition in Central Europe. In P.S. Wells (ed.) *The Archaeology of Spatial Organization in Early Europe*. Oxford. Oxbow Books.

n.d. b. "The Development of Iron Age Landscapes in Central Europe: Discursive Strategies and Archaeological Places of the Final Millennium B.C." Unpublished Ph.D. thesis: Harvard University.

Mytum, H. 1992. *The Origins of Early Christian Ireland*. New York: Routledge.

Nash, D. 1976. Reconstructing Poseidonius' ethnography. *Britannia* 7:111–27.

1978. Territory and state formation in Central Gaul. In D. Greene, C. Haselgrove and M. Spriggs (eds.) *Social Organization and Settlement*, pp. 455–75. British Archaeological Reports Supplementary Series 47. Oxford: British Archaeological Reports.

1987. Imperial expansion under the Roman Republic. In M.J. Rowlands, M. Larsen and K. Kristiansen (eds.) *Center and Periphery in the Ancient World*, pp. 87–103. Cambridge: Cambridge University Press.

Nicholls, K.W. 1972. *Gaelic and Gaelicised Ireland in the Middle Ages*. Dublin: Gill and MacMillan.

1978. *Land, Law and Society in Sixteenth-Century Ireland*. Dublin: The O'Donnell Lecture.

Niesiołowska-Wedzka, A. 1974. Anfänge und Entwicklung der Burgen der Lausitzer Kultur. *Polskie Badania Archeologiczne* 18. Warsaw: Ossolineum.

Nisbet, R. 1980. *History of the Idea of Progress*. New York: Basic Books.

Oaks, L.S. 1987. Epona in the Aeduan landscape: transfunctional deity under changing rule. In C.L. Crumley and W.H. Marquardt (eds.) *Regional Dynamics: Burgundian Landscapes in Historical Perspective*, pp. 295–333. San Diego: Academic Press.

O'Brien, M.A. 1976. *Corpus Genealogiarum Hiberniae*. Dublin: The Dublin Institute for Advanced Studies.

Ó Corráin, D. 1971. Irish regnal succession: a reappraisal. *Studia Hibernica* 11:7–39.

1972. *Ireland Before the Normans*. Dublin: Gill and Macmillan.

1973. Dál Cais – church and dynasty. *Ériu* 24:52–63.

O'Corráin, D., L. Breatnach and A. Breen 1984. The laws of the Irish. *Peritia* 3:382–438.

Oeftiger, K. 1984. Mehrfachbestattungen im Westhallstattkreis: zum Problem der Totenfolge. *Antiquitas* 3(26). Mainz: Rudolph Habelt Verlag.

Olivier, L. 1988. Le tumulus à tombe à char de Marainville-sur-Madon (Vosges). Premiers résultats. In J.P. Mohen, A. Duval and C. Eluère (eds.) *Les Princes celtes et la Méditerranée*, pp. 271–301. Paris: La Documentation Française.

O'Neill, R. V., D. L. DeAngelis, J. B. Waide and T. F. H. Allen 1986. *A Hierarchical Concept of Ecosystems*. Princeton: Princeton University Press.

O'Rahilly, C. (ed. and trans.) 1967. *Táin Bó Cúailnge*. Dublin: Dublin Institute for Advanced Studies.

Ó Ríain, P. 1972. Boundary association in early Irish society. *Studia Celtica* 1: 12–29.

O'Shea, J. 1984. *Mortuary Variability*. New York: Academic Press.

Overbeck, B. and P.S. Wells 1991. Vier neue keltische Münzen vom Kelheimer Mitterfeld. *Bäyerische Vorgeschichtsblätter* 56:163–8.

Oxford Latin Dictionary [OLD] 1982. Oxford: Clarendon.

Pader, E.-J. 1982. *Symbolism, Social Relations and the Interpretation of Mortuary Remains*. British Archaeological Reports International Series 130. Oxford: British Archaeological Reports.

Pare, C. 1991. Fürstensitze, Celts and the Mediterranean world: developments in the West Hallstatt Culture in the 6th and 5th centuries BC. *Proceedings of the Prehistoric Society* 57:183–202.

1992. *Wagons and Wagon-Graves of the Early Iron Age in Central Europe*. Oxford: Oxford University Committee for Archaeology Monograph 35.

Partridge, E. 1983. *Origins: A Short Etymological Dictionary of Modern English*. New York: Greenwich House.

Parzinger, H. 1986. Zur Späthallstatt- und Frühlatènezeit

in Nordwürttemberg. *Fundberichte aus Baden-Württemberg* 11:231–58.

Pattee, H.H. (ed.) 1973. *Hierarchy Theory: The Challenge of Complex Systems.* New York: George Braziller.

Patterson, N.W. 1981. Material and symbolic exchange in early Irish clientship. *Proceedings of the Harvard Celtic Colloquium* 1:53–61.

——— 1989. Brehon law in the late middle ages: "antiquarian and obsolete" or "traditional and functional." *Cambridge Medieval Celtic Studies 17* (Summer): 43–63.

——— 1990. Patrilineal groups in early Irish society: the evidence of the law-tracts. *Bulletin Board of Celtic Studies* 37.

——— 1991 and 1994. *Cattle-lords and Clansmen: Kinship and Rank in Early Ireland.* New York: Garland (1991); second edition: Notre Dame University Press (forthcoming 1994).

Pauli, L. 1971. Die Golasecca-Kultur und Mitteleuropa: ein Beitrag zur Geschichte des Handels über den Alpen. *Hamburger Beiträge zur Archäologie* 1. Hamburg.

——— 1972. *Untersuchungen zur Späthallstattkultur in Nordwürttemberg.* Hamburg: Helmut Buske.

——— 1975. *Keltischer Volksglaube: Amulette und Sonderbestattungen am Dürrnberg bei Hallein und im eisenzeitlichen Mitteleuropa.* Munich: C.H. Beck Verlag.

——— 1978. *Der Dürrnberg bei Hallein III.* Munich: C.H. Beck Verlag.

——— 1981. Review of H. Jankuhn, N. Nehlsen and H. Roth (eds.) *Zum Grabfrevel in vor- und frühgeschichtlicher Zeit: Untersuchungen zum Grabraub und "haugbrot" in Mittel- und Nordeuropa.* Bericht über ein Kolloquium der Kommission für die Altertumskunde Mittel- und Nordeuropas vom 14. bis 16. February 1977. In *Abhandlungen der Wissenschaften in Göttingen* 113. *Germania* 59(2):467–75.

——— 1984. Die westliche Hallstattkultur: Aufstieg und Niedergang einer Randkultur der antiken Welt. *Archäologie und Kulturgeschichte* 2:46–61. Saerbeck: Symposium Saerbeck.

——— 1985. Early Celtic society: two centuries of wealth and turmoil in central Europe. In T.C. Champion and J.V.S. Megaw (eds.) *Settlement and Society: Aspects of West European Prehistory in the First Millennium B.C.*, pp. 23–43. New York: St. Martin's Press.

Paynter, R. 1989. The archaeology of equality and inequality. *Annual Review of Anthropology* 18: 369–99.

Pearson, M.P. 1982. Mortuary practices, society and ideology: an ethnoarchaeological study. In I. Hodder (ed.) *Symbolic and Structural Archaeology*, pp. 99–113. Cambridge: Cambridge University Press.

Peebles, C. and S. Kus 1977. Some archaeological correlates of ranked societies. *American Antiquity* 42:421–8.

Peschel, K. 1988. Germanen und Kelten. In B. Krüger (ed.) *Die Germanen*, Vol. I, pp. 241–63. Berlin: Akademie-Verlag.

Peyre, C. 1979. *La Cisalpine gauloise du IIIe au Ier siècle avant J.-C.* Paris: Presses de l'Ecole Normale Supérieure.

Piggott, S. 1968. *The Druids.* London: Thames and Hudson.

——— 1983. *The Earliest Wheeled Transport from the Atlantic Coast to the Caspian Sea.* Ithaca: Cornell University Press.

Pion, P. n.d. De la chefferie à l'état? Territoires et organisation sociale dans la Vallée de l'Aisne aux âges des métaux (2200–20 av. JC). *Acts du Colloque d'Antibes 1989.* In press.

Pleiner, R. 1982. Untersuchungen zur Schmiedetechnik auf den keltischen Oppida. *Pamatky Archeologické* 73:86–173.

——— 1993. *The Celtic Sword.* Oxford: Clarendon Press.

Polenz, H. 1982. Münzen in latènezeitlichen Gräbern Mitteleuropas aus der Zeit zwischen 300 und 50 vor Christi Geburt. *Bayerische Vorgeschichtsblätter* 47: 27–222.

Pommeret, C. 1992. Nuits-St. Georges, Les Bolards (Côte d'Or). In M. Mangin (ed.) *Colloque Bliesbruck-Reinheim-Bitche: les agglomerations secondaires de Gaule belgique et des Germains*, 21–24 Octobre 1992. Atlas.

Pounds, N.J.G. and S.S. Ball 1964. Core areas and the development of the European state system. *Annals of the Association of American Geographers* 54(1): 24–40.

Powell, T.G.E. 1958. *The Celts.* London: Thames and Hudson.

——— 1966. *Prehistoric Art.* London: Thames and Hudson.

Py, M. 1968. Les influences méditerranéennes en Vaunage du VIIIme au Ier siècle avant J.C. *Bulletin de l'Ecole Antique de Nîmes* 3:39–91.

——— 1978. *L'Oppidum de Nages (Gard) 35e suppl. à Gallia*, p. 361. Paris.

——— 1979–80. Ensayo de clasificación de un estilo cerámica de Occidente: los vasos pseudojonios pinta dos. *Ampurias* 41–2:155–202.

——— 1985. Les amphores étrusques de Gaule méridionale. In M. Cristofani, P. Moscati, G. Nardi and M. Pandolfini (eds.) *Il Commercio Etrusco Arcaico. Atti dell'Incontro di Studio*, 5–7 Dicembre 1983. Quaderni del Centro di Studio per l'Archeologia Etrusco-Italica 9, pp. 73–94. Rome: Consiglio Nazionale delle Ricerche.

1988. Sondages dans l'habitat antique de Lattes: les fouilles d'Henri Prades et du Groupe Archéologique Painlevé (1963–1985). In G. Barruol, C. Landes, A. Nickels, M. Py and J. Roux (eds.) *Lattara* 1, pp. 65–146. Lattes: Association pour la Recherche Archéologique en Languedoc Oriental.

1990. *Culture, économie et société protohistoriques dans la région nimoise*. 2 vols. Rome: Ecole Française de Rome.

Qviller, B. 1981. The dynamics of Homeric society. *Symbolae Osloenses* 56:109–55.

Raftery, B. 1972. Irish hill-forts. In C. Thomas (ed.) *The Iron-Age in the Irish Sea Province*. Council of British Archaeology Research Report 9. Oxford: Oxford University Press.

1975. Dowris, Hallstatt and La Tène in Ireland: problems of the transition from bronze to iron. In S.J. de Laet (ed.) *Acculturation and Continuity in Atlantic Europe*. Fourth Atlantic Colloquium, pp. 189–97. Ghent: Brugge.

1976. Rathgall and Irish hillfort problems. In D. W. Harding (ed.) *Hillforts: Late Prehistoric Earthworks in Britain and Ireland*, pp. 339–57. London: Academic Press.

1991. Horse and cart in Iron Age Ireland. *Journal of Indo-European Studies* 19 (1/2):49–71.

Ralston, I.B.M. 1984. Les caractères de l'habitat à La Tène III: les structures urbaines et leurs correspondances avec les entités politiques. In *Recherche sur la Naissance de l'Urbanisation au I^e Siècle avant JC dans le Centre de la France*, pp. 169–98.

1992. *Les Habitats fortifiés du Limousin*. Paris: Documents d'Archéologie Française.

Rambaud, M. 1953. *L'Art de la déformation historique dans les Commentaires de César*. Paris: Presses Universitaires de France.

Ramseyer, D. 1990. Amphores massaliètes en territoire helvétique. In M. Bats (ed.) *Les amphores de Marseille grecque*, Etudes Massaliètes 2, pp. 259–261. Aix-en-Provence: Publications de l'Université de Provence.

Randsborg, K. 1974. Social stratification in Bronze Age Denmark: a study in the regulation of cultural systems. *Praehistorische Zeitschrift* 49:38–61.

1980. *The Viking Age in Denmark: The Formation of a State*. New York: St. Martin's Press.

Rankin, H.D. 1987. *Celts and the Classical World*. London: Areopagitica Press.

Rathje, W.L. 1975. The last tango in Mayapan: a tentative trajectory of production-distribution systems. In J.A. Sabloff and C.C. Lamberg-Karlovsky (eds.) *Ancient Civilization and Trade*, pp. 409–48. Albuquerque: University of New Mexico Press.

Rawson, E. 1985. *Intellectual Life in the Late Roman Republic*. Baltimore: Johns Hopkins University Press.

Reim, H. 1988. *Das keltische Gräberfeld bei Rottenburg am Neckar: Grabungen 1984–1987*. Archäologische Informationen aus Baden-Württemberg 3. Stuttgart.

Reinecke, P. 1935. Bodendenkmale spätkeltischer Eisengewinnung an der untersten Altmühl. *Bericht der Römisch-Germanischen Kommission* 24–5:166–228.

1965. *Mainzer Aufsätze zur Chronologie der Bronze- und Eisenzeit*. Bonn: Habelt.

Reinhard, W. 1988. Das hallstattzeitliche Gräberfeld von Rubenheim. *Führer zu Archäologischen Denkmälern in Deutschland. Saar-Pfalz Kreis* 18:89–96. Stuttgart: Konrad Theiss Verlag.

1990. Die hallstattzeitlichen Hügelgräber von Rubenheim-Wolfersheim, Saar-Pfalz-Kreis. *Archäologie in Deutschland 1990* 2:44–5.

Renfrew, C. 1973. Monuments, mobilization and social organization in Neolithic Wessex. In C. Renfrew (ed.) *The Explanation of Culture Change: Models in Prehistory*, pp. 539–58. Pittsburgh: University of Pittsburgh Press.

1973. *Before Civilization*. New York: Alfred A. Knopf.

1976. Megaliths, territories and populations. In S.J. de Laet (ed.) *Acculturation and Continuity in Atlantic Europe*, pp. 198–220. Bruge: de Tempel.

1979. *Investigations in Orkney*. London: The Society of Antiquaries.

1984. *Approaches to Social Archaeology*. Edinburgh: Edinburgh University Press.

1987. *Archaeology and Language*: The Puzzle of Indo-European Origins. Cambridge: Cambridge University Press.

Renfrew, C. and P. Bahn 1991. *Archaeology: Theories, Methods and Practice*. New York: Thames and Hudson.

Renfrew, C. and E. Level 1979. Exploring dominance: predicting polities from centres. In C. Renfrew and K.L. Cooke (eds.) *Transformation: Mathematical Approaches to Culture Change*, pp. 147–67. London: Academic Press.

Richards, E. and M. Clough 1989. *Cromartie: Highland Life 1650-1914*. Aberdeen: Aberdeen University Press.

Ricklefs, R.E. 1987. Structural ecology: a review of O'Neill *et al. A Hierarchical Concept of Ecosystems*. In *Science* 236:206–7.

Rieckhoff, S. 1992. Überlegungen zur Chronologie der

Spätlatènezeit im südlichen Mitteleuropa. *Bayerische Vorgeschichtsblätter* 57:103–21.

Robbins, R.H. 1973. Alcohol and the identity struggle: some effects of economic change on interpersonal relations. *American Anthropologist* 75:99–122.

Röder, J. 1948. Der Goloring, ein eisenzeitliches Heiligtum vom Henge-Charakter im Koblenzer Wald (Landkreis Koblenz). *Bonner Jahrbücher* 148: 81–132.

Rousseau, J. 1985. The ideological prerequisites of inequality. In J.M. Claessen, P. van de Velde and M.E. Smith (eds.) *Development and Decline: The Evolution of Socio-Political Organization*, pp. 36–45. South Hadley: Bergin and Garvey.

Rowe, J.H. 1963. Urban settlements in ancient Peru. *Nawpa Pacha* 1:1–27.

Rowlands, M.J. 1980. Kinship, alliance and exchange in the European Bronze Age. In J. Barrett and R.J. Bradley (eds.) *Settlement and Society in the Later British Bronze Age*, pp. 15–55. Oxford: British Archaeological Reports 83.

1984. Conceptualizing the European Bronze and Early Iron Age. In J.L. Bintliff (ed.) *European Social Evolution: Archaeological Perspectives*, pp. 147–55. Sussex: Chanctonbury Press.

Roymans, N. 1990. *Tribal Societies in Northern Gaul: An Anthropological Perspective*. University of Amsterdam: Cingula 12.

Rybová, A. and B. Soudský 1962. *Libenice: sanctuaire celtique en Bohème centrale*. Prague: Ceskoslovenske Akademie Ved.

Sahlins, M. 1958. *Social Stratification in Polynesia*. University of Washington Press.

1968. *Tribesmen*. Englewood Cliffs: Prentice-Hall.

Said, E.W. 1978. *Orientalism*. New York: Pantheon Books.

Sanders, W.T. 1974. Chiefdom to state: political evolution at Kaminaljuyu, Guatemala. In C.B. Moore (ed.) *Reconstructing Complex Societies: An Archaeological Colloquium. Bulletin of the American Schools of Oriental Research Supplement* 20:97–113.

Sanders, W.T. and J. Marino 1970. *New World Prehistory: Archaeology of the Americas*. Englewood Cliffs: Prentice-Hall.

Sanders, W.T. and D. Webster 1978. Unilineality, multilineality, and the evolution of complex societies. In C. Redman *et al.* (eds.) *Social Archaeology: Beyond Subsistence and Dating*, pp. 249–302. New York: Academic Press.

Sangmeister, E. 1969. Die Hallstattkultur im Hagenauer Forst und die relative Chronologie der jüngeren Hallstattkultur im Westen. *Fundberichte aus Hessen Supplement* 1:154–87.

Saxe, A.A. 1970. *Social Dimensions of Mortuary Practices*. Ph.D. dissertation, Ann Arbor: University of Michigan Microfilms.

Scabell, J. 1966. Die Rinderknochen von der Heuneburg, einem frühkeltischen Herrensitz bei Hundersingen an der Donau. Grabungen 1959 und 1963. *Naturwissenschaftliche Untersuchungen zur Vor- und Frühgeschichte in Württemberg und Hohenzollern* 1.

Schaaf, U. 1969. Versuch einer regionalen Gliederung frühlatènezeitlicher Fürstengräber. *Fundberichte aus Hessen Supplement* 1:188–202.

Schiek, S. 1977. Zur Viereckschanze bei Hundersingen, Gde. Herbertingen, Kr. Sigmaringen. *Archäologische Ausgrabungen 1977*:39–43.

1981. Bestattungsbräuche. In K. Bittel, W. Kimmig and S. Schiek (eds.) *Die Kelten in Baden-Württemberg*, pp. 118–37. Stuttgart: Konrad Theiss Verlag.

1982. Zu Viereckschanzen und Grabhügeln: Eine Ergänzung. *Fundberichte aus Baden-Württemberg* 7:221–31.

Schindler, R. 1975. Die Altburg von Bundenbach und andere spätkeltische Befestigungen im Trevererland. *Ausgrabungen in Deutschland 1950–1975*, Vol. I, pp. 273–86. Mainz: Römisch-Germanisches Zentralmuseum.

Schönberger, H. 1952. Die Spätlatènezeit in der Wetterau. *Saalburger Jahrbuch* 11:21–130.

Schwab, H. 1983. Châtillon-sur-Glâne, Bilanz der ersten Sondiergrabungen. *Germania* 61:405–58.

1990. *Archéologie de la 2e correction des eaux du Jura*, Vol. I: *Les Celtes sur la Broye et la Thielle*. Fribourg: Editions Universitaires.

Scott, J.C. 1985. *Weapons of the Weak: Everyday Forms of Peasant Resistance*. New Haven: Yale University Press.

1990. *Domination and the Arts of Resistance*. New Haven: Yale University Press.

Sellar, D.W.H. 1981. Marriage, divorce and concubinage in Gaelic Scotland. *Trans-Gaelic Society of Inverness* 51:464–95.

Service, E. 1971. *Primitive Social Organization*. Second edition. New York: Random House.

1975. *Origins of the State and Civilization: The Process of Cultural Evolution*. New York: Norton.

Seyer, H. 1988. Die regionale Gliederung der Kulturen der vorrömischen Eisenzeit – Stammesgebiete – erste Wanderungen. In B. Krüger (ed.) *Die Germanen*, Vol. I, pp. 191–203. Berlin: Akademie-Verlag.

Shefton, B.B. 1979. *Die "Rhodischen" Bronzekannen*.

Marburger Studien zur Vor- und Frühgeschichte 2. Mainz: Philipp Von Zabern.

Sherratt, A. 1984. Social evolution: Europe in the late Neolithic and Copper Ages. In J. Bintliff (ed.) *European Social Evolution: Archaeological Perspectives*, pp. 123–34. Bradford: University of Bradford Press.

Shipton, P.M. 1984. Strips and patches: a demographic dimension in some African land-holding and political systems. *Man* 19:613–34.

Simms, K. 1978. Guesting and feasting in Gaelic Ireland. *Journal of the Royal Society of Antiquaries of Ireland* 108:67–100.

Skene, W.F. 1877. *Celtic Scotland*, 3 vols. Edinburgh: Edmonston and Douglas.

Small, D.B. n.d. Elite economic separation and the development of heterarchy in state level societies. In C.L. Crumley and R.M. Ehrenreich (eds.) *Heterarchy and the Analysis of Complex Societies*. Under consideration by the Archaeology Division, American Anthropological Association.

Smith, C.A. 1976. Regional economic systems: linking geographical models and socioeconomic problems. In C.A. Smith (ed.) *Regional Analysis*, Vol. I, pp. 3–63. New York: Academic Press.

Smith, C.E. 1952. The "Bellum Gallicum" as a work of propaganda. *Latomus: Revue de Etudes Latines* 11:3–18; 166–79.

Smith, M.E. 1985. Introduction. In J.M. Claessen, P. van de Velde and M.E. Smith (eds.) *Development and Decline*. South Hadley: Bergin and Garvey.

Smyth, A.P. 1982. *Celtic Leinster*. Blackrock: Irish Academic Press.

Southall, A.W. 1968. Stateless society. *International Encyclopedia of the Social Sciences* 15:157–68. New York: Macmillan and The Free Press.

Spindler, K. 1983. *Die Frühen Kelten*. Stuttgart: Reclam.

Sproule, D. 1984. Origins of the Éoganachta. *Ériu* 35:31–7.

Steer, K.A. and J. Bannerman 1977. *Late Medieval Monumental Sculpture in the West Highlands*. Edinburgh: HMSO.

Steponaitis, V. 1978. Location theory and complex chiefdoms: a Mississippian example. In B.D. Smith (ed.) *Mississippian Settlement Patterns*, pp. 417–53. New York: Academic Press.

Steuer, H. 1979. Frühgeschichtliche Sozialstrukturen in Mitteleuropa. In H. Jankuhn and R. Wenskus (eds.) *Geschichtswissenschaft und Archäologie*, pp. 595–637. Sigmaringen: Jan Thorbecke.

1987. Gewichtgeldwirtschaften im frühgeschichtlichen Europa. In K. Duwel *et al.* (eds.) *Untersuchungen zu Handel und Verkehr der vor- und frühgeschichtlichen Zeit in Mittel- und Nordeuropa*, Part 4, *Der Handel der Karolinger-und Wikingerzeit*, pp. 405–527. Göttingen: Vandenhoeck and Ruprecht.

Steward, J. 1949. Cultural causality and law: a trial formulation of early civilization. *American Anthropologist* 51:1–27.

1979 [1955]. *Theory of Culture Change*. Urbana: University of Illinois Press.

Storrie, M.C. 1961. Islay: the Hebridean exception. *Geographical Review* 51: 87–108.

Strathern, A. 1971. *The Rope of Moka: Big-Men and Ceremonial Exchange in Mount Hagen, New Guinea*. Cambridge: Cambridge University Press.

Svobodová, H. 1985. Antike Importy z Keltskych Oppid v Cechach a na Morave (Antike Importe aus den keltischen Oppida in Böhmen und Mähren). *Archéologicke Rozhledy* 37:653–88.

Syme, R. 1939. *The Roman Revolution*. Oxford: Oxford University Press.

Szabó, M. 1991. Mercenary activity. In S. Moscati *et al.* (eds.) *The Celts*, pp. 333–6. New York: Rizzoli.

Tainter, J.A. 1978. Mortuary practices and the study of prehistoric social systems. In M.B. Schiffer (ed.) *Advances in Archaeological Method and Theory* 1:105–41. New York: Academic Press.

Taylor, L.R. 1966. *Party Politics in the Age of Caesar*. Berkeley: University of California Press.

Tchernia, A. 1983. Italian wine in Gaul at the end of the Rebublic. In P. Garnsey and C.R. Whittaker (eds.) *Trade in the Ancient Economy*, pp. 87–104. London: Chatto and Windus.

1992. Résumés des discussions. In M. Bats, G. Bertucchi, G. Congès and H. Trézing (eds.) *Marseille grecque et la Gaule*. Etudes Massaliètes 3, p. 475. Lattes: ADAM Editions.

Tierney, J.J. 1960. The Celtic ethnography of Poseidonius. *Proceedings of the Royal Irish Academy* 5(60C).

Tilley, C. 1982. Social formation, social structure and social change. In I. Hodder (ed.) *Structural and Symbolic Archaeology*, pp. 26–38. Cambridge: Cambridge University Press.

Timpe, D. 1985. Der keltische Handel nach historischen Quellen. In K. Duwel *et al.* (eds.) *Untersuchungen zu Handel und Verkehr der vor- und frühgeschichtlichen Zeit in Mittel- und Nordeuropa*, Part 1, *Methodische Grundlagen und Darstellungen zum Handel in vorgeschichtlicher Zeit und in der Antike*, pp. 258–84. Göttingen: Vandenhoeck and Ruprecht.

Todd, M. 1992. *The Early Germans*. Oxford: Blackwell.

Tolstoy, P. 1989. Chiefdoms, states and scales of analysis.

The Interpretation of History. Essays from the *Quarterly Review of Archaeology* 10(1):72–8.

Torbrügge, W. 1971. Vor- und frühgeschichtliche Flussfunde. *Bericht der Römisch-Germanischen Kommission* 51–2:1–146.

Trigger, B. 1982. Ethnohistory: problems and prospects. *Ethnohistory* 29(1):1–19.

Uenze, H.-P. 1964. Zur Frühlatènezeit in der Oberpfalz. *Bayerische Vorgeschichtsblätter* 29:77–118.

Upham, S. 1987. A theoretical consideration of Middle Range Societies. In R. Drennan and C. Uribe (eds) *Archaeological Reconstructions and Chiefdoms in the Americas*, pp. 345–68. New York: University Press of America.

van de Velde, P. 1979. Bandkeramik social structure. *Analecta Praehistorica Leidensia* 12. The Hague: Leiden University Press.

1985. Early state formation in Iron Age Central Europe. In H. Claessen, P. van de Velde and M.E. Smith (eds.) *Development and Decline: The Evolution of Sociopolitical Organization*, pp. 170–82. South Hadley: Bergin and Garvey.

van den Boom, H. 1990. Amphoren der Heuneburg. In M. Bats (ed.) *Les Amphores de Marseille grecque*, pp. 263–6. Etudes Massaliètes 2. Aix-en-Provence: Publications de l'Université de Provence.

van der Leeuw, S. 1981. Information flows, flow structures and the explanation of change in archaeology. In S. van der Leeuw (ed.) *Archaeological Approaches to the Study of Complexity*. Amsterdam: Cingula VI.

n.d. Chaos, information and urban systems. Iron Age symposium, Cambridge, 1988.

Villard, F. 1960. *La Céramique grecque de Marseille (VIe–IVe siècle).* Essai d'Histoire Économique. Bibliothèque des Ecoles Françaises d'Athènes et de Rome 195. Paris: Boccard.

Vullierme, J.-L. 1989. *Le Concept de système politique.* Paris: Presses Universitaires de France.

Waldhauser, J. 1978. *Das Keltische Gräberfeld bei Jenišův Újezd in Böhmen.* Teplice: Krajske Muzeum.

1981a. Keltske Rotacni Mlyny v Cechach (Keltische Drehmühlen in Böhmen). *Pamatky Archéologicke* 72:153–221.

1981b. Organisation de l'habitat celtique en Bohème du Hallstatt final à La Tène III: enquête sur la region celtique du cours moyen du fleuve Bilina. In O. Büchsenschütz (ed.) *Les Structures d'habitat à l'âge du Fer en Europe Temperée*, pp. 139–43. Paris: Maison des Sciences de l'Homme.

1987. Keltische Gräberfelder in Böhmen. *Bericht der Römisch-Germanischen Kommission* 68:25–179.

1992. Keltische Distributionssysteme von Graphittonkeramik und die Ausbeutung der Graphitlagerstätten während der fortgeschrittenen Latènezeit. *Archäologisches Korrespondenzblatt* 22:377–92.

Wallerstein, I. 1974–80. *The Modern World-System*, 2 vols. New York: Academic Press.

Wamser, G. 1975. Zur Hallstattkultur in Ostfrankreich. Die Fundgruppen im Jura und in Burgund. *Bericht der Römisch-Germanischen Kommission* 56:1–178.

Webb, M. 1973. The Peten Maya decline viewed in the perspective of state formation. In T.P. Culbert (ed.) *The Classic Maya Collapse*, pp. 367–404. Alberquerque: University of New Mexico Press.

Weber, G. 1989. Neues zur Befestigung des Oppidums Tarodunum, Gde. Kirchzarten, Kreis Breisgau-Hochschwarzwald. *Fundberichte aus Baden-Württemberg* 14: 273–88.

Webster, G. 1990. Labor control and emergent stratification in prehistoric Europe. *Current Anthropology* 31(4):337–66.

Weingrod, A. 1968. Patrons, patronage and political parties. *Comparative Studies in Society and History* 10:1–22.

Wells, P.S. 1980. *Culture Contact and Culture Change: Early Iron Age Central Europe and the Mediterranean World.* Cambridge: Cambridge University Press.

1984. *Farms, Villages and Cities: Commerce and Urban Origins in Late Prehistoric Europe.* Ithaca: Cornell University Press.

1991. Zur Verbreitung der späteisenzeitlichen Siedlungsreste am Kelheimer Mitterfeld. *Archäologisches Korrespondenzblatt* 21:517–22.

Wells, P.S. (ed.) 1993. *Settlement, Economy, and Cultural Change at the End of the European Iron Age: Excavations at Kelheim in Bavaria, 1987–1991.* Ann Arbor: International Monographs in Prehistory.

Wenke, R.J. 1989. Egypt: origins of complex societies. *Annual Review of Anthropology* 18:129–55.

Wenskus, R. 1961. *Stammesbildung und Verfassung: Das Werden der frühmittelalterlichen Gentes.* Cologne: Böhlau.

Werner, J. 1978. Zur Bronzekanne von Kelheim. *Bayerische Vorgeschichtsblätter* 43:1–18.

White, L.A. 1949. *The Science of Culture.* New York: Grove Press.

1959 *The Evolution of Culture.* New York: McGraw-Hill.

Whittlesey, D. 1944. *The Earth and the State.* New York: Henry Holt and Co.

Wightman, E.M. 1978. Peasants and potentates: an investigation of social structure and land tenure in

Roman Gaul. *American Journal of Ancient History* 3:97–128.

Will, E.L. 1987. The Roman amphorae from Manching: a reappraisal. *Bayerische Vorgeschichtsblätter* 52: 21–36.

Willaume, M. 1985. *Le Berry à l'Age du Fer, HaC – La Tène.* British Archaeological Reports International Series 247. Oxford: British Archaeological Reports.

Winter, F. 1986. The Celtic boar feast: how barbaric was it really? *Archaeology* 39 (July/August):48–52.

Woolf, G. n.d. Assessing social complexity in the final Iron Age of central France. Iron Age seminar, Cambridge, 1987.

Wormald, P.J. 1985. *Lords and Men in Scotland: Bonds of Manrent 1442-1603.* Edinburgh: J. Donald.

Young, M.W. 1971. *Fighting with Food: Leadership, Values and Social Control in a Massim Society.* Cambridge: Cambridge University Press.

Ziegaus, B. 1993. Das keltische Münzwesen. In H. Dannheimer and R. Gebhard (eds.) *Das Keltische Jahrtausend,* pp. 220–7. Mainz: Philipp von Zabern.

Zürn, H. 1952. Zum Übergang von Späthallstatt zu Latène im südwestdeutschen Raum. *Germania* 26:116–24.

1987. *Hallstattzeitliche Grabfunde in Württemberg und Hohenzollern.* 2 Vols. Stuttgart: Konrad Theiss Verlag.

Index

Printed in the United Kingdom
by Lightning Source UK Ltd.
102411UKS00002B/127